DEVELOPING GESTALT
COUNSELLING

A field theoretical and relational
model of contemporary Gestalt
counselling and psychotherapy

Developing Counselling, edited by Windy Dryden, is an innovative series of books which provides counsellors and counselling trainees with practical hints and guidelines on the problems they face in the counselling process. The books assume that readers have a working knowledge of the approach in question, and, in a clear and accessible fashion show how the counsellor can more effectively translate that knowledge into everyday practice.

Books in the series include:

Developing the Practice of Counselling
Windy Dryden and Colin Feltham

Developing Counsellor Supervision
Colin Feltham and Windy Dryden

Developing Counsellor Training
Windy Dryden and Colin Feltham

Developing Person-Centred Counselling
Dave Mearns

Developing Psychodynamic Counselling
Brendan McLoughlin

Developing Rational Emotive Behavioural Counselling
Windy Dryden and Joseph Yankura

Developing Cognitive-Behavioural Counselling
Michael J. Scott, Stephen G. Stradling and Windy Dryden

Developing Transactional Analysis Counselling
Ian Stewart

DEVELOPING GESTALT COUNSELLING

A field theoretical and relational
model of contemporary Gestalt
counselling and psychotherapy

Jennifer Mackewn

SAGE Publications
London • Thousand Oaks • New Delhi

SAGE Publications Ltd
6 Bonhill Street
London EC2A 4PU

SAGE Publications Inc.
2455 Teller Road
Thousand Oaks, California 91320

SAGE Publications India Pvt Ltd
32, M-Block Market
Greater Kailash – I
New Delhi 110 048

British Library Cataloguing in Publication data

A catalogue record for this book is available from the British Library

ISBN 0 8039 7860 X
ISBN 0 8039 7861 8 (pbk)

Library of Congress catalog card number 97–066577

Typeset by Mayhew Typesetting, Rhayader, Powys
Printed in Great Britain by Biddles Ltd, Guildford, Surrey

Contents

Preface

This book has been written with three aims in mind. Firstly, I hope to provide a view of contemporary integrative Gestalt which will go some way to offset and counterbalance the oft repeated and sometimes reductionist descriptions of Fritz Perl's demonstration work in the 1960s. The Gestalt approach to counselling and therapy has been consistently misrepresented and misunderstood by people who have not differentiated between Gestalt and 'Perlsism' (Clarkson and Mackewn, 1993; Dublin, 1977). Contemporary integrative Gestalt is a complex intersubjective approach based in phenomenological field theory. I especially want to convey how flexible and adaptable Gestalt can be, allowing the practitioner to incorporate all manner of ideas and insights from other forms of therapy and from different fields of expertise, within the integrative frame of field theory. Gestalt is not, at heart, a matter of developing new tricks and techniques but of creatively adapting the approach and the practitioner to meet the other person or people where they are available for meeting.

Secondly, I have attempted to meet a need for an overview of contemporary integrative Gestalt. In recent years many counsellors, psychotherapists and trainees have approached me saying that they know Gestalt has evolved and developed enormously since the 1960s but they have found it hard to get a comprehensive sense of its evolution. To gather relevant and necessary information about contemporary Gestalt (as opposed to Perlsian 1960s Gestalt which still predominates in the minds of many) they have had to find and read material from a wide range of sources, not all of which are easy to get hold of or absorb. This book integrates many of the important developments of the last decade.

Thirdly, I have wished to provoke some new thinking within the field of counselling and therapy. In this context I am proposing a model of counselling and therapy as complex processes which are not linear in nature but iterative, recursive and spiralling – see the Introduction. I am also suggesting that counselling and therapy need to go beyond individualism, beyond even human intersubjectivity and address issues of the field in which we live – our interdependence with the natural world, our responsibilities for the economic and cultural conditions of our times as well as our responsibilities towards the other species which co-habit our earth.

In tune with most other Western developments of the century, counselling and psychotherapy have persistently recommended a 'person-centred' approach. The result is that we human beings now participate predominantly with other humans and with human made technologies and experiences. Most of us have lost a sense of our interdependent place in the universe. This is a precarious situation both for our survival as a species and for our psychological health. We have become estranged from the animate earth (Abram, 1996). We need connection and contact with the elements of earth, sky, water, fire and a lived sense of relationship to rocks, trees, flowers and wild creatures in order to live meaningful, sustainable lives.

Counselling and psychotherapy do not seem to have fulfilled their early promise. Far from improving the world, we have had a hundred years of psychotherapy and the world is getting worse. Indeed psychotherapy and counselling may have contributed to the fostering of a narcissistic culture (Lasch, 1979) which emphasises the rights of individuals without fully taking account of their responsibilities and the entitlements of other peoples, cultures, species and life forms or indeed of the earth herself. Counselling and psychotherapy have undoubtedly helped many individuals but they have also upset many individuals and bypassed many more.

Above all, therapeutic counselling has contributed relatively little to the care of the world or the interaction between individuals and the ecological, social and economic conditions of our times. Counselling and psychotherapy have emphasised the hurts which older generations and society have inflicted and they have shown some useful ways that individuals can alleviate these wounds. But they have offered little guidance about how we can tend the wounds of society, of our ancestors or of the world.

Gestalt is perhaps uniquely placed to redress this imbalance because of its emphasis upon field theory and existential phenomenology. I propose that contemporary integrative Gestalt offers a different basis for counselling and psychotherapy. It does not emphasise the person but the person in context. It places as much emphasis upon the environment or field as upon the person coming for counselling. Field theory shows how we are shaped by our environment but it also indicates how we individually contribute towards shaping our environment and are responsible in many respects for choosing our reality. It invites us to experience our interdependence with the world and challenges us to feel our responsibility for the field conditions in which we live. It therefore seems a useful approach to counselling at a time when the ecological balance of the world is immediately threatened and a continued emphasis upon 'humanistic' and 'person-centred' approaches is proving fatal to many species and habitats and is likely to be fatal to the human species as well.

Existential phenomenology suggests that there is not one but many realities, not one but many perspectives, not one but many truths. It reminds us of the inherent subjectivity of any one person's view and the humbling limits of our human perceptions. It opens us to multiple levels of reality, reconnects us to the direct sensuous nature of our bodily experience and puts us back in touch with the interdependent world. Only through such lived experience of interconnection can we start living as one of earth's animals, equally conscious of our responsibilities as of our rights.

Developing Gestalt Counselling and Psychotherapy makes no claims for being either authoritative or comprehensive. Rather, what I have set out to do is outline the various areas which I feel have been under- or misrepresented in the general books published on Gestalt so far. It is inevitably a subjective view of the Gestalt approach even though tempered by the subjective comments of the many colleagues and trainees who have been kind enough to read and help me with the typescripts.

The book can be read as a whole, but it is equally intended to be treated as a reference and a support, to be dipped into at different places. Each section is fairly complete in itself and is amply cross-referenced so I hope you will feel free to pick and choose to meet your needs and follow your interests. I hope you enjoy the book and find it of use.

Acknowledgements

This book is not in any way an isolated entity and cannot be understood in isolation but only as an interactive part of the whole field from which it has emerged. It has evolved through my interdependent experiences with many other people, situations and creatures and I would like to acknowledge and appreciate the wonderful teachings and support that I have received from all of these.

In particular this book could not have been written without the active as well as background support of my partner, Philip Raby and the tolerance of my children and friends. I would also like to offer my warmest thanks and appreciation to my patient and unflappable secretary and assistant, Michelle Challifour, whose help has been invaluable at all times.

I thank colleagues and friends who have kindly and patiently read and commented upon several versions of the typescript, including Annie Blackbum, Hazel Elliott, Jenifer Elton Wilson, David Evans, Iris Fodor, Maria Gilbert, Judith Hemming, Jude Higgins, Philip Lapworth, Peter McCowen, Malcolm Parlett, Peter Philippson, Felicity Stretton, Jenny Thompson, Mary WiLkins.

I thank and honour my many teachers. Gestaltists and non-Gestaltists; teachers I have known in person and teachers I have read, dreamt or heard stories about; teachers who are human and teachers who are non-human, I thank you all. In particular I would like to mention David Abram, Arwyn Dreamwalker, David Boadella, Petrūska Clarkson, Maria Gilbert, Pat Grant, Elinor Greenberg, Deb'bora John-Wilson, James Masterson, Thich Nhat Hanh, Malcolm Parlett, Clarissa Pinkola Estes, Gabrielle Roth, Nicholas Spicer, Marie-Louise von Franz, Gordon Wheeler.

I appreciate and honour my colleagues and friends who have supported me, discussed, debated and creatively challenged me especially: Elizabeth Adeline, Bill Critchley, Jenifer Elton Wilson, Dave Gowling, Fran Lacey, Phil Lapworth, Val Magna, Peter Reason, Paul Roberts, David Rooke, Judy Ryde, Patricia Shaw, Charlotte Sills, Kirti Wheway. I thank all the members of the Gestalt Institute of Cleveland writing conference who have encouraged me to write each year, especially Ed and Sonia Nevis, Gordon Wheeler and Jo Melnick who have made this event happen. I thank also Windy Dryden, the series editor, Rosemary Campbell and Susan Worsey from Sage, who have all been wonderfully encouraging, patient and supportive.

My thanks to the trainees with whom I have worked. This book is written because of you and for you. Your interests, feedback, searching questions, humorous affection and challenges have been a constant source of nourishment and inspiration. I appreciate the generous support of the various organisations who have invited me to work with them and thus given me the opportunity to be in continual interaction with hundreds of trainees over many years. In particular I appreciate The Metanoia Trust, The Institute for the Arts in Therapy in Education, Gestalt South West, Roffey Park Management Institute.

Finally I thank the people who have come to me for counselling, psychotherapy or supervisory consultation in individual or group, private or organisational settings. The book could not have been written without you and your courage, your integrity, your sense of adventure, your willingness to keep going even when this felt hard. I dedicate the book to all of you – all of us – who are willing to risk ourselves and our self image in the adventure of honest exploration of self, soul and otherness, facing ourselves and our responsibilities in the world.

Introduction: A field theoretical and relational model of contemporary integrative Gestalt

I address this book to counsellors and psychotherapists and trainee counsellors or psychotherapists of all orientations, and especially to those of you who are or wish to become Gestalt counsellors and psychotherapists; or who wish to integrate Gestalt into your current practice. The book is primarily designed for those who already have knowledge both of counselling and of Gestalt. However I have provided an optional section of this introduction on theoretical background (p. 14ff.) and I suggest that if you do not have any previous knowledge of Gestalt counselling and psychotherapy you might find it helpful to read this before the main body of the book.

Attempts to distinguish between counselling and psychotherapy are never wholly successful (Nelson-Jones, 1982) and rarely satisfy the professionals concerned. Indeed Truax and Carkhuff (1967) have argued that the terms can be – and frequently are – used interchangeably. For the purposes of this book, I shall follow the lead of Clarkson and Carroll (in Clarkson and Carroll, 1993) and use counselling and psychotherapy to mean two interrelated disciplines with substantial overlap or as two stages on a continuum of therapeutic counselling.

◄ – ►

counselling   therapeutic counselling   psychotherapy

The book may thus be considered to be exploring the continuum of Gestalt counselling, therapeutic counselling *and* psychotherapy; and I alternate randomly between the words counsellor and therapist.

A field theoretical and relational model of integrative Gestalt

This book describes a relational and field theoretical model of contemporary integrative Gestalt counselling and psychotherapy. The model presented suggests that counselling is a complex process which requires the counsellor/psychotherapist to be intuitive, self aware and in touch with their bodily and emotional selves. Yet at the same time therapeutic counselling involves a number of interrelated component tasks which require counsellors and psychotherapists to develop a wide range of knowledge and skills and an ability to envisage what they are doing and why in terms of several conceptual frameworks, as well as to meet their clients person to person in a meaningful relationship and blend the component skills into a subtle and versatile art form.

The component aspects of Gestalt counselling and psychotherapy include:

Attending to beginnings and initial conditions (Part I);

Understanding and exploring the holistic field, while appreciating the paradoxical theory of change (Part II);

Developing a dialogic relationship as the crucible for self development (Part III);

Observing process and developing diagnostic perspectives from these observations. Differentiating different styles of making and moderating contact in the relationship and evolving therapeutic strategies in the light of such diagnostic perspectives (Part IV and Appendix 2);

Exploring awareness and contact (Part V);

Integrating creative, experimental and transpersonal dimensions (Part VI);

Working with body process, energy, resistance and impasse (Part VII);

Attending to support and background processes in clients' lives: exploring life themes and internalisation processes (Part VIII);

Shaping counselling over time: shaping the overall counselling process while remaining open to the immediacy of the spontaneous moment (Part IX).

Each of these component aspects of therapeutic counselling can of course be subdivided into further complex systems of skills which interact with all the other aspects. The component tasks and skills of Gestalt counselling and therapy are not separate but inherently interdependent. They are interwoven and cannot be understood or meaningfully practised in isolation from each other but only as essential aspects of the whole; for one of the most important concepts of Gestalt is the notion of the whole, which cannot be broken without destroying its very nature. Describing the Gestalt

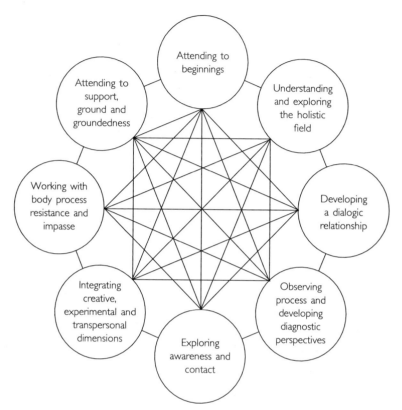

Figure I.1 *Interrelated component tasks of Gestalt counselling and psychotherapy*

approach therefore poses a challenge which is intrinsic and peculiar to any holistic approach: an understanding of any one aspect of the theory and practice of Gestalt counselling and therapy presupposes and requires a simultaneous understanding of the other aspects and indeed of the whole. Figures I.1 and I.2 attempt to capture the holistic spirit of the Gestalt approach to counselling and therapy by illustrating diagrammatically how all of the component tasks listed above are interconnected and form a whole.

Certain of these aspects or tasks of counselling and psychotherapy will be more present or in focus at certain times and so will organise the counselling work at that time. But all other aspects of counselling are also always present and being worked on to some degree. A field theoretical and relational model of

Attending to beginnings	Attending to beginnings	Attending to beginnings	Attending to beginnings	Attending to beginnings	Attending to beginnings	Attending to beginnings	Attending to beginnings
Exploring the holistic field	Exploring the holistic field	Exploring the holistic field	Exploring the holistic field	Exploring the holistic field	Exploring the holistic field	Exploring the holistic field	Exploring the holistic field
Developing a dialogic relationship	Developing a dialogic relationship	Developing a dialogic relationship	Developing a dialogic relationship	Developing a dialogic relationship	Developing a dialogic relationship	Developing a dialogic relationship	Developing a dialogic relationship
Observing process developing diagnostic perspectives	Observing process developing diagnostic perspectives	Observing process developing diagnostic perspectives	Observing process developing diagnostic perspectives	Observing process developing diagnostic perspectives	Observing process developing diagnostic perspectives	Observing process developing diagnostic perspectives	Observing process developing diagnostic perspectives
Exploring awareness and contact	Exploring awareness and contact	Exploring awareness and contact	Exploring awareness and contact	Exploring awareness and contact	Exploring awareness and contact	Exploring awareness and contact	Exploring awareness and contact
Integrating creative and experimental approaches	Integrating creative and experimental approaches	Integrating creative and experimental approaches	Integrating creative and experimental approaches	Integrating creative and experimental approaches	Integrating creative and experimental approaches	Integrating creative and experimental approaches	Integrating creative and experimental approaches
Working with body process, resistance & impasse	Working with body process, resistance & impasse	Working with body process, resistance & impasse	Working with body process, resistance & impasse	Working with body process, resistance & impasse	Working with body process, resistance & impasse	Working with body process, resistance & impasse	Working with body process, resistance & impasse
Attending to ground	Attending to ground	Attending to ground	Attending to ground	Attending to ground	Attending to ground	Attending to ground	Attending to ground and support

Figure I.2   *Holographic model of Gestalt counselling as a non-linear network or a complex adaptive system. The shaded boxes represent those tasks that are more in the foreground, while the unshaded boxes represent tasks that are in the background*

Gestalt is not a linear process which leads directly from A to Z, moving sequentially through each of the intervening stages. It is more of a spiral process in which client and counsellor together explore life themes and undertake various aspects of the therapeutic process not once but several times, and where each successive exploration contributes to the support available for the next spiral of the overall process.

Figure I.2 offers a holographic model of Gestalt counselling and therapy as a field theoretical and relational approach (the original idea of a holographic model comes from Kepner, 1995). This model suggests that counselling and psychotherapy, growth and development are cyclical, multi-focal processes. Although counselling and psychotherapy do move through all the aspects indicated in Figure I.1 and described in this book, the movement is not a simple linear sequence but a complex interactive, spiralling and recursive process.

Any one of the aspects of therapeutic counselling which are illustrated in Figures I.2 and I.3 may become the focus for a while and will organise and shape the work while it is the focus. Subsequently that aspect or conceptual framework may recede into the background and be superseded by another aspect, task or framework which then organises the therapeutic work for the next phase. Even when one aspect or task is foreground, the other aspects are also present and can still inform the therapeutic counsellor's thinking and practice (although probably to a lesser degree).

For example when the counsellor first meets the client he or she may be concentrating on attending to the initial conditions and the need to develop rapport and clarify what the client wants. Thus *attention to beginnings* organises and shapes the counselling work at that time. But at the same time the counsellor may also be *observing the client's processes* of contacting the environment, *formulating some initial diagnostic hypotheses*; and *integrating some creative approaches*. Thus attention to observing process, formulating diagnostic hypotheses and integrating creative and bodily approaches are also present and shape and inform the counsellor's thinking and practice (although to a lesser degree). Figure I.3 illustrates how one or two main tasks or aspects of the therapeutic process organise the work for a time while others recede into the background, but remain present.

Each task or conceptual framework of counselling will be visited not once but many times in a spiralling and recursive fashion. Each spiral of work builds the foundation or support for the next spiral within the overall process. While it is fairly self-

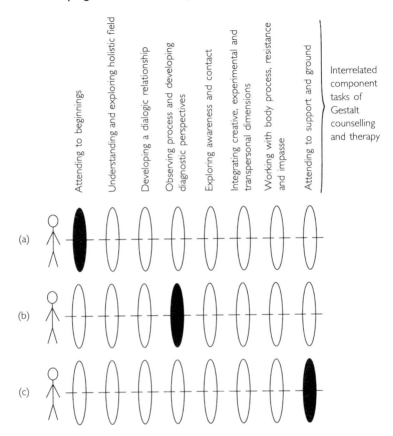

Figure I.3   *Cross-sections through the holographic model of Gestalt as a complex adaptive system. The shaded discs represent the task or aspect of the therapeutic process which is most in the foreground and organises the therapeutic work at that time. The unshaded discs represent tasks that are in the background but remain present and continue to influence the counsellor or therapist's thinking to a lesser degree*

evident that attending sensitively to beginnings lays the foundation for the future development of trust and may well influence the quality and outcome of the therapeutic experience, it is perhaps less commonplace to suggest (as does this model) that attending to background features in clients' lives (such as exploring and developing their support network and/or the ways they assimilate the insights of counselling episodes) may provide a better and sometimes essential foundation for the development

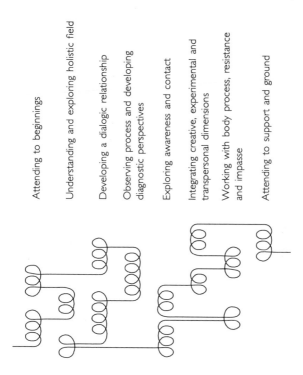

Figure I.4 *Example of the complex spiralling and often recursive movement through the different interrelated tasks or aspects of Gestalt counselling or therapy*

of awareness. Figure I.4 shows an example of how each aspect or conceptual framework of counselling may be visited not once but many times in this spiralling and recursive fashion.

Some discrete and sequential tasks and skills are, of course, associated with the beginning and ending of counselling and psychotherapy and these are described at the beginning and end of the book (see pp. 31, 209). However, even these tasks and skills will often be used in a spiralling and recurring, rather than a purely sequential manner, for beginning and ending skills are of course needed at the beginning and ending of each therapeutic session, before and after holiday breaks and so on.

This sort of holographic model for Gestalt counselling and therapy represents a non-linear network or complex adaptive system and is resonant with the latest developments in the new science of complexity (Stacey, 1995; Chia, 1994; Tsoukas, in press).

Multiple conceptual lenses or frameworks

Such a model of Gestalt illustrates how a field approach to counselling and therapy is by its very nature multi-dimensional and requires the therapeutic counsellor to be able to survey and experience the field through many possible lenses or conceptual frameworks, sometimes sequentially, sometimes concurrently. A metaphorical way of envisaging this is to imagine that counsellors wear a pair of optician's testing glasses into which they can slot different lenses: sometimes the same lenses for both eyes, sometimes different lenses for each eye, sometimes several lenses at a time, in order to get a multi-dimensional picture of what is happening and what they need to do or how they need to be.

The counsellor slots in one or several lenses at a time and works through those lenses (or with those conceptual frameworks) for a time. Then the counsellor may add a new conceptual framework or substitute one conceptual framework for another and thus apprehend what is now required differently. For example he/she may be working through the frame of observing the client's styles of making and moderating contact and looking for ways to support the client's development of awareness. This work may reveal that the client is isolated or undersupported – so the counsellor may now slot in the lens of support systems and self functions and, experiencing the work through this frame, may stay with developing these functions before doing any further development of awareness. Alternatively the awareness work may reveal some deeply embedded life patterns and the therapeutic counsellor may slot in the lens of life themes and, looking through that framework, may begin to investigate how the client's life themes can be identified and unravelled, before attempting any further awareness work. Then again, the counsellor may discover that the client has little memory of previous work done, so he/she may slot in the lenses of reinforcement, reconsolidation and assimilation and see what needs to be done through that conceptual framework to help the client anchor awareness gained before carrying on with developing any new awareness.

Interweaving theory and practice

Throughout the book I have tried to help the practitioner understand how theory applies to practice and how practice can be illuminated by theory. I have concentrated especially upon discussing practice in terms of theory and upon illustrating theory by clinical examples. I have borne in mind the need of the practitioner and trainee to understand the practical implication of the theory, for it is this area of overlap which is consistently challenging and yet centrally important. Informal research using the Myers-Briggs type indicator[R] (MBTI[R]) suggests that most people who are attracted to the practice of Gestalt counselling and therapy are naturally intuitive, and Gestalt has always valued intuition very highly. But intuition alone is not enough – therapeutic counsellors also need the ability to conceptualise what they are doing and why, so as to ensure that they work safely with different clients at different stages and so that they can explain and be ethically accountable for their work:

> This is a paradoxical and perplexing profession because the therapist must be able to deeply empathise with the client – must be able to enter the client's world and feel the world from the client's perspective – and yet the therapist is always professionally challenged to understand the client's experience in the format of theory . . . The paradox is that if the therapist is too theoretical, he can't apply this knowledge . . . On the other hand if the therapist is too applied, he will be deprived of the broad depth that theory can provide. (Hycner, 1988: 14)

Theoretical presentations are illustrated by client examples adapted from many different clinical settings and practitioners, including examples from the Gestalt literature. Many of the examples are accompanied by a theoretical commentary to further illustrate how the theory is demonstrated by the example. (All original examples are inspired by real people but for reasons of confidentiality and respect none are *based* upon real people, but upon a composite of the many different people I have worked with, supervised or read about.)

The book is not intended to be a comprehensive survey of Gestalt counselling and therapy but a discussion of selected aspects of contemporary integrative Gestalt. I have concentrated especially on those aspects of Gestalt theory and practice which have been least explored, where there has been most evolution in recent years, or on those aspects which have (in my experience as a trainer of Gestalt counsellors and therapists) been least well understood. Throughout I have endeavoured to show how field theory is not just a background idea (as it has often been presented in previous books) but a practical integrating frame which informs all our work. In particular I illustrate how the fact that we all organise (and can therefore reorganise) our perception of our circumstances or reconfigure our story or sense of self is crucial to counselling and to therapy; and to show how paying attention to all aspects of the intersubjective field and relationship is as much Gestalt therapy and counselling as the better known dramatic episodic demonstration work of Fritz Perls in the 1960s.

Gestalt as an art form

One of the most important themes of Gestalt theory is that the whole is greater than and different from the sum of the component parts. So the whole that is Gestalt counselling and psychotherapy is of course also greater than and different from the sum of the component tasks shown in the holographic diagram (Figure I.2) or described in this book.

Gestalt counselling and psychotherapy are elegant, and can be practised as an art form which requires knowledge of technique, practice and a sense of aesthetic style. All aspects of the therapeutic process, the therapist's openness, ability to relate, manner of talking, responding or moving, the timing of interventions, assessment and diagnostic skills, ability to link one session with another and to relate the moment by moment exploration with the client's background and problems, are part of the overall creative process. Each therapeutic session is like a canvas, a lump of raw clay or a blank piece of paper, through which the client and therapist will co-create a work of art for that day, which will be one creation within the interconnected series of works of art of the whole therapeutic experience between that client and that practitioner.

Each session and each therapeutic relationship has its own flow, shape and form. It is my job as a counsellor or psychotherapist to immerse myself in the craft, science, technique and tradition of my profession, to read, to study, watch and analyse the art of the masters of my craft in the same time-honoured way as artists in the visual or musical arts have always studied. Then standing on the shoulders of my predecessors and drawing on all the technique I have acquired, I try to create my own form and style through the discipline of continual practice, the education of feedback from others, trial and error, willingness to take risks, try things out, make a fool of myself, pick myself up and start all over again in a continual fresh creative learning cycle.

Versatility of Gestalt

Field theoretical integrative Gestalt is an exceptionally versatile approach to counselling and psychotherapy, which can be adapted to most people in many settings. It has, for example, been successfully used with depressed and alcoholic clients,[1] in psychiatric settings, for focused counselling in medical settings and GP surgeries, for people who have eating disorders, for survivors of sexual abuse, in organisational and educational settings and in consultancy. Its interrelational and systemic emphasis makes it particularly suitable for couples counselling and the exploration of family systems and for work with group, organisational and larger community or political systems

Gestalt can be exquisitely finely calibrated, so that the practice of Gestalt may include sitting in silence as a companion to someone who is dying, discussing study skills with a student, offering minuscule amounts of contact to a victim of abuse who trusts no one, playing the fool with someone who never got to play when they were a kid, designing a counselling at work scheme, or becoming involved in social, political or organisational action.

Occasionally people who are new to Gestalt will say that they 'can't do Gestalt with *their* clients' because their clients are 'too fragile', 'too nervous', 'too formal' or 'too fixed in their ways'. This sort of observation is based on a misconception which usually arises from mistaking some of the methods for the approach. Quite rightly they are feeling that they cannot do some of the things which they saw demonstrated in their training workshop with their clients in their work setting, but that does *not* mean that they cannot do Gestalt in that work setting. For Gestalt is not about practitioners getting clients to do things (experiments or any other techniques). It is always about practitioners finding out how and where clients are available for meeting and exploration and then imagining how they can best manifest themselves to meet the person at that point.

In one residential setting I worked with a client who had recently been hospitalised because she was seriously self harming and unable for the time being to lead an ordinary life in the community. She had frequently been physically and mentally abused and deeply shamed, as well as having been

---

1. With alcoholic clients, Carlock et al. (1992); with psychotics, Harris (1992); for focused counselling, Scott in Sills et al. (1995); with people suffering from eating disorders, Merian (1993); with survivors of sexual abuse, Kepner (1995); with organisations, Nevis (1987), Clark and Frazer (1987); with couples and family systems, Wheeler and Backman (1994); Zinker (1978, 1994), Kempler (1973), Papernow (1993); with group and larger community or political systems, Parlett and Hemming (1996).

involved in illegal trading. She certainly wasn't open to any active experimentation and viciously dismissed the psychodrama group which she was
offered as 'stupid' and 'childish'. Nor was she apparently available for contact or
relationship with me or others as she maintained a stony silence most of the
time, looking stormy but denying she had any feelings at all. It could have been
ineffective and possibly even harmful at this stage to ask this young woman to
experiment with seeing what it would be like to make better eye contact with
me or breathe more deeply, or hold a 'two-chair dialogue between different
aspects of herself' (interventions which many Gestaltists would think of as
common 'Gestalt interventions' that attend to present process).

However, she was in residential care voluntarily and coming to see me
more or less regularly; so I decided to believe that she came for something and
to see my job as finding out what she did have energy for and how, if at all, I
could reach out to her. I had to try and try again and be prepared to fail –
which I frequently did – and yet I needed to be open to learn from her as I
failed. Eventually I did find that she could make contact with me by letters in
between the sessions and then by writing and drawing during sessions as well,
that she could externalise her rage by filling the tiny sheets of the only art pad
she would use with solid black and by cutting viciously through the pages of
this same pad with the sharpened points of her pencils. Occasionally she could
visualise herself doing what she wanted to do with me, such as speaking
fluently to me, sometimes thumping my head against the wall, sometimes
approaching me for the attention and affection she yearned for. Our discoveries of how I could be of service to her were infinitely slow and infinitely
painful. Sometimes I had the impression of using a dropper feeder: one tiny
drop of human contact or increased awareness at a time was all she could
stand. Yet we did build some sort of a relationship and she did stop cutting
herself.

This sort of delicate, painstaking, tentative work (or the very
varying work with managers described on p. 114, for instance) is
field theoretical and relational Gestalt because it emerged from
the field conditions that the client and I co-created between us
and because it met the client where she was available for meeting.
Gestalt practitioners of all sorts need to attune themselves to
clients and try to meet clients where clients are available for
meeting. It is intrinsic to the Gestalt approach that practitioners
adjust themselves, their approach and their methods to meet the
client: 'It is the task of the therapist to build a "bridge" to where
the client is. It is certainly not the responsibility of the client to
build a bridge to where the therapist is' (Hycner, 1988: 108).

Historical context

The reader may find that the model presented here differs sub-
stantially from some previous accounts of Gestalt which have

given less emphasis to field, self and relational theories as central and practical dimensions of self exploration and development. For contemporary Gestalt has deepened and matured its own theory and practice in response to changing circumstances in the world, to the changing needs of clients and to the changing climate in the field of counselling and psychotherapy (Yontef, 1991; Parlett and Hemming, 1996).

In the past Gestalt has too often been primarily associated with the style popularised by Fritz Perls in large demonstrations in the 1960s, so that many practitioners have mistakenly believed that Gestalt consists primarily of exercises, experiments and techniques. Brilliant though Fritz Perls's demonstration work often was, it was only one person's style of doing Gestalt and did not represent the theoretical and practical discipline as originally conceived by the founders of Gestalt in the 1940s and 1950s or as it has evolved in the 1970s, 1980s and 1990s.

In the last ten to fifteen years, Gestaltists have taken important and far reaching steps to retain and develop the original creative complexity of Gestalt therapy; to fill the holes or lacks inherent in the Perlsian 1960s style by integrating new developments in counselling and psychotherapy, including some psychoanalytic and psychiatric perspectives. Overall, Gestalt has evolved a system of counselling and psychotherapy which meets the complex and varied needs of the 1990s.

For example, Gestaltists have developed the theory and practice of group therapy (Kepner, 1980; Zinker, 1980) and organisational consultancy (Nevis, 1987; Nevis et al., 1996). They have integrated recent research on child and adult development (Stern, 1985). They have articulated a theory of intersubjective relationships as the essential vehicle for healing and self development (Jacobs, 1989, 1992; Hycner, 1985, 1988, 1990; Yontef, 1993; Jacobs and Hycner, 1995). They have reconsidered field theory as a practical integrating framework that informs all our work, as well as the concepts of contact and moderating contact within the evolving field (Parlett, 1991; Wheeler, 1991). They have evolved systems of diagnosing habitual patterns of behaviour that are compatible with the Gestalt emphasis upon process and immediacy (Delisle, 1988, 1991, 1993b; Yontef, 1993; Melnick and Nevis, 1992). They have attended to the increasing number of clients with fragile self process who came for counselling in all settings, and have developed specialist Gestalt approaches for working with people who manifest varying styles of psychological fragility (such as narcissistic and borderline characteristics) (Tobin, 1982; Greenberg, 1989, 1991, 1995).

Gestaltists have shown how Perlsian Gestalt of the 1960s tended to favour dramatic, episodic pieces of work without paying sufficient attention to the ground that supported those contact episodes or to the reintegration of individual contact episodes into the ground of the self (Wheeler, 1991); and have evolved various models of doing Gestalt therapeutic exploration over time, which ensure that contact episodes are seen within and integrated into the overarching structures and general context of the clients' life process (Shub, 1992; Kepner, 1995).

The relational and field theoretical model of Gestalt described in this book attempts to encompass some of these important recent developments in Gestalt theory and practice.

Theoretical background

If you are already familiar with Gestalt theory, or if you dislike reading theoretical background, you may wish to go straight to section 1 on p. 29.

Gestalt therapy is rooted in a range of creative and theoretical disciplines as varied as modern physics, Eastern religion, existential phenomenology, theatre, psychoanalysis, Gestalt psychology, systems and field theory, bio-energetics and expressive movement. Elsewhere I have traced the origins, evolution and interweaving of these multiple influences upon Gestalt counselling and therapy in some detail (see Clarkson and Mackewn, 1993). Here I offer the briefest description of the evolution of holism, field theory, systems theory and those Gestalt principles of perception which underlie Gestalt therapy and counselling.

Principles of perception within a field orientation

The concept of systems and fields came from early twentieth-century physics which discovered and described the electromagnetic forces of the field surrounding objects, people and creatures. Field theory was adopted by other disciplines such as philosophy, social sciences and psychology. Of particular relevance to the development of Gestalt therapy were the adoptions of field theory by the holistic politician and philosopher Jan Smuts (1995), by the physician Goldstein (1939), by the Gestalt psychologists Koffka (1935), Wertheimer (1925 and 1938) and Kohler (1970), by the social scientist Kurt Lewin (1926, 1935, 1952)

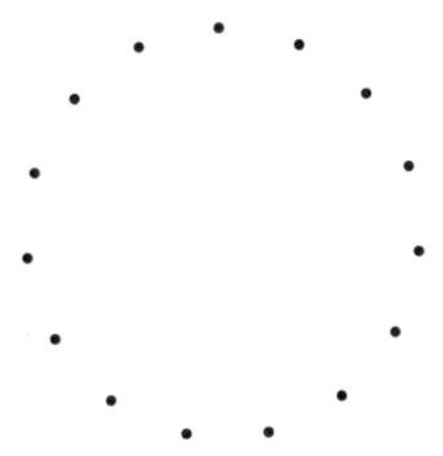

Figure I.5 *Example of an incomplete form or gestalt which we automatically complete or make sense of*

(who developed field theory) and the biologist Ludwig von Bertalanffy (1950) who developed systems theory.

Jan Smuts (1995) developed the physicists' concept that everything has a field, proposing that things, ideas, animals, plants and persons like physical forces have their fields, and are unintelligible if considered without those fields. The Gestalt psychologists, in particular Wertheimer, explored and developed theories of perception within a field orientation, discovering principles of perception which were adopted and adapted both by Kurt Lewin in his subsequent exposition of field theory and by Fritz and Laura Perls in their innovative new approach to psychotherapy. Amongst these principles of perception the human urge to complete and the process of figure and ground are fundamental to Gestalt therapy and are now briefly described.

The urge to complete When we look at individual items and incomplete patterns we automatically and spontaneously complete them, supplying or guessing at the missing parts in order to complete or make meaning of the partial form. Thus when we look at Figure I.5 we do not see fifteen disconnected or meaningless dots, we see a circle or a dotted circle. We see a completed 'figure' or gestalt. The German word gestalt means a whole or a complete pattern, form or configuration, which cannot be broken without destroying its nature. We make patterns and wholes of our experience: we have a spontaneous urge to complete or make meaning out of perceptual stimuli.

Psychologically also we organise our world (or field) in a similar fashion – we organise experience into meaningful wholes and we have a strong and inherent urge to complete or make meaning of our emotional life. We want to see completed emotional 'figures' or 'gestalten' against the background of the rest of the field. When we do so, we experience closure – we feel emotional satisfaction, integration, insight and completion or alternatively we experience grieving, insight, letting go and subsequent closure. When we are unable to organise our experience to make sense or to achieve some sort of closure, we feel dis-ease or discomfort. People tend to remember unfinished situations better than finished ones (Zeigarnik, 1927) and they have a natural tendency to resume and complete unfinished tasks (Ovsiankina, 1928) and make meaning out of incomplete information and situations.

Principle of figure and ground   The concept of figure and ground explains the process by which people organise their perceptions to form configurations which they endow with meaning. People don't apprehend the whole of themselves and their surroundings in one undifferentiated mass; they select and focus upon something they are interested in and this thing, person or process then appears as a bright figure against a dim background. People differentiate the field into those things which are relevant to the object of their interest and those which are not. As soon as their interest changes, they reconfigure the field, so that the first object of interest recedes into the background while something else becomes figural. This principle of perception has often been explicated and illustrated by the well-known picture of the vases/ faces. This book concentrates on exploring the psychological differentiation or organisation of the field according to people's past experience and expectations (see pp. 54 and 93).

Kurt Lewin took the Gestalt psychology model beyond the world of laboratory testing, developing the Gestalt psychologists' concept of the field and principles of visual perceptions and applying them to the more complex realm of everyday life. In particular, Lewin emphasised the fact that individuals actively organise or constellate their field and make meaning of their experience, according to their current needs and to the prevailing conditions in which they find themselves, and he underlined that events and people can thus only be understood as a whole and in context.

The founders of Gestalt therapy – Fritz and Laura Perls and Paul Goodman – extended the Gestalt principles of perception and Lewin's field theory. Gathering holistic field notions from a wide range of sources, they applied them to the field of psychological health and disturbance, developing a practical form of psychotherapy based on their extension of these principles. For example they developed the psychological concepts of self–other regulation, contact, interruptions to contact, unfinished business and fixed gestalt to explain psychological health and disturbance and created a therapy which offered uniquely imaginative and creative ways to complete or resolve people's unfinished business and free them up to move on with their life. I will briefly describe these concepts, as a knowledge of them is an essential background to this book.

Self–other regulation and the emotional organisation of the field

People have physical and emotional needs and a natural urge to regulate themselves and meet those needs. They organise their experience, sensation, images, energy, interest and activity around their needs until they have met or otherwise resolved them. Once a need is met or resolved, it recedes into the background, allowing people to be at rest until a new need or interest emerges and the cycle starts over again. The process of self–other regulation does not ensure that people can always satisfy their needs. Often the environment simply does not currently offer the needed element or quality. Closure can also be achieved by acknowledging the unfulfilled need and experiencing and expressing the emotions evoked by the impossibility of meeting the need. Such emotions might include frustration, grief, disappointment.

Perls used to claim that if the individual had a conflict of needs then the dominant need would take precedence, citing the example of the dehydrated corporal in the desert whose need for water completely obliterated his interest in promotion. However, recent Gestalt therapists have extended and greatly enhanced the concept of self–other regulation by describing the complexity of our human needs and desires: in a complex field people often don't have one dominant desire but experience genuinely competing values and desires and they are thus sometimes unable to resolve their desires but may seek acceptable and sometimes painful compromises in complex field conditions. Melnick et al. (1995) give the example of Ilsa and Rick in the movie *Casablanca*. Ilsa, who is married to another man has finally agreed to run off with Rick. Just as they are about to achieve their longed for escape together, Rick does a dramatic turnaround, telling a stunned Ilsa that she must go with her husband, explaining that if they go off together she would regret it, 'maybe not today, maybe not tomorrow, but soon and for the rest of your life'. Melnick et al. add a new twist to the plot by reminding their audience that things aren't that simple because Rick could equally have said 'if we do *not* go off together, we'll regret it, maybe not tomorrow, but soon, and for the rest of our lives'. Either decision is likely to generate joy as well as sorrow. Sometimes there is no way out, no dominant need or satisfactory conclusion.

In the 1960s Fritz Perls expounded a rather self-centred version of self–other regulation, which seemed to prioritise the hedonistic needs of the individual over those of the community. However, the early Gestalt literature recognised that as people are essentially social and relational beings, forming an interactive whole with their environment, their self regulation must inherently involve consideration of other people and of that environment. The Gestalt theory of self regulation encompasses, and has always encompassed, the whole irreducible complexity of the individual within the field and could perhaps more consistently be called self–other regulation, as it is here.

The individualistic stance that Fritz Perls glorified in his ode to Gestalt 'I do my thing and you do your thing' is a reductionistic misrepresentation of Gestalt self–other regulation, probably meant to shock or shake fixed attitudes. Even Perls at other times spoke in terms of the interdependence of individual and community:

> The man who can live in concernful contact with his society, neither being swallowed up by it nor withdrawing from it completely, is the well-integrated man . . . Our approach . . . sees the human being as simultaneously and by nature both an individual and a member of the group. (Perls, 1976: 26, 52)

The needs of the group and of the environment are as much the subject matter of Gestalt field theory as the needs of the individual (Clarkson, 1991b; E. Polster, 1993). Commonality and individuality are interconnected polarities within the field and we need to be open to and prepared to explore both poles of the individual–communal continuum in the therapeutic relationship (Fox, 1994).

Cycle of self/other contact

Perls crystallised the sequence of organismic self–other regulation into what he called the 'cycle of the interdependency of organism and environment' (1969a). This cycle has since been renamed 'the process of contact', 'the cycle of contact', 'the cycle of awareness' and 'the cycle of gestalt formation and destruction'. Long-winded though it is, I like Perls's original name because it reminds us of

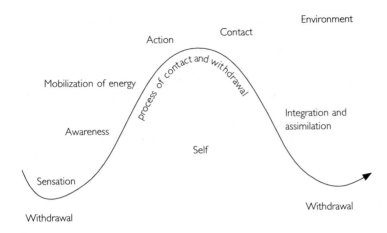

Figure I.6 *Interactive cycle of contact – withdrawal of organism and environment (inspired by Zinker, 1978)*

the intrinsic interdependence of people and their environment in a way that has been rather lost in the subsequent titles.[2]

The cycle of the interdependence of the organism and environment (or the interactive contact cycle)[2] describes the phases in the formation of a single figure of interest/need against the background of the rest of the field in the overall process of self–other regulation (see Figure I.6). It illustrates the phases of a single episode of contact between the individual and the environment. Although it has frequently been illustrated as a circle, I propose that Zinker's diagram of a wave better illustrates the fluid, organic rising and falling of the formation and destruction of a figure of interest.

Waves of contact and withdrawal can be short – for example when we hug another person or do our teeth – or longer, as when we engage or are engaged with a large experience such as writing a book, studying for a degree, mourning the loss of a parent or raising a child. The longer cycles of contact and withdrawal will encompass many shorter cycles within the overall undertaking or experience. Human life is made up of waves of contact and withdrawal – we all go through many waves every day, responding to the stimulus of an inner sensation, such as hunger or loneliness, or to an outer disturbance such as noise, or a call from a friend.

2. Zinker (1994) has recently called it the interactive cycle, which does capture the interdependence of the original title.

The phases of figure formation and destruction in a single contact episode have been differentiated as sensation; awareness; mobilisation; action; contact or expression; integration and assimilation; withdrawal. We pass or flow through each of these phases in each wave of contact. A simple example of brushing teeth illustrates the sequence of the phases in the interaction with the environment: I feel a stale sensation in my mouth and at the same time register that it is 8 a.m. and I have not done my teeth (sensation and awareness phase); I go upstairs to the bathroom and put toothpaste on my brush (mobilisation phase); I start to brush my teeth (action phase); I become temporarily absorbed in the brushing, aware of the white foam, the freshness in my mouth and the urge to clean all the hidden surfaces (contact phase); I finish brushing, rinse my mouth, run my tongue over my teeth and enjoy the sensation of smooth cleanliness (integration and assimilation). I put my toothbrush away and leave the bathroom (withdrawal phase).

A more personal and emotional example illustrates the phases of the emotional cycle of contact and withdrawal: Later in the day I remember that my son is about to leave home and suddenly my heart aches with sadness and loneliness (sensation and awareness); I turn to my friend and tell her what I feel (awareness, mobilisation and action) and as I do so hot tears well up in my throat, I cry and describe how nineteen years seem to have flown by in a second (contact); my crying complete, I feel a return of the sense of excitement and anticipation with which I have also been viewing this life transition (integration and assimilation) and I turn my attention to other matters for the time being (withdrawal). The interactive cycle of contact and withdrawal has been well explicated elsewhere (Zinker, 1978, 1994; Polster and Polster, 1974; Clarkson, 1989; Clarkson and Mackewn, 1993) and is further illustrated in practical examples in this book, especially p. 104.

An individual's process of figure formation and destruction is complex, lively and continually flowing, and it interacts with the other elements and processes of the field, which are of course also in continual flux. Sometimes people's interest will change spontaneously and the first figure will recede to be replaced by a new more absorbing aspect of themselves or their field. Other times they will be obliged to interrupt themselves and temporarily set aside the figure of interest, especially if it involves a long project.

A series of waves, as shown in Figure I.7 illustrates this sort of continual ebb and flow of the individual's process of contact with the environment in a never-ending sequence of gestalt formation and destruction. In each wave of contact, the individual manifests the self differently in response to each different aspect of the

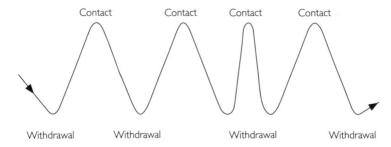

Figure I.7 *Waves of contact and withdrawal or figure formation and destruction in contact episodes*

environment. Of course there are also often mini waves of contact within one larger cycle of contact (see p. 77 and Appendix 6).

Complex cycles of self/other contact in group, system and organisational work

Over the years many Gestalt theorists (Nevis, 1987; Nevis et al., 1996; Kepner, 1980; Zinker, 1980, 1994; Bentley, 1997; Clayton, 1997) have developed this simple Gestalt cycle of contact and withdrawal into a more complex model of contact and withdrawal, which attempts to map the complexities of human experience in real-life situations. These more complex models of the process of contact and withdrawal are used to describe and illustrate the processes in small systems (such as families and couples) groups and organisational life. They have thus broadened the possible application of the Gestalt cycle of contact and withdrawal from the individual to group, system and large system processes in organisations and communities – Appendix 6 discusses and illustrates the complex representations of the process of contact and withdrawal, in group, systems and organisational work.

Health

From a Gestalt viewpoint, psychologically healthy people are self-regulating individuals, able to respond flexibly to changing circumstances and to support themselves in many respects while accepting mutual interdependence with other people and the environment. They can strike a balance between looking after their own individual needs and caring for the needs of other people and their community, recognising their interdependence with the environment and caring for it as well. They take responsibility for the choices they make in life and especially for the meaning they give their life and they experience their ability to actualise themselves within the limits of their life circumstances. They are potentially aware of and in touch with many aspects of themselves and their environment and are continuously making creative adjustments at the contact boundary between themselves and the world around them, responding to, acting upon, influencing, interacting with and withdrawing from the environment in order to meet their own needs, without either being swallowed up by society or impinging too heavily upon it: 'The ordinary state of affairs for the normal organism is to move fluidly from a state of need arousal to a state of need satisfaction, from tension to relaxation, from figural attention to homogenised disinterest. Well-functioning people are the ongoing process itself and do not experience themselves as static objects' (Zinker, 1994: 50).

Health is not just personal and intrapsychic but is also contextual and interrelational (or intersubjective). The novel *David Copperfield* offers a fine illustration of the intersubjective nature of health and character assessment. David is found by most of his family and acquaintances to be good humoured, generous and flexible, and he behaves accordingly. But his stepfather and step-aunt repeatedly condemn him as sullen, withdrawn, bad and mad. In these circumstances the young David does of course become extremely withdrawn and eventually runs away, undoubtedly convincing his stepfather (but not the reader) that he is indeed bad and mad. David eventually finds and lives with his aunt, Betsy Trotwood who adores him. In these circumstances he flourishes and comes to love her in return.

Some people seem to be able to retain their ability to function creatively even in adverse conditions (such as opposition from others, family breakdown, captivity, starvation) while others have less self support (or inner strength) and require a more encouraging environment before they can act and react creatively and cohesively. But all of us (if sufficiently supported) have the innate ability to develop greater and more flexible skills for interacting with our circumstances.

Psychological disturbance or the interruption of self–other regulation

Disturbance is the loss of flexibility to adjust creatively to changing conditions (or to contact and interact creatively with the environment). Psychological disturbance, like psychological health, is not purely individual but also contextual and inter-relational and therefore varies in different circumstances. Thus individuals may mainly function in an aware fashion, in touch with the reality of their world, other people and themselves and responding flexibly. But in certain specialised conditions, those same individuals may lose touch with the reality of the present and fall back on fixed or habitual patterns of behaviour which were once creative solutions to some past difficulties but which do not relate to present events.

Perls, Hefferline and Goodman suggested that psychological disturbance results from chronic interruption to contact or disruption in organismic self–other regulation. They developed the concepts of unfinished psychological business and emotional fixed gestalts and proposed that people have six main styles of interrupting (or modifying) their self–other regulation. Here I describe the concepts of unfinished business, fixed gestalt and the interruptions or moderations of contact as they apply to Gestalt counselling and therapy.

Many of us have been taught to ignore our own unfolding process of awareness and the ebb and flow of our own naturally arising interest and excitement within the field, in favour of external regulation or internal pressures associated not with the reality of the present but with messages from our past which are now often out of our awareness. These messages may develop into fixed patterns of behaviour which were once useful but are now automatically continued even though they have become redundant or even counter-productive.

Such fixed patterns of behaviour arise as the result of an accumulation of unresolved situations from the past (unfinished business) and of premature solutions to problems which have become habitual and unaware (fixed gestalts). The concepts of unfinished business and fixed gestalts will now be explained in more detail as they are the key processes by which the individual's development may become disturbed.

Unfinished business

The urge to complete the cycle of contact and withdrawal is natural and compelling. Ideally people take action to make full contact with their current need or interest. If they are able to be in full contact with the subject of their interest, they will withdraw satisfied. If for some reason people are *not* able to make contact with whatever is attracting them, the gestalt will be incomplete. Until they are able to complete, acknowledge or mourn the interrupted cycle, individuals are likely to interpret their world in terms of the incomplete gestalt. The need (whether in or out of awareness) organises the field (see pp. 49 and 54).

Of course in everyday life, human beings do experience multiple ordinary interruptions to the fulfilment of their needs and they are able to tolerate a considerable delay in the need fulfilment cycle. By bracketing off the need which cannot immediately be met, they are able to divert their attention to other things. However, if the need is important, the incomplete gestalt of the interrupted need exerts a strong attraction and influence – as long as it remains unfulfilled, or unacknowledged, it is calling out for attention. So bracketing it off for later attention requires energy. The more times people are forced to interrupt their needs, the more energy is required to bracket off the unfinished business which is now accumulating. People who are using energy (awarely or unawarely) in ignoring the urgency of a number of pressing unresolved situations do not have all their attention for the current situation. The accumulation of unfinished business is thus instrumental in the development of growth disturbance or neurosis. As long as people remain in touch with the original need, however, there is still a possibility of it being resolved (or acknowledged and mourned) quite naturally some time in the future.

Fixed gestalt

If on the other hand people's needs are consistently ignored or misinterpreted, an emotional rupture occurs in the relational field between themselves and others. When such a rupture occurs, people are likely to feel awkward, misunderstood, embarrassed, or as if they are 'wrong' – which are all feelings closely associated with shame. Initially people thus thwarted will probably strive to meet the unmet need, or close the incomplete gestalt. But if the ruptures in the relationship between say children and their caretakers persist, the original need loses dynamism, is distorted or 'fixed' in an adaptation or fixed gestalt. Not feeling sufficiently supported or met by those around them to stick with their own needs and feel them to be legitimate, people adapt as best they can in the difficult circumstances: 'The unfinished situations cry for solutions, but if they are barred from awareness, neurotic symptoms and neurotic character formation will be the result' (Perls, 1948: 573).

If the loss of support for the children's real needs and feelings is perpetuated, the children may lose touch with their primary needs and feelings and persistently respond to circumstances in this adapted way that is false to their true nature. A 'false' (Tobin, 1982) adapted or introjected sense of self develops:

> George's mother and father died when he was a child and George spontaneously clung to his grandfather, begging him not to leave. When his clinging fingers were disengaged and his echoing wails hushed, he at first increased his efforts to hold on to his grandfather, but when these were repeatedly dismissed, he lost hope and gave up. Many similar experiences occurred in George's early life in which his need to express his grief and be comforted was dismissed. To the best of his ability, he killed off or 'fixed' the needs to weep or depend on others when he was deeply distressed.

Because people are holistic organisms, Gestalt stresses that the fixing of the gestalt involves their whole being, that is the physical, emotional and cognitive (or meaning-making) processes. Physiologically people may restrict their breathing as a way of cutting off from a sensation of emotional or physical pain; cognitively they explain the lack of support as best they can with little information. The original feeling of need to be held and comforted in his loss is replaced by a substitute feeling, such as 'I'm too much for other people' which the child finds easier to tolerate and which protects him from the pain of rejection.

> George breathed shallowly and believed that he would only be loved if he was good and controlled. Experiences of sadness were associated with people's disappearance or desertion and thus cut off or diverted almost before they began.

When a natural need is not met but becomes fixed in the manner described, the need may be distorted, exaggerated, denied or displaced. If the original need is denied, it is pushed out of awareness and forgotten;

> So as an adult George still said, 'I'm fine' even when his father-in-law died and his wife left him alone to care for his dementing mother-in-law while she went away on an extended holiday.

If the original need is displaced on to others it may then be 'met' by looking after and supporting them. So George looked after everyone in his family.

Such experiences of being misunderstood, ignored or shamed for legitimate human needs are likely to occur in the lives of most people at some time to a greater or lesser extent. The more intense the experience of mismatch between the felt need and the environmental response, the more frequently reinforced the sense of shame or lack of support, the greater is likely to be the impact upon people's development and habitual ways of reaching out to others and contacting their environment (see Appendix 6).

Even though the psychological disturbance, adaptation or fixed gestalt may have originated in past circumstances, it is perpetuated in the present, in that the fixed patterns of contacting are manifested in the present and can therefore be studied and undone in the present. Themes associated with the denied need are likely to come up again and again in a person's life and he or she is likely to keep getting into situations in which the denied need is unconsciously reactivated – as though it is clamouring for attention. George for example became involved in bereavement counselling without any awareness that this was because of his own unresolved feelings, as well as because of his genuine wish to help others.

These situations restimulate the traumatic past experience and all the associated environmental conditions and feelings. When this happens, people's immediate response is often to avoid getting any deeper into the problematic areas, while their learned adapted responses may emerge automatically as a way to deflect from painful old feelings being reawakened. They are no longer reacting to the present as it is but they are projecting their past experience on to the present and reacting as though the present circumstances were as dangerous, as potentially unsupported and shaming as the past ones. They are out of touch and their behaviour, thinking and feeling have become less flexible, more rigid and stereotyped. Their unaware preoccupation with the denied need is a healthy innate urge to seek resolution and closure. But because the original need has been 'fixed' and pushed out of awareness, the automatic adapted response usually carries the seeds of its own failure and people often complete the adapted need cycle repetitiously, experiencing no real sense of resolution or closure because the denied need remains untouched.

People's fixed patterns of adapting and reacting to present circumstances as though they were the past are often so habitual and unaware that they do not realise that they are responding in a rigid fashion or that they may now have alternative choices which could be more effective or life enhancing. A central part of the art of Gestalt therapy lies in helping people recognise for themselves how, when and to what extent their present styles of configuring (or interpreting) and contacting the environment are reality based and flexible and how and when they are out of touch, rigid or ineffective.

Styles of contact

Gestalt counselling and therapy study the individual at the contact boundary between the self and the environment, the relationship between the person and the situation, for it is here that client and counsellor can notice the patterns of how people connect (or fail to connect) to their surroundings and circumstances and thus learn about how they meet (or fail to meet) their needs. A fixed gestalt involves denying or displacing a human need and requires effort and energy, even though the active effort, like the original need, is kept out of awareness. People maintain fixed gestalts by unconsciously developing individual styles of contact on the contact continuums shown in Figure I.8.

These styles of moderating contact have frequently been described as disturbances or interruptions to contact, and have been extensively explained as such elsewhere.[3] Here I will give only the briefest of definitions of the specialist terms for anyone who is not familiar with them and then I will introduce a radical change in perspective in how these contact processes are now viewed in Gestalt theory and practice. *Projection* involves denying or repressing a quality or feeling and attributing it to other people or institutions. *Introjection* involves taking into our system aspects of the environment (such as food or ideas) without assimilating them. *Confluence* occurs when two people or two parts of the field flow together with no sense of differentiation. *Retroflection* means doing to oneself what one would really like to do to other people or the environment. *Deflection* involves a turning aside from direct contact with other people or aspects of the environment. It may involve indirectness in outgoing overtures which the person initiates or a turning aside from overtures of contact from others. *Desensitisation* is the process by which we numb ourselves to the sensations in our bodies or to external stimuli. *Egotism* is the slowing down of spontaneity by deliberate introspection and self vigilance to make sure that there is no risk of making a mistake, being silly and so on.

Traditionally in the Gestalt literature, these styles of contact have been seen as processes that are primarily interruptive of

---

3. Polster and Polster (1974); Zinker (1978); Clarkson and Mackewn (1993: 72–8).

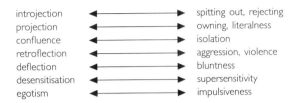

Figure I.8   *Bipolar continuums of contact style*

contact. Wheeler (1991) and Melnick and Nevis (1992) have pointed out that people do not actually interrupt contact but rather moderate the flow of their contact, giving them a particular contact style (see p. 105). This book argues that the so-called 'interruptions' to contact can more meaningfully be seen as dimensions or styles of contact within the overall field, where either the traditional 'interruption to contact' or its polar opposite (as shown in Figure I.8) or any position along the bipolar continuum between the two may interrupt or support contact (see p. 106 for a fuller discussion of this changed perspective). The perspective of bipolar continuums of contact style makes Gestalt a much more flexible and adaptable approach, suitable for a wide range of people and circumstances. The new perspective allows practitioners and clients to consider and explore the client's contact styles from moment to moment and discover how and in what ways they may be supporting or undermining the client's intentions at any given time.

So, for example, retroflection is seen as neither intrinsically good or bad but just one style of moderating contact. Whether it is useful or dysfunctional will depend upon the circumstances of the individual. Retroflection is usually useful to a person who feels murderous rage and contains it. But it may not be useful to someone who is tense and sleepless because they are unable to cry or safely express frustration. Either retroflection, or its opposite, aggression, may support or interrupt contact. Some people retroflect too much and need to learn to undo retroflection in therapy while others who are prone to explosions of violent or damaging rage may need to explore and learn how to retroflect, or contain themselves, in the therapy process.

Similarly, both confluence and individualism can be important parts of our full repertoire of behaviours and feelings. But if we are habitually and unawarely either confluent or isolated, the rigidity of the response is likely to interfere with our varied and lively living in the moment.

I

Attending to Beginnings: Initial
Conditions and Existential Meeting

1 Using initial session(s) for meeting, clarification and two-way assessment

The beginning stages of counselling and therapy are especially significant as initial conditions and people's first impressions of each other generally make a great impact and may set the tone for much of the subsequent interaction between them. The beginning of any significant life experience can stir up people's memories of previous beginnings (such as the first day at school, significant meetings or interviews). Sometimes these earlier memories were very emotional – so the new beginning of counselling in the present may carry some of the emotional charge of those past events and the participants may be unusually sensitised to the present conditions and to the verbal and non-verbal interactions. If such past memories are triggered in a defined way then people can articulate them clearly but frequently these memories may not yet have emerged into full awareness and may therefore influence the present in broad or unconscious ways.

Furthermore some clients may feel nervous about making an initial contact with a counsellor and may well be coping with the unhappy feelings or difficult problems which bring them to counselling or therapy. All are likely to be highly sensitive to the response of the counsellor or therapist that they approach for help.

Although each therapeutic counsellor evolves their own particular style of handling the delicate stages of initial contact and initial sessions, some universal skills and qualities are identifiable (see Rowan, 1983; Kopp, 1977; Yalom, 1985 and Clarkson, 1989 for some varying accounts of this stage). These universals include sensitivity to the importance of the initial contact and initial sessions, receptivity, warmth, the ability to put the other person at their ease, to build rapport, to show empathy and acceptance, to draw people out, to clarify expectations; the capacity to explain what you can offer and help clients articulate what they want, to negotiate terms and conditions and establish some sort of a contract for working or to make a good referral (if appropriate), to explore issues of trust and mistrust and to think about the person's likely capacity to benefit from the therapeutic counselling you can offer.

Of course initial contact between counsellor and client often begins before you meet. The client and counsellor may have heard about each other through other people or may even have met before. They may speak on the phone. Clients will see the building where you work and your waiting room before they meet you. Be aware that all of these pre-impressions will effect your reactions to each other:

> One woman contrasted her two experiences of going for counselling – the first time she went to a pleasant counselling agency where the walls were painted in neutral colours and there were a few prints on the wall which to her seemed 'bland'; the second time she went to a family centre with a multi-cultural philosophy where the walls were painted in bright colours and there were pictures of people from different races, quotations from Martin Luther King and Nelson Mandela. She described her totally different reaction. In the first setting she had felt, 'OK, but where am I?' In the second setting she felt a strong bodily reaction of 'Yes'.

Other clients might have exactly the opposite response to these two settings. There is no one way to decorate or organise your work room but it is important to realise that the way you do so is likely to have varying impact on different clients.

From the very beginning of your actual meeting, whatever you do or say (and *how* you do or say it) is likely to make a significant impact and provide a model for subsequent exchanges that can be helpful or otherwise to the overall process.

In any initial contact, people often unawarely reveal their key issues and their crucial patterns of interacting with others; so it is important to be especially attentive to the way clients approach you and negotiate a meeting, to their mannerisms, facial expressions, gestures and body language, while also noticing your own ongoing emotional and physiological responses. These may offer a flavour of how this person approaches the world and how other people react to him or her (see p. 47). It is also worth being aware that you are likely to be drawing upon your own typical patterns of relating in a similar manner and thus unconsciously influencing the way that the client enters into the dance of relationship with you.

You can use the initial session(s) to meet a wide variety of important and complex interrelated responsibilities (see Box 1.1).

Box 1.1   Complex interrelated tasks of initial session(s)

Mutual tasks or responsibilities
Meeting existentially person to person;
Establishing consensus about the client's needs and aims for coun-
    selling, whether these are specific or broad;
Discussing possible ways of exploring those needs and aims;
Discussing possible forms of therapy (e.g. group; individual; family,
    etc.) as well as possible methods and approaches;
Establishing initial contracts and working conditions.

Counsellor tasks or responsibilities
Explaining the counselling process; modelling the Gestalt approach (if
    appropriate);
Assessing whether counselling is likely to be helpful to the client and
    whether you are the right counsellor
Assessing the client's suitability for counselling with you in your
    working circumstances;
Noticing first impressions of client's process of contacting, supporting
    self, etc. (see pp. 104 and 224).

Client tasks or responsibilities
Explaining what brings you to counselling and what you hope to gain
    from it;
Assessing whether this is a suitable approach to counselling and
    whether this is the right counsellor for you;
Asking any questions you want or need to ask in order to help you
    decide: about counsellor's qualifications, experience, ways of
    working, attitudes, fees, etc.

*No hierarchy of importance is implied. All of these aspects need to be
attended to throughout initial session(s).*

When possible allow yourself some flexibility regarding the
number of exploratory session(s), so that you can prioritise
meeting the individual and yet have time to explore the necessary
areas. Often one exploratory session is sufficient but sometimes
the client's need to be heard is so great that you may decide to
postpone some of the negotiating of conditions; other times either
you or the client may still not be certain about suitability or
compatibility by the end of one exploratory session, and a second
exploratory session or a mini-commitment (Elton Wilson, 1996)
can be useful.

Existential meeting between two people

Gestalt counselling and therapy are seen as a dialogue, existential meeting or encounter between two people. It is thus central to the Gestalt approach that we do not have a pre-established agenda but endeavour to start the therapeutic process afresh with each new client, allowing the 'between' (p. 80) to emerge in a person to person relationship, for there can be no prescription for existential meeting (Clarkson, 1989). So we try to meet clients where they are available for meeting, accepting and exploring their individual phenomenological truth (p. 58) about themselves and their reasons for coming to counselling or therapy. You can show that you are willing to try to see things from their viewpoint by entering imaginatively into their reality and problems. From the beginning, you can meet the client person to person by experimentally sharing some of your own responses (see p. 86) and noting how clients respond. You can model an active partnership (where clients share responsibility for the counselling process) in various ways, such as by consulting clients about how they think counselling could best help them, what has helped them in life so far, etc.

Aims, contracts and commitments

Awareness and specific goals: two poles of a continuum

The primary aim of Gestalt counselling and therapy is the development of awareness through a sustained enquiry into clients' subjective experience, honouring all aspects of their being and their circumstances, rather than just focusing upon their problems or symptoms (see pp. 61, 65, 113, 133, 152 and 179).

This emphasis upon the development of awareness does not preclude the need for Gestalt counsellors to clarify what clients are searching for or hoping to gain from the counselling process. It is, of course, important to establish a sense of rapport and model attention to awareness. But these can be balanced with an exploration of clients' current needs and some negotiation of the likely means of exploring those needs.

Some clients come with clear agendas and specific goals but many clients come with broad feelings of dis-ease, unhappiness, confusion or dissatisfaction and have a rather general hope that counselling or therapy may be able to help. One way to help such clients articulate their aims is to listen to their stories, summarise what you have heard and say what you understand to be their longing or need, checking whether or not the client feels you have 'got' what he or she is saying. Other ways of exploring clients' needs include asking them to describe how they are currently feeling, what life circumstances have contributed to their coming for counselling now or what they hope to gain from it.

Some form of contracting is ethical, practical and therapeutic. It is often helpful to distinguish in your own mind whether a client has come in order to achieve specific outcomes or to explore their overall process in a broader way – some practitioners distinguish between outcome or goal-oriented contracts and process-oriented contracts, which explore broad aspects of the clients' process (Sills, 1997). This distinction is not clear-cut, for many people start counselling with clear goals and when they have fulfilled those goals they decide that they want to explore in a broader way, while others are quite content to finish once they have achieved their initial specific goals (see Dryden and Feltham, 1994 and Sills, 1997, for much fuller discussions of contracting).

Initial discussion can only surface those needs of which the client is already conscious and ready to speak. However skilled you become at facilitating initial sessions, clients' less conscious wishes will only surface after time and as you establish a trusting relationship. By encouraging the articulation of specific wishes and two-way negotiation at an early stage, you will be modelling the respectful, active and equal partnership which is central to Gestalt counselling.

Clarify boundaries and conditions (form of therapy times, place and fees) for counselling, indicating which conditions are negotiable and which are non-negotiable. It is often a good idea to arrange an initial time commitment, with a review at the end of those sessions and a decision about where next – recommitment/ finish/referral. New aims and goals tend to emerge as the therapeutic exploration proceeds and as previously unconscious wishes come to awareness (see Shub, 1992), so you will probably need to review your work and the therapeutic contract at intervals (Dryden and Feltham, 1994; Elton Wilson, 1996). Reviews give you both a chance to reconsider your overall work together, recontract as new and previously unconscious wishes surface, and they give clients an opportunity to voice dissatisfactions, celebrations or requests which they might otherwise overlook.

Leaving contract

I also suggest you discuss the client's eventual leaving at or near the beginning of counselling and establish a simple leaving contract. For example I ask clients who come for focused counselling to agree not to leave without notice but to return for at least one full session if they decide they want to leave, in order to give themselves and me a chance to check out (and resolve if possible) any misunderstandings which may have arisen between us. If people come for long-term therapy, or switch to long-term therapy, I arrange a proportionately longer period for leaving.

The example given below illustrates just one client's way of negotiating and using a counselling process and is not meant to be typical.

> Margaret wanted to get a better sense of herself. The therapeutic counsellor accepted this broad aim and then later in the session (when some rapport had been established between them) asked some exploratory questions to find out what Margaret meant by the phrase. It turned out that Margaret had difficulty in saying no to people and wanted to 'learn to protect' herself. The counsellor proposed that they start with a short commitment of six sessions and the quite limited goal of seeing whether or not Gestalt counselling as it evolved between them could effectively help her to learn to protect herself. Margaret was very relieved to be able to start work on something tangible and related to her overall aim, which had seemed important but overwhelming to her.
>
> At the sixth session, they reviewed the work done. Margaret had by now got a much greater awareness of what therapeutic exploration could offer and had also increased her awareness of how she failed to protect herself in her everyday interactions and she decided that the counselling *could* help her learn to protect herself better. So she and the counsellor renegotiated a further three-month commitment with the agreed extended aim of developing Margaret's *means* of self protection. At the end of this three-month period Margaret decided to take a break and then six months later continued in longer term, broader therapeutic exploration in order to find out how better self protection could contribute to a more definite sense of herself.

It is important to balance your exploration of clients' goals with discussion of the fact that Gestalt's primary aim is the development of awareness as a means of increasing people's choice and flexibility. You may also wish to explain that our experience suggests that attention to the whole person and the development of their awareness of their overall way of interacting in the world is a more effective means of bringing about change than just concentrating on their specific goals or the bits that they want to change (see pp. 61, 65, 113, 133, 152 and 179).

Explaining counselling and psychotherapy

Research (Walker and Patten, 1990) indicates that clients value being given explanations about counselling and therapy highly, whereas counsellors tend to underestimate this need. How much you explain depends on the clients. If an individual knows very little about counselling, they may not need to know much about the nuances of the different approaches. But they will normally appreciate some information about what counselling and therapy are and what to expect. At some point you may also choose to say a few sentences about Gestalt and to make interventions which model the rich, holistic range of the Gestalt approach and notice how clients respond to this range as part of your assessment of whether or not you are likely to be a suitable counsellor for them and of how you may need to modify or enhance your style to work with them (Mackewn, 1995). Don't overwhelm clients with information, but don't overlook the need to explain.

Assessing clients' and your own suitability

It is not in the client's interests for you to take on and work with people for whom you do not have the training, background, skills or appropriate level of environmental support needed. Some Gestalt (and other humanistic) counsellors and therapists feel hesitant to assess clients' suitability for counselling or therapy with them because they fear that assessment is incompatible with developing a dialogical relationship. I suggest that such a hesitation is based upon a misunderstanding of the dialogical relationship which includes a rhythmic alternation between 'I–It' and 'I–Thou' styles of relating (Hycner, 1985) (see pp. 81–5).

When making an assessment of a client's suitability, multiple factors in the interpersonal field need to be considered, such as the realism of their goals and expectations, the quality of their contact with you, their contact with consensual reality, their level of self support and of environmental support, their ego strength, their ability to invest energy and commitment in the therapeutic process, any levels of risk to themselves or others; diagnosis (see pp. 103 and 226); your cultural and social background, your training and experience, your environmental support and the setting in which you work.

In order to consider the factors mentioned you will probably need to find out both background and current information about clients during the initial session(s), as well as attending to intuitive hunches and non-verbal information. Appendix 1 offers an example of a Gestalt intake sheet, which may help you think in Gestalt terms about the relevant factors and both the verbal and non-verbal information you gather. It also provides an example of a simple initial contract form.

Clients are not simply suitable or unsuitable for counselling or therapy – the question of suitability is very complex and involves an interaction between the client's needs and what you can offer. When thinking about a client's suitability you need to be clear about the range of your skills and your ability to decide what type or level of therapeutic counselling is suitable for which clients and to put your decision into action. While anyone in difficulties can benefit from support, not everyone can benefit from deeper exploratory therapeutic work. Brown and Pedder (1991) for example have defined supportive counselling as supporting and building on clients' strengths and avoiding challenging their frame of reference, while they describe exploratory therapeutic work as addressing the whole personality structure and exploring the possibilities for change and reintegration in that structure and in the person's functioning.

If you are a counsellor or therapist in training or in any doubt, it is often safer to consult a supervisor before deciding whether or not you can work with a client. Many training courses require such consultation. There can be no ultimate prescriptions for who you can or cannot work with. It depends upon the overall conditions prevalent in the field (see p. 219).

Clients' assessment of your suitability as a counsellor or therapist

Clients also need to assess whether or not you are a suitable practitioner for them. I suggest that as a general principle you explicitly tell clients at the beginning of initial sessions that this is a two-way exploration designed for you both to decide whether or not you are a suitable counsellor or therapist for the client, as well as whether or not you feel you can work with the client. Encourage clients to voice their fears, doubts and expectations as well as their hopes for counselling. Support them in asking questions and clarifying their understanding of what is or may be possible. You may want to say that you are open to the idea of clients meeting other potential counsellors and therapists (if this is feasible) and that you can offer alternative referrals, so that they feel they have a choice. You can develop a good referral list of counsellors, therapists and agencies and see referral as an essential skill in its own right (see Dryden and Feltham, 1994).

Sometimes there really is no choice, in which case you may want to make that explicit.

Forms of therapy

There are several potential forms of counselling and therapy (individual; group; family therapy or couples counselling, for instance). Be aware of these possibilities and consider their suitability for clients, discussing their advantages and disadvantages if appropriate. Examples of individual, group and couples counselling as well as of innovative outreach approaches to therapeutic work are included throughout this book. The complex interactive dynamics of groups are discussed in Appendix 6.

Therapeutic frame, boundaries and containment

The initial conditions arranged for counselling or therapy are sometimes called the therapeutic frame or container. The therapeutic frame holds the therapeutic process and provides containment for self development and the exploration and working through of difficult feelings. It is therefore generally considered advisable to keep the therapeutic frame and the therapeutic role as consistent as possible throughout the counselling process. Sometimes clients want counsellors to alter the initial arrangements or the therapist's role and the therapist often feels tempted to do so out of humanity. Credible though this flexibility is, counsellors need to be aware that too much flexibility regarding boundaries may prevent clients' more intense feelings from emerging in the therapeutic relationship and may mean that strong feelings are dissipated rather than brought into awareness and explored.

At the same time we need to be aware of the inevitable cultural bias of many therapeutic concepts and expectations and may need to be open to sometimes developing new forms of innovative therapeutic work to meet the requirements or values of clients from different cultures and belief systems.

If clients ask you to alter the initial conditions, the holding frame, or your role, I suggest that even very experienced practitioners benefit from asking for time to think about the client's needs and then talking through the complexity of boundary, culture and power issues in consultation or supervision before either acquiescing or refusing.

Key point

Your initial contact and encounter with clients is important and the tone you establish now can crucially affect the subsequent relationship. So prioritise meeting the other person as a person, establishing an initial rapport between you and developing your awareness of their wants, longings and needs. But don't forget to negotiate working conditions and contracts.

II Exploring the Client's Context and Culture

2 Attending to the whole person

Forming a holistic impression of clients in relation to others

A person is at all times a whole person, whose body, emotions, thoughts and perceptions function interrelatedly as one complex relational whole. You cannot divide a person into parts in order to study or treat that person without rendering meaningless the very entity you hope to get to know; for the whole is always more than and different from the sum of its parts. Gestalt's holistic approach affirms the complexity of persons and events within a 'whole-making' universe (Smuts, 1995) and, resisting reductionism, tries to include all the possibly relevant dimensions of the human beings who meet in the counselling or therapy situation. In this way Gestalt differs from some other approaches which emphasise only a few aspects of individuals (such as their current problems *or* their childhood issues, their social problems *or* their birth experiences, their body armour *or* their words).

To work holistically, you could try beholding clients with fresh curiosity and wonder, rather as you might gaze at a beautiful tree, mountain stream or seascape. For to do therapy that is truly responsive to the needs of the other we need to allow ourselves to be touched by the mystery of their whole being. Working in such a profoundly holistic way can feel almost like a form of meditation in which you allow yourself to be fully receptive to clients and how they impact upon you. Although it sounds simple, developing this sort of openness to the other person as a whole is not easy because most of us are trained to make suppositions and classifications, using the knowledge that we have acquired over many years. We are often so full of ideas about what is wrong or how to help that there is little room for just being with the other person as a whole person.

Excluding nothing, remain open to all the possibilities of the experience of meeting this other person. Let yourself experience how their total being touches your essential being, take in their rhythms, hear their voice tones. Each person is like a complex musical composition waiting to be heard. Often the composition has been lost or hidden away through years of abusive or miserable experiences so that the individual is now only playing one or two fragments of the many possible melodies which make up the whole symphony. You need to be open and available to help the beauty of the full orchestral version to emerge in its own way and in its own time.

One good way of developing a holistic overall impression of the individual in their environment is to think of both the individual and their relationship with the environment symbolically. How would you describe this person metaphorically? The symbol or metaphor often conveys the essence or the whole of the person better than an analysis of the individual parts.

> One counsellor described a client as 'a medieval king barricaded in his castle and not realising that the danger had passed'; another saw the client as 'a life split in two'; while another counsellor explained how the client experienced himself as a 'dolphin who is swimming in shark infested waters'.

Observing holistically

You could start by concentrating upon your ability to holistically *observe* and *experience* clients, shuttling your attention from one aspect to another of the rich complexity of the interaction between you. It's important to notice the process as well as the content of the therapeutic exchange, which means paying as much attention to *how* clients talk to you as to what they say; noticing *how* clients enter the room; observing *how* they move, sit, breathe or fidget; being aware of clients' facial expressions and gestures and of how and when these seem to interrelate with the story they are telling. For human beings communicate through their whole beings not just through their words – and their body language may communicate those aspects of themselves that they are less aware of. Each person's whole self conveys distinctive personal messages; so we don't categorise body language by deciding in advance that certain gestures convey certain meanings (in the manner of some popular books). Instead we explore the unique meaning of each individual person's non-verbal as well as verbal self in relationship to the environment.

Sometimes you may just want to notice and register these observations of the client's holistic process; other times you may choose to share your observations with the client. Sharing observations about how clients are talking, breathing or sitting may seem very alien or odd to you if you are new to working actively with people's holistic process and indeed doing so *can be* unhelpful or interruptive; but it can also be extremely revealing and often enriches the work or leads clients to expand their awareness dramatically. There are no fixed rules about whether, when or how it is advisable to share your observations of non-verbal process. Interventions are always field dependent (see p. 48).

Working with microcosms of the whole

It is important not to start attending to different aspects of people's being in an over-analytical or reductionist way but to notice and work with these large and small details of clients' beings *in relationship to the whole person*. Holism proposes that all parts of a person function in a coordinated fashion in the interests of the whole, and that all the different parts are interrelated so that change in any one part will affect the whole of that person. Change in one part creates change in the whole, while change in the whole engenders change in the parts.

Thus if a client learns a new personal melody, completes an unfinished tune or refines an existing one, this will contribute to and change the overall musical composition that makes their whole self. It will also have an impact on those who live in relationship to them – they may have to learn a different song in order to respond. You and clients may explore either the macrocosm of the individual's family or economic history *or* the microcosm of how they use their breathing to support themselves, believing that in both cases the whole of the person will be affected by the work.

You could try imagining that small aspects of a person's current interactions are a microcosm or a fractal of that person's experience in the world – they may represent an underlying pattern of the way they perceive or contact the environment or other people. So for example the way a client relates to food, or to you, or the way a client initiates or ends a session may sometimes be a metaphor for their whole interaction with the environment. If you can help clients work with such fractals of their existence and transform these microscopic processes, they may similarly transform the greater wholes or macroscopic processes of their existence. Figure 2.1 illustrates fractal patterns in the natural world.

Shelley, a tense young woman, was talking to the counsellor in her local medical practice. She sat on the very edge of her chair, leaning anxiously

Figure 2.1   *Self-similar or fractal patterns repeated from the largest to the smallest scale in natural systems. (Katsushika Hokusai,* The Great Wave, *William S. and John T. Spaulding Collection; courtesy, Museum of Fine Arts, Boston.) A fractal is an irregular curve which occurs repeatedly in natural systems from their largest to their smallest scale. The study of fractal geometry reveals that many natural systems involve an interweaving of several fractal or self-similar patterns which are both orderly and chaotic, iterative and complex (Mandelbrot, 1982; Bohm et al., 1987; Briggs and Peat, 1989).*

towards the counsellor. The counsellor asked her if she would be interested in experimenting with sitting back in her chair just to see how, if at all, that would change her experience in their exchange. Although she couldn't particularly see the point, Shelley decided to try making this small change in her behaviour and sat back in her chair. By the third meeting the counsellor noticed that Shelley relaxed back in her chair from the beginning of the session. She remarked upon this very different style of sitting and Shelley explained with some surprise that this apparently tiny change which she had made experimentally was having quite far-reaching consequences. She felt more open in this position – and her friends and family had actually told her that she seemed more relaxed and confident, which of course made her feel more confident still. She had reconfigured herself and in doing so had reorganised her relationship to others. *Raising awareness of the microcosm of Shelley's way of supporting herself as she sat had affected the macrocosm of her life.*

Attention to small details of a person's way of being does not always have such an impact upon the whole because people have often developed their habits as complicated survival strategies and an exploration of and respect for the complex web of their internal processes is important (see p. 188).

Conversely, recent Gestaltists have developed means of working with the larger scale dynamics of family systems over several generations in order to support healing and creative living in the present. Hellinger (1991) has developed a systemic psychotherapy that mobilises the dynamics of family systems to work with constellations of family systems over several generations.

> For example Ed felt unsure as a man, father and stepfather. Ed's father had been fatherless and Ed had experienced himself as subtly responsible for his dad, who somehow felt frail to Ed. The group counsellor offered Ed an experience of working with the larger dynamics of his family background. Ed said he wished he had had a line of men – father, grandfathers and great-great-grandfathers – behind him, whom he could lean on. Group participants volunteered for various manly roles and Ed and his 'father' were experimentally 'given' a long line of men behind them. Not only did Ed feel a tremendous sense of relief but he immediately experienced himself as able to be a more substantial father to his own son and stepson, who, knowing nothing of the work Ed had done, made several remarks about his changed manner to them.

Being aware of yourself as part of a relational system

To work holistically you need equally to be aware of your own whole person in relationship to clients, paying attention to all your own reactions and responses. Exclude nothing; dismiss nothing as irrelevant. What is your body doing involuntarily in the presence of this other person? Are your muscles tightening up or relaxing and opening? Does your attention wander or is your interest riveted? If you begin to daydream, *when* do you do so and *of what* are you daydreaming? What ideas and suppositions are you making? What is your response to this person? What are your images, intuitions and hunches?

> ultimately the therapist's self is the 'instrument' which will be utilised in therapy. This 'instrument' needs to be kept 'tuned' in order to be responsive to the ever-changing rhythms of the human encounter. It is not the therapist's theoretical orientation that is as crucial in the healing process as is the wholeness and availability of the self of the therapist. In that meeting a wholeness is engendered in the client which was absent before this meeting. (Hycner, 1988: 12)

Many approaches to counselling, psychology and therapy have emphasised intellectual understanding and rational analysis and have proportionately *undervalued* the counsellor's intuition, imagination, fantasy and play.[1] The Gestalt approach encourages you to listen to and use *all* aspects of yourself – your playful creativity, your unexpected and sometimes inexplicable images, your intuitions and subjective experience *as well as* your theoretical analysis and intellectual understanding. Part III discusses the relationship in Gestalt counselling and psychotherapy; while Parts VI and VII discuss the integration of creative and body process.

Key point

Meet the whole of the other person (or people) with the whole of yourself, being open and receptive to how their being touches yours, taking in their essential rhythm and hearing their personal melody. A holistic encounter involves attending to all the different aspects of the people who are meeting and to the interaction or dance that occurs between them. Working with either smaller or larger aspects of clients or of the relational system can affect the whole system.

---

3   Understanding field theory and meeting clients from a field perspective

Gestalt counselling and therapy are based in field theory. This is a set of principles that emphasises the interconnectedness of events and the settings in which those events take place. In Gestalt the individual–environment entity is known as the field, *where the field consists of all the complex interactive phenomena of individuals and their environment.* Gestalt field theory looks at the total situation,

---

1. Ornstein (1982) associated the first list of activities with the left-hand side of the brain and the second list of activities with the right-hand side of the brain, although subsequent neurological research has suggested that this may be an oversimplification (see Table 16.1, p. 132).

Box 3.1 Main principles of Gestalt field theory

1. People cannot be understood in isolation but only as integral and interactive wholes with their socio-cultural background and ecological environment (see p. 50).
2. The field consists of all the interactive phenomena of individuals and their environment and all aspects of that field are potentially significant and interconnected (see pp. 52 and 58).
3. Human behaviour cannot be attributed to any single cause but arises from the interlocking forces of the field (or as a function of the organisation or constellation of the field as a whole) (see pp. 58 and 181–2).
4. The field and the forces operating in the field are in continual flux. Individuals are constantly changing their perspective of the field as they organise and understand it differently, from moment to moment (see pp. 54 and 93).
5. People actively organise and reorganise their perception of their circumstances (or field) by continually making some aspects of that field focus while others become background, and vice versa. The need or interest organises the field (see pp. 16 and 17).
6. People endow the events they thus experience with individual meaning (see p. 59).
7. In these ways they contribute to the creation of their own circumstances or lived experience (they co-create the field and have existential responsibility for their own lives or at least the meaning they give to their lives) (see pp. 54 and 124).
8. Human behaviour and experience happen in the present and a person's behaviour can only be explained in terms of the present field (see pp. 115–16).
9. As all aspects of the field are interconnected, change in any part of the field is likely to affect the whole field (see pp. 45 and 188).

The page numbers indicate the pages where each principle is discussed in more detail.

---

affirming and respecting wholeness and complexity, rather than reducing that situation by piecemeal, item by item analysis. To work from a field perspective, you need to understand and know how to apply the main principles of Gestalt field theory, which are listed in everyday language in Box 3.1 In this section I discuss the first principle of field theory shown in Box 3.1. The other principles listed in the table are intrinsically connected to the first one, and will be discussed later.

People cannot be understood in isolation

We cannot understand ourselves or other human beings in isolation but only as interactive wholes with the complex ecological and cultural system of our environment. The gestalt or whole of an individual includes the whole person, together with their context and the relationship between the two. So we need to start by getting a feel for the client's total situation; and keep viewing all subsequent events of the therapeutic counselling process within the context of the client's overall life space.

A client and counsellor jointly create a relational field, which consists of all the interconnected aspects of themselves and their environment. These multiple aspects include the ecological, cultural and economic environment, the client's current functioning, the client's and the counsellor's background and past experience, including such factors as age, appearance, religion, gender, sexual orientation, ethnicity, social class, economic and social circumstances, and the character structure of both participants. The field of an individual entering group counselling or therapy is even more complex, as the cultural fields of many individuals come together to co-create the field of the group (see Appendix 6 for a discussion of group processes).

Understanding people in context involves paying attention to what lies in the background of their lives, as well as to what is uppermost in their attention or in the foreground of the counselling or therapy session. You can do this by listening to clients' stories (Polster, 1987), getting to know their belief systems, developing an open, investigative attitude to their background and an actively enquiring mind about the culture in which they grew up (John-Wilson, 1997).

Culture and diversity

'A psychotherapeutic process that does not take into account the person's whole life experience, or that denies consideration of their race, culture, gender or social values, can only fragment that person' (Kareem and Littlewood, 1992: 16).

Gestalt therapy is in some ways well suited to work with differences in race, skin colour, cultural perspective, gender and sexual orientation because of its emphasis upon the individual in the field and the phenomenological method of investigation. Gestalt's insistence upon the fact that the individual cannot be understood in isolation but only as part of their historical and social context means that in theory at least we have the capacity to take into account and attend to cultural difference, historical background and social perspectives. And one of Gestalt's primary methods – phenomenological investigation (which involves the therapist bracketing their past assumptions) – offers excellent opportunities for exploring in collaboration with clients what their beliefs and needs are. Gestalt is thus often thought to avoid the pitfalls (inherent in some therapeutic approaches) of sliding into interpretations based on faulty assumptions about the other person's culture.

However, Kareem and Littlewood (1992) have argued that counselling and therapy (including Gestalt therapy) are inherently culture-bound, having developed within a Jewish cultural frame and subsequently evolved in a Western bourgeois milieu. They have shown that many people from ethnic minorities have been reluctant to use traditional therapeutic services (including Gestalt) because of the perceived cultural bias of almost all approaches to therapy and of therapeutic concepts and theories. They show that Western theories of child development, child rearing, family, self and mental health – which underlie therapeutic approaches – are culturally limited and suggest that if professionals remain set in their beliefs, then people from other cultures with their own experiences are unintentionally placed in an inferior position.

They propose that it is the therapist's responsibility to address and acknowledge issues of race, class or gender and to be able to facilitate and hear clients' negative feelings where these emerge from historical or cultural experiences of discrimination. They suggest that white therapists can do intercultural work but they need to be prepared to learn how to and they underline that it takes a great deal of effort to gather sufficient knowledge of the other person's culture in order to really respect the values and background of that culture.

Taking account of the client's current field and of the therapeutic setting

You will need to consider the total situation of the client in order to gauge how to work safely with them. For example if the client's partner is violent, you need to take this into consideration before encouraging the client to experiment with assertiveness skills at home. If you guess that a client is in debt or drinking excessively, you need to take these factors into account when reviewing whether or not the client should continue therapeutic exploration and in what setting.

The setting in which you undertake counselling or therapy will also influence and set a context for your work – there will be limitations and freedoms in a counselling service within a medical practice or a university campus which are different from the limitations and freedoms of a private therapy practice. Counselling in a commercial workplace or in a hospital setting will require attention to still other background forces in the field. These different background field conditions will have an important effect upon the whole therapeutic process from beginning to end. They will be a prime factor in deciding which clients you can work with (see pp. 37–8) and will influence the style and timing of the interventions you choose to make.

To avoid being reductionist in your understanding of field theory, we need to take account of all nine principles of field theory given in Box 3.1 (p. 49), not just the first one. The field has multiple possibilities and complexities. These complex phenomena are interconnected and we cannot separate them without destroying or changing the meaning of the whole. Thus the individual's cultural background cannot be studied and understood in isolation, but *only in relationship to all other aspects of the field*.

Addressing issues of racial, cultural or ethnic diversity (Kareen and Littlewood, 1992) is a matter not only of content but also of process. It means more than trying to learn about other cultures from our own perspective; it also means trying to imagine and empathetically respect the other person's perspective. 'Multicultural counselling [or therapy] is not an exotic topic that applies to remote regions, but is the heart and core of good counselling with any client' (Pedersen et al., 1989: 1). Individuals are unique and distinct from each other and thus there is always an 'intercultural' dimension to any encounter between two people.

Our responsibility for the field

Field theory is a radical discipline which highlights both the importance of the context for understanding individuals and the responsibility of individuals for co-creating and giving meaning to their environment. So by implication field theory not only involves counsellors and therapists in exploring the political, economic and cultural background of clients but also requires all of us to review our personal contribution to and accountability for the cultural, social and economic circumstances in which we and clients live. It may cause us to look for ways of working actively to improve conditions at a global and local level, taking

Gestalt from the counselling room into the community and working with larger groups and systems such as community groups, political parties, pressure groups, spiritual or therapeutic communities. As counsellors our leadership is needed to influence the media and our educational institutions to embrace the variety of sizes and shapes, colours and belief systems of people in our multi-cultural society.

> A multi-disciplinary and multi-racial team of counsellors, therapists and social workers who worked in a community family centre became aware that significant numbers of boys of Caribbean origin were being excluded from school but very few of them were following up their opportunities for referral to the family centre. Investigation suggested that referrals for anything which sounded like 'help' or 'counselling' were alien and unpopular in their culture. The team decided that they needed to take responsibility for making themselves better known and for altering their approach so as to more genuinely meet the needs of the community. They suggested to one of the affected schools that some of their counsellors and therapists would cooperate with the drama teachers in the school to offer courses within school hours. These courses fast became very popular and allowed the young men to explore the tensions they experienced without having to 'lose face' by saying they had problems, needed help or by coming to the family centre.

We are working at a time of ever-growing alienation between human beings and the earth. If we are to take seriously a field theoretical approach, we must acknowledge the limitation of any person-centred psychotherapy or counselling. We must honestly face and grapple with the differing needs, experiences and perspectives not only of different human cultures, but also of the different species and essential eco-structures of our universe. We need to take responsibility for exploring the possibilities for meaningful human re-connection to earth, rock, air, water, fire, feathered bird, mighty tree, creature of the land and sea (see also pp. 150–6).

Key point

The field perspective encourages you to occasionally stand outside the current situation, whatever it is, and see alternative ways of understanding it. From this standpoint you will inevitably lose any sense of certainty about *one* right way to do counselling; for in the Gestalt approach the value of any therapeutic intervention is field dependent (p. 219). Ideally you need to be constantly adjusting your approach to take into account the many possible and variable dimensions of the field.

---

4 Understanding how people organise their psychological field

This section explores how people organise their emotional and psychological field and describes how counselling and therapy can help them to reorganise their perception of their field. It elaborates on principles 4, 5 and 6 of field theory (see Box 3.1). The field and the forces operating in the field are in continual flux. People are constantly changing their perspective of the field as they organise and understand it differently, from moment to moment. People actively organise and reorganise their perception of their circumstances (or field) according to their needs/interests and to the prevailing conditions, and endow the events they thus experience with individual meaning.

The way people organise their perceptual field through the free functioning process of figure formation is briefly described on p. 16 and has frequently been explored. Here I concentrate upon describing the way people organise their field psychologically and emotionally, and explore how people may sometimes organise their field in self-limiting or fixed ways.

Research (see Spinelli, 1989) indicates that people form impressions of their situations based to a large extent on their own subjective perspective, rather than purely on the objective characteristics of the data. The meaning we give to people and situations and the manner we perceive them depends on our own mental framework of beliefs and habits generated from personal and cultural experience. Thus a group of people who were asked to describe a photograph of a man went well beyond the description of obvious physical characteristics and inferred (very different) psychological features, such as his personality, occupation, moods and motives. People organise their field and endow the events they experience with individual meaning. A group of people who were attending a funeral attended the same/a different event. One woman saw it mainly as a celebration of her sister's deliverance from terrible suffering; a young man saw it as a harrowing reproach to him for not finding time to spend with his mother before she died and for being unemployed and unable to afford a 'decent' coffin; while a friend of the family who was in charge of the teas was preoccupied with her fear that she would not have enough cups for the guests.

People's present experience of reality is coloured by their mood, their past experiences, their need, their personal preferences, their expectations. People's need or expectation is like a special lens through which they perceive and give meaning to the field. Their expectations or attitudes especially colour the way they experience their psychological life. For example people who are in the habit of interpreting things optimistically will tend to interpret neutral or even negative situations optimistically. If they are inclined to feel loved, then they may well interpret neutral remarks as loving. If on the other hand they have frequently been rejected and have come to expect rejection, then they may easily interpret neutral remarks, gestures and situations as rejecting, whether or not they were intended to be so.

Understanding how fixed gestalts (temporarily) organise the field

As already discussed in the Introduction, people usually organise and reorganise their perception of the field through the processes of self–other regulation and free functioning figure and ground formation, giving their attention to one thing after another in a fluid and evolving way, according to the need or interest of the moment (see p. 17). This section discusses what happens when that fluid self–other organisation gets more rigid or fixed.

People often look at life through the lens of a fixed attitude, or experience life through a whole network of fixed beliefs or gestalts (see p. 24) which they formed in earlier life and continue to apply unawarely to their present circumstances even though the attitude is now out of date: For instance they may have formulated a belief that they are unlovable because they were unloved and they go around actively but unawarely configuring their field to fulfil this belief. They may interpret remarks addressed to them as slighting or insincere; they may behave in ways that ensure that they are unloved or unconsciously invite people who *do* love them to think badly of them. People often reproduce these webs of fixed attitudes or beliefs in many areas of their life including in the counselling relationship – either interpreting the counsellor's responses in the light of their fixed belief or unconsciously inviting the counsellor to behave towards them in the way that significant others have done in the past.

People may be generally quite good at staying in touch with the reality of current circumstances but certain specialised situations may trigger a fixed attitude which may suddenly loom very large and dominate their perception of their field.

> John had been badly bullied at school. Normally an easygoing, humorous man who liked to tease and be teased, he was extremely sensitive to a few key phrases or certain voice tones. So when his young son said, 'Nya Nya, look at Daddy, he's dropped his toast, or forgotten his keys or . . .', John's face reddened, his temper escalated and he roared like a bull, terrifying his son. Exploration revealed that his son's teasing reminded John of the miserable bullying he'd endured as a child and triggered a reaction in him which made him believe he had to fight back with all his strength (even though his son was only five and posed no threat). John was also sometimes super-sensitive to the remarks of the counsellor. He and the counsellor had a similar sense of humour and would often share a joke but at times John would suddenly flinch and accuse the counsellor of laughing at him. Exploration revealed that the tone of the counsellor's laughter triggered a similarly defensive reaction.

Implications for counselling

The fact that we actively organise and give meaning to our field has important implications for the practice of counselling and therapy. Firstly therapeutic exploration can help people become aware that they *are* currently organising and interpreting their experience in personal or subjective ways (often people really do believe that their interpretation of reality is the only possible one – especially if this interpretation is born from a fixed gestalt or web of interconnected fixed gestalts, p. 189). Secondly, therapeutic exploration can help people realise *how* they are interpreting their reality. Thirdly, it may enable people to loosen fixed ways of experiencing the field, to reshuffle the way they organise their field, to remake the relationship between figure and ground and to choose to *interpret* their experience differently as well as possibly changing their circumstances. It can allow them to realise that they are active and selective in some of the ways they choose to lead their lives. Finally it can enable people to realise how they are active and selective in most of the ways they choose to tell their life stories both to themselves and to others. Those aspects of their life story which they choose to focus on and to repeat have a profound effect upon how they configure themselves and feel their circumstances. If we genuinely learn to tell our story differently, we may change our subjectively experienced reality. Alternatively, when we change our subjectively experienced reality, we change our life story.

> Peter was depressed. Despite having creative work, a loving wife, two beautiful children and a decent home, he dwelt upon the fact that his mother had been depressed and occasionally hospitalised so that from early childhood he had spent periods with family aunts. He seemed caught in the spell of his own story — or the way he told his story — and felt doomed to be depressed like his mother. In counselling he at first dwelt upon his tale of abandonment and with the counsellor's support grieved fully for the losses of his life. Gradually the therapeutic counsellor became interested in what was missing from the story and began to enquire about other aspects of Peter's childhood and present life. It turned out that Peter had been an only child who had been offered many opportunities that his friends had lacked. He had done well at the local school and made many friends, some of whom he was still in contact with; and as an adult he had developed a tremendous capacity for gathering people around him and creating a sense of community for himself and his family. But he had consistently discounted these aspects of himself.
>
> At the counsellor's invitation Peter experimentally tried telling his story by selecting and focusing on different aspects of his life events. Rather to his surprise, he discovered he felt differently about himself when he did so. He was learning to loosen the fixed way he had configured himself and his life and to allow for the possibility of reconfiguring both. Further examples of ways clients reorganise their field or reconfigure their life story are given on pp. 126, 186 and 192.

People's fixed ways of configuring their sense of self, interpreting their reality or telling their story were almost always formed for reasons that were good at the time: they were often generated as a way of surviving difficult individual experience or responding to family or cultural beliefs. So it is important that you hear people's stories and accept the current meaning they give to their lives – as Peter's counsellor did – as well as challenging the way they see things. Reconsidering and loosening fixed ways of perceiving ourselves and our lives can precipitate internal conflict; and therapists need to accept and respect clients as they currently are and to be prepared to explore the complex internal processes (such as the system of introjects and projections) which support their fixed perceptions. The concept of exploring the introjection–projection system is discussed on pp. 189–92; the concept of exploring internal conflict on pp. 169–74; and the concept of self responsibility is discussed further on pp. 124–28.

Key point

Listen to and accept clients' ways of understanding themselves and their circumstances without becoming confluent with the way they configure things. People experience their lives from a personal perspective which may sometimes be creative and flexible and at other times fixed, unaware and obsolete. Through respectful exploration you can help them discover how their more automatic attitudes may be self-limiting and introduce them to a wider variety of possible viewpoints from which to choose.

---

5 Using phenomenological methods to describe and investigate the field

This section focuses on two more principles of field theory and discusses how the phenomenological approach can offer practical methods of investigating the whole field which are in tune with these principles. The interrelated principles of field theory discussed here are: All aspects of the field are potentially significant and interconnected (principle 2, p. 49); human behaviour cannot be attributed to any single cause but arises from the interlocking forces or the constellation of the field as a whole (principle 3, p. 49).

The Gestalt approach is a form of phenomenological field theory.[1] Gestalt shares the concerns of phenomenology, which are to study the multiple possibilities of a given field or situation as it is experienced subjectively by the people co-creating it at

---

1. I am indebted to E. Hüsserl (1931, 1968), David Abram (1996), Gary Yontef (1993) and to Ernesto Spinelli (1989) for many of the ideas in this section.

any moment in time.[2] It shares the phenomenological premise that it is not possible to establish a single objective or absolute truth but only to be open to a multiplicity of subjective interpretations of reality, for each of us experiences a uniquely interpreted reality – because people form highly individual impressions of situations and endow events with subjective meaning.

We need to be aware that our own way(s) of perceiving clients or their situations are likely to be different from the clients' ways of perceiving themselves. We try to avoid unawarely projecting our perspectives on to the clients and instead hold an exploratory dialogue in which we investigate and as far as possible enter into their world, in order to uncover their unique sense of the meaning of the events in their life, and the events in the counselling process. Be open to the multiple possibilities of the relationship that arises between you, consult clients and listen to how things are seen and experienced from their point of view.

The phenomenological method

The phenomenological method offers you a practical method of setting aside your own inevitably limited perspectives and opening yourself up to a wide range of alternative perspectives of the intersubjective field. It allows you to explore all aspects of the field and to set up a form of mini cooperative enquiry in which you and clients study the ways clients function and interact with you and interpret their circumstances (and thus may or may not contribute to their own difficulties). There is no one objective truth – only a multitude of subjective perceptions. The aim is to reveal many aspects of the numerous perceptual possibilities and

2. Spinelli (1989) has argued that Gestalt psychology's emphasis upon an experimental approach and holistic stance means that it is implicitly dependent upon the phenomenological method as a means to psychological investigation. He has further argued that the aims of Gestalt therapy (increased awareness, acknowledgement of responsibility for subjective experience, self acceptance and reintegration of disowned aspects of self) are essentially the same as those of phenomenological therapies. However, he has also suggested that Gestalt's optimistic stance on human nature, its emphasis on liberation and its sometimes high degree of active exploration differentiate it from phenomenological psychology, as Spinelli describes it. In his later book Spinelli (1994) presents a more reductionistic view of Gestalt therapy, quoting the outdated Gestalt prayer – which has been repudiated by many major Gestalt theoreticians (Dublin, 1977; L. Perls, 1991; Clarkson and Mackewn, 1993) – as an example of the approach.

thus obtain a more adequate perception of overall relational situations.

To use the phenomenological method in counselling and therapy, we:

- bracket previous assumptions;
- track and describe immediate experience;
- equalise or treat all aspects of the field (including those which are currently in the background) as initially equally significant;
- enquire.

Bracketing previous assumptions

Bracketing previous assumptions means suspending habitual perspectives and concentrating instead on the primary data of your experience so that your subsequent understanding of the clients and their situations may be fuller. Setting aside expectations you have formulated about clients before meeting them try to base your impressions on your immediate experience of the person. You can also periodically practise bracketing your previous assumptions about clients you have been seeing for a while and meet them anew in the freshness of the moment. Similarly, try bracketing your prejudgements about the general meanings of body language (see p. 162), setting aside preconceptions about what are suitable topics for counselling and suspending even your assumptions about what are appropriate attitudes or behaviour for a counsellor (while of course honouring the ethical boundaries of the therapeutic relationship).

Tracking and describing

Having opened up the possibilities in this way, track the client's and your own holistic process. Tracking holistic process involves noticing (and sometimes describing) your immediate impression of the variable aspects of the field you are co-creating. For example, you might notice (and possibly choose to describe) how the client is flushing, moving or turning away. Or you might notice (and possibly choose to describe) how you feel or what you are imagining. The choice of intervention will depend upon a variety of factors such as the client's character, past experience, need to tell the story, understanding of the usefulness of such interventions, vulnerability to shame, the stage of the therapeutic process and so on. Describe what you perceive and invite clients to do the same. Simple description offers a powerful way of working which often allows people to be in touch with the raw data and essence of their existence (Clarkson and Mackewn, 1993).

When you are working phenomenologically, as far as possible describe what you observe and experience rather than explaining or interpreting. If you interpret, you tend to make sense of the other person's subjective experience in terms of the hypotheses *you* habitually use and thus may inadvertently make the other person's experience fit into *your own world view*, so you may close down the very sense of multiple possibilities that you opened up by bracketing your assumptions.

Preventing ourselves from explaining or interpreting can be surprisingly hard – most of us have been trained to feel we need to help or provide answers. And clients themselves frequently *ask* us to offer explanations or interpretations. If clients do ask for these we can try to find a way which involves a balance between falling immediately into line with their request and denying it. Gestalt involves meeting people where they are available for contact, while also staying in touch with our own phenomenological training and perspective.

Equalising

'Equalising' means treating all aspects of the field that you are describing as initially equally significant. You can do this by noticing (and possibly reporting) what you are seeing, experiencing or imagining in a descriptive way without imposing any hierarchy of assumptions about what is important. Following and reporting immediate experience in this way allows you to explore the clients' and your own functioning with far less prejudice or personal limitation. On the other hand treating all the possibilities of the field as equally significant can be extremely challenging. If, for instance, you have been trained to pay most of your attention to clients' words, you may find it difficult to attend to their bodily process or to your own sensations or feelings.

Treating all aspects of the field as equally significant means paying as much attention to what is in the background of the field as to what is currently focus or figure – to what is missing as well as to what is present. You will need to attend to (and may sometimes describe) not only what the client and you are saying or doing but also what the client and you are *not* saying or doing:

whatever polarity is not focus must be in the background of the field. For example if a client is describing how horribly someone else has behaved to them, you might enquire what part they themselves played in creating the situation; or vice versa. And if clients are very admiring of you, you might wonder aloud what they do with their more negative judgements about you. (See Clarkson and Mackewn, 1993 for a detailed example of Fritz Perls working with what was missing from the field.)

Counsellors and therapists who have been trained to track the client's verbal process often find it especially difficult to switch their attention to what the client is not doing or saying in this way, i.e. to what is missing in the field, because it seems to go against tracking the client's process. In Gestalt we *do* need to develop a fine ability to track (see p. 60) the client's process phenomenologically but we do *not* do so exclusively. It is not in the interests of a full phenomenological investigation of the field to become entirely identified (or confluent) with the client's figure of interest or viewpoint of what is important. We want to enter the client's subjective world but also to stay in touch with our own experience and the other aspects of the field which are not currently figural. The balance is very fine and subtle. The choice of when we track the client's process and when we switch our attention to other aspects of the field depends on many factors, such as the client's and our own level of energy, our background knowledge of the client's issues, timing and so on. The choice of intervention is always field dependent (see p. 49).

Enquiring

I suggest that you adopt an attitude of sustained enquiry throughout the therapeutic process. Such an attitude can help you foster an active partnership with clients, a form of cooperative enquiry in which both of you explore the clients' ways of being in a persistent fashion. You can do this by developing curiosity and fine skills of observation and by asking open questions, which concentrate more on the clients' process than on the content of their words, for such questions can help clients heighten their awareness of how they function. How? and what? questions are especially useful in that they invite clients to undertake their own phenomenological exploration and description of their process, whereas too many why? questions can encourage clients to formulate speculations which are far from their lived experience.

The phenomenological approach seeks to reveal our actual lived experience, the embodied nature of perception. It explores the sensuous and sentient nature of life as an active participant in the world or field. Although it can focus on the individual, it can also go beyond the individual, acknowledging and exploring the diversity of experience. For the world or intersubjective field may be quite different for different peoples and different cultures and it is almost certainly even more different for different species. Deeply embraced, a phenomenological approach can help us acknowledge that we are one of the earth's animals and remember the limits of our human awareness, as well as the interdependent basis of out rights to life (see pp. 150–6).

Key point

The phenomenological approach is a discipline which requires you to empty your mind of past assumptions, and be open and fresh. However experienced a counsellor you become, keep a beginner's mind for 'in the beginner's mind there are many possibilities, in the expert's mind there are few' (Suzuki, 1970: 21).

---

6 Understanding the paradoxical theory of change

Present awareness and the paradoxical theory of change

Gestalt's theory of change is known as the paradoxical theory of change because it is based on the apparently paradoxical premise that people change by becoming more fully themselves not by trying to make themselves be something or someone they are not: 'Change occurs when one becomes what he is, not when he tries to become what he is not' (Beisser, 1970: 77).

People change when they give up trying or struggling to be what they would like to become; when they allow themselves to be currently what they are now at this moment in time; and when they become fully aware of who or what that is. This view of change involves supporting the client's self acceptance and the development of their holistic awareness of themselves and their field and of how they are currently functioning and interacting with other people in that field. It grows out of the Gestalt theory of contact or self–other regulation,[1] which proposes that awareness and contact are the natural means by which people develop and grow (see Clarkson and Mackewn, 1993: 55–6) and that when contact is vital and assimilation is complete this automatically leads to change. Each time people move to the edge of their present self concept and take risks with what they are willing to be aware of and make contact with, they grow. If they are genuinely able to feel their authentic self and let go of their self image (i.e. who they would like to be), they change.

This view of change represents a radical paradigm shift from the more commonly accepted tradition of change which puts much emphasis upon trying to change in order to conform to moral, family or cultural standards by a process of willpower and determination. Promotion of external imperatives or 'shoulds' is inclined to set up an inner conflict between the aware, controlling part (or willpower) of the individual (which Fritz Perls often called the top dog) and the spontaneous, impulsive or unaware parts of the self (often called the underdog). The more the aware or controlling part tries to change, the more the unaware parts may resist; so change which is driven by willpower, coercion or persuasion is likely to be short-lived, because it is inherently divisive and dualistic and engenders a split in the vital energies of the person between unassimilated introjects of externally imposed rules and the other aspects of the self which can manifest as rebellion, passive aggression or apparent but lifeless conformity. Those parts of ourselves that we disown or try to deny have great unacknowledged power and the 'underdog' is inclined to win, as anyone who has ever made New Year's resolutions and then 'found' that they have dropped them a week later may well recognise.

Working with the paradoxical theory of change is challenging and it requires discipline and skill. Clients usually come for counselling or therapy wanting change and often doing so from

---

1. Discussed briefly in the Introduction and described in great detail elsewhere (see Perls et al., 1994; Zinker, 1978, 1994; Polster and Polster, 1974; Clarkson and Mackewn, 1993; Kepner, 1987).

the standpoint of wanting to be what they are not; for they have been taught to embrace external standards of behaviour or to have a 'shouldistic' attitude to their own functioning. They are thus frequently in the state of inner conflict described in the previous paragraph: they are divided against themselves and expect you to take sides in their intrapsychic battle. Some counsellors and therapists do go along with this expectation and side with the part of the client that wants to effect a change, and many clients and counsellors who adopt this path suggest that they have achieved their aim. However, they do so at the cost of reinforcing the process of inner conflict and although the result may be superficially successful, the side of the client which did not want to change has not been valued or integrated and is likely to make its power felt in covert ways such as a lack of spontaneity or zest for life and lack of enthusiasm for the chosen path or sometimes in more serious symptoms such as illness or depression.

Declining the role of change agent

A practical implication of the paradoxical theory of change is that we need to decline the role of ordinary change agent, refusing the invitation to join with the client's coercive side in cajoling or persuading the other aspects of the client's self into obedience, change or action. The more we push for change, the more we are likely to activate a counter-force within the individual or their field which pushes against change and seeks to maintain the status quo. In addition, if we join with the side of the client which wants to change, we will be joining forces with one part of the client only; so we will have abandoned the position of working with the whole person of the client (see p. 43) and although clients may temporarily express satisfaction, in the long run they are less likely to feel *confirmed in their whole being*. To be of service to the whole person, we need to avoid getting locked in with any one aspect of the client.

This unwillingness to accept the role of change agent differentiates Gestalt from many other approaches and it may well go against clients' expectations. Wheeler (1991) gives an example where the client, Josh, persistently tried to put the therapist in the role of change agent by expecting the therapist to express disapproval of his drinking. The therapist persistently declined to take on this role, while at the same time extending warm support to the whole of Josh's person and carefully investigating all the factors in the field contributing to Josh's lifestyle, including his drinking. Josh eventually became his own change agent, taking on responsibility for monitoring his own behaviour.

Instead of taking on the role of change agent, you can become an active research partner by collaborating with clients to study and find out about their ways of being in the world and how these support or undermine their desires and intentions and by using phenomenological methods to investigate all the forces for and against change within clients and their field (p. 172). Together with clients, you can thus undertake a form of cooperative enquiry (Reason and Rowan, 1981) to develop greater awareness of all the forces operating in the field. In this sense, Yontef has suggested that the sole aim of Gestalt is the development of awareness (see pp. 34, 61, 65, 113, 133, 152 and 179).

Creative indifference or non-attachment

Perls, Hefferline and Goodman proposed adopting a neutral position, or a position of 'creative indifference' (Friedlander, 1918; Perls et al., 1994; Perls, 1969a). This is *not* a position of indifference. It is a position in which you can be warmly involved with the whole person of clients and their life dilemmas while not being *invested* in the success of any single aspect or the outcome of your joint investigation. If you take up a position of 'creative indifference' you can lean in any direction (or non-attachment) – helping the client to investigate now this aspect of self, now that one; to explore now this force within the field, now that one.

From a position of creative indifference you can see how all aspects of the client have had some value or are potentially valuable to their whole self system. You can explore with clients what (hidden) value of those aspects of themselves seem to undermine their apparent desire for change. For it is usually only when the whole person feels understood in this way that they are able to transform habits which were once useful but are now anachronistic. In this way you can support clients to develop their awareness even of those aspects of themselves or their environment which they are currently disowning. They can eventually get to know more of themselves and may choose to reintegrate the energy locked in disowned aspects of self and develop self functions that were not completely learned in earlier relationships and environments. Through these processes they may achieve a better integration and a more cohesive sense of self, which can allow them to actualise themselves more fully.

Often this sort of phenomenological enquiry into the forces for and against change can precipitate or reveal an impasse where clients experience themselves as locked in inner conflict. Section 23 further explores how to work with inner conflict, 'resistance' and the impasse and provides an illustration of forces for and against change operating within the field (p. 172).

Don't underestimate the radical challenge embedded in the paradoxical theory of change or the discipline required to work with it. Developing awareness of self in relationship instead of staying with attachment to a self concept of how we 'should' be is not easy in this society, where almost all approaches to education put great emphasis upon self image and security or safety. Awareness and contact with self is anxiety-provoking, for each time people allow themselves to know themselves and grow through awareness and contact, they destroy part of their old habits, identity or self image (the old gestalt). Fuller holistic awareness and contact thus inevitably arouse existential anxiety because they involve knowing and letting go of the old limited or fixed 'character' and risking the unpredictability of becoming the new self. In reasonably healthy people, the anxiety provoked by the unknown is tolerated because the disturbing anxiety can be converted to energy and excitement which flow into the new configuration of the self.

In the following example, Arthur finally allows himself to be fully in contact with who he currently is, as opposed to who he wished he was:

Arthur was being teased by Rachel, another group member. He felt hurt and embarrassed about his dislike of teasing, so at first he said nothing. Then he decided to risk telling Rachel that he didn't like her teasing him. Rachel apologised and said she'd just felt playful. The counsellor, Jim, asked Arthur how he was feeling and the following exchange ensued:

Arthur: I can feel my stomach clenching. My adult self knows that she was feeling playful but another part of me didn't like it. I felt uncomfortable.
Jim: Is there any place in your body where you feel discomfort now? [*phenomenological enquiry*]
Arthur: Yes, here. [*Rubs his stomach*]
Jim: You are rubbing your stomach. [*phenomenological description*] Would you describe how your stomach feels? [*invitation to client to develop phenomenological description*]
Arthur: All clenched up and tight and sore.

Jim: What does your 'stomach self' need? [*phenomenological enquiry oriented to increasing Arthur's support and inner connection*]
Arthur: Reassurance and comfort.
Jim: How could you reassure and comfort yourself now? [*phenomenological enquiry, oriented towards increasing Arthur's support*]
Arthur: I am doing that by rubbing my stomach – it feels warmer when I do that.
Jim: What else do you need? [*sustained phenomenological enquiry*]
Arthur: I need your attention just as you are right now. I need to hear something. I think I need to hear that it's all right to dislike teasing. [*environmental support and present relationship*]
Jim: How could you hear that? [*phenomenological enquiry*]
Arthur: [*speaking to himself*] 'It's quite all right that you didn't like being teased, even though Rachel only meant to be playful. You're entitled to feel whatever you want.' [*Arthur breathes out and looks different.*]
Jim: You look different. What happened then? [*Counsellor notices and draws attention to ongoing holistic process with phenomenological enquiry. He also shows that he is finely attuned to Arthur with a view to strengthening his sense of relatedness, which is especially important because of the theme of shame: see Lee and Wheeler, 1996 and Appendix 7.*]
Arthur: The knot in my stomach just melted. I don't feel uncomfortable any more.
Counsellor: So what you said and did made a difference. [*Counsellor affirms the client and his ability to make a difference.*]
Arthur: Yes – You see this has happened many times before – people have teased me and I have felt uncomfortable. But I have always chided myself for feeling like that. I wanted to be cool; so I pretended I didn't mind. Today I admitted to myself how uncomfortable I felt and then to Rachel and you as well. That's very different. Only when I did that could I realise that that uncomfortable part of me needed kinder treatment from me. [*Client elaborates upon and makes sense of his experience, sharing his increased awareness of how he has habitually limited himself by adhering to an idea of how he should be rather than acknowledging how he is. With the counsellor's support, he increases his self support.*]
Jim: How do you want to complete this? [*sustained phenomenological enquiry*]
Arthur: [*turning to Rachel*] I don't like being teased; please don't tease me.

Throughout this exchange, the counsellor maintained an attitude of creative indifference and sustained enquiry, thus developing an active partnership with the client and supporting the client's self support. The counsellor put particular emphasis upon support, self support and relatedness because Arthur appeared to be feeling some degree of shame which often indicates a rupture in relationship and inadequate support (Lee, 1995 and Appendix 7).

Key point

People often believe that change involves trying to get rid of various qualities within themselves. The paradoxical theory of change suggests that when people allow themselves to be fully and awarely in touch with who they currently are, change and growth then emerge as the inevitable and natural outcome of such contact and genuine self knowledge. So support clients to discover more about who they are rather than joining forces with the part of them that says they ought to be different.

III

Developing a Dialogic Relationship as a Crucible for Self Development

7 Understanding Gestalt theories of self and their implications

This section describes and illustrates various Gestalt theories of the self in relationship. If you don't enjoy theoretical discussion, you may prefer to skip straight to section 8.

Your view of the self must profoundly affect your approach to counselling and therapy and to the interventions you make at any given time. In this Part I describe some of the main Gestalt theories of the self (which relate to and further explore principle 5 of field theory: see Box 3.1, p. 49);[1] and of relationship.

Intersubjective self as changing process in the evolving field

The founders of Gestalt (in particular Paul Goodman in Perls et al., 1994) proposed that the self is not a structure but a changing process. The self varies according to the different people or things it encounters and in the ever-changing circumstances of the field in which it exists. The self is the experiencer and organiser of contact at the boundary between self and other and plays the crucial role of organising our perceptions of people and circumstances and making meaning out of the perceived world in which we live. *The activity of the self is the forming and dissolving of meaningful figures of interest against the background of the individual's changing field or world* – gestalt formation and destruction (related to field theory principle 5). The self is thus intersubjective – it is the process of contacting and relating. It evolves and grows through contact and assimilation of experiences with other aspects of, or people in, the environment.

The self is inherently relational, it exists or manifests itself in the interaction between the person and their environment or between one person and another. We discover and find out who

---

1. The self is an elusive and controversial concept and is the subject of much lively debate amongst theoreticians of Gestalt and other orientations.

we are in relationship to others. The self is not aware of itself abstractly but only as contacting something or someone. 'I' exists in contrast to 'you' or 'it'. This intersubjective phenomenological conception of the self sees the self 'that we interpret and believe in at any given moment in time [as] both temporary and, at best a partial expression of an infinity of potential interpreted selves' (Spinelli, 1989: 84). See Appendix 7 (pp. 247–50) for further discussion of the significance of an intersubjective concept of self.

The self is active in the choosing and organisation of itself and its environment. We are therefore able to take existential responsibility for ourselves and many aspects of our lives, especially the meaning we give our lives. Human beings have an innate tendency to self actualise – their primary motive to realise their unique potential, to become who they really are.

The means by which the self experiences, organises and modulates the process of contact are the contact functions (movement, speech, seeing, hearing, tasting, etc.: Polster and Polster, 1974) and the self functions, which include all our qualities and capacities for managing our experiences of self and others, such as our capacity to negotiate interpersonal boundaries and bodily boundaries; our experiencing functions (such as sensing, imaging, pacing, moderating and soothing); our self support functions (see p. 183); our feeling functions; our differentiating functions; our assimilating and reconsolidating functions (Kepner, 1995).

Implications for counselling and therapy

A positive implication of the self as variable process is that people are not predetermined but are free to choose from moment to moment amongst their possibilities – they construct themselves and the meaning they give their existence. To some extent all counselling and therapy depend upon the world view that people can develop and remake themselves, especially when the conditions – as in the authentic and supportive conditions of the therapeutic relationship – are ameliorated.

However distressed or even dysfunctional people may seem when they first come for counselling, their distress is not merely individual but arises in an intersubjective and contextual field; so they are not necessarily permanently distressed but can remake themselves in the changed conditions of the next moment.

> One client was permanently depressed at home and showed this aspect of herself in the counselling situation, slumping over, with very low energy, droning voice and barely able to articulate her words; whereas at work she

seemed to be dynamic and successful. Therapist and client investigated the conditions which allowed and supported her to be one way in one place and another in the other place. People can often change their life circumstances and they can always change the meaning they give themselves and their lives by reorganising their perception of their field, by altering the relationship they make between figure and ground.

A further inference of this view of self is the importance of the relationship between client and counsellor or therapist. We define and learn about ourselves in relationship to the 'other'. We invent and shape ourselves, as well as finding out who we are and how we are experienced, in relationship to others. We evolve our contact functions and develop our self functions in relationship to others in our childhood and adult environment. So Gestalt counselling and therapy study the processes of contact and withdrawal, the functioning of the contact boundary between self and other in the therapeutic relationship, as well as in other relationships in the client's life.

The unfolding dialogue between yourself and clients is a fundamental way in which clients can show, share and develop different aspects of themselves. The therapeutic relationship (Jacobs, 1989; Yontef, 1980, 1993; Hycner, 1985, 1988, 1990) offers a crucible in which, with the counsellor's support, clients can study their processes of contact and withdrawal, discover who they currently are and explore who they may become. People develop a huge range of aspects of self through ongoing relationship with others (Stern, 1985). If the counselling or therapy environment is conducive to interpersonal learning and experimentation, clients who did not acquire a full spectrum of self functions because of impoverished or damaging interpersonal environments may develop new self functions and experiment with new styles of contact (see also p. 247).

Self as ground as well as process of contact

Some later Gestalt theorists have suggested that Goodman's view of the self as variable process does not pay enough attention to the qualities of cohesion, groundedness, continuity and connectedness that are so essential for individuals to function in an effective way within the shared field. They have argued that Perls, Hefferline and Goodman did not sufficiently underline the fact that the variable self also has – and needs to have – enduring characteristics. In fact, Goodman's view of self as the process of contact did always include a personality function or consistent aspect of the self – which he called the personality function. According to Goodman, the personality is what one is or *has consistently become*; it is the responsible *structure* of the self that can be used for every kind of interpersonal behaviour. It provides some of the ground and support from which activity and each individual contact episode emerges.

But the 1960s emphasis upon the *figure* of contact has sometimes obscured the fact that the assimilating and integrating processes are as important in the overall process of contact as the earlier phases in the cycle. For several decades much Gestalt practice has tended to focus on those aspects of the self which are figural and changing rather than on what is consistently in the ground of the self; on what is present in the moment rather than in the background processes of a person's life. Wheeler (1991) has argued that this form of practice of Gestalt therapy is 'figure-bound', in that it concentrates upon observation and analysis of the figure of contact without an equivalent attention to those habitual features of contact functioning which are embedded in the life of the individual and organised over time and in the background of the field. He proposes that contemporary Gestalt therapy explore the structured ground and processes of people's overall lives. (Of course as soon as we do attend to aspects of the structure of ground, these will cease to be ground, for by turning our attention to them, we will make them figural for ourselves.)

Self as both changing process and enduring features

Integration of the two views of self is necessary and possible. Self *is* process. It does vary as it encounters each new person, remaking itself as each fresh figure of contact emerges in unique response to different aspects/people in the environment. Yet self *also* encompasses consistent personality, enduring characteristics, habitual styles of contact, learned self functions, self organisation and so on. Self as changing process and self as enduring identity and groundedness need not be seen as mutually exclusive but as two poles along a continuum, as illustrated in Figure 7.1. Gestalt counselling and therapy need to pay attention to both poles of the continuum and to their interaction. By its very nature Gestalt embraces complexity and must therefore attend not just to the variability of the self but also to the continuity of self, not just to the contact episode but also to the ground from which it arises; not just to self regulation at the contact boundary but also to the internal self organisation of the individual.

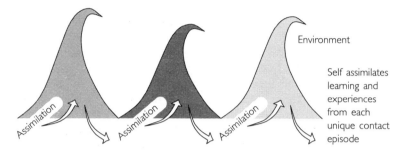

Self as process (or waves) of contact, changing and remaking itself differently as each fresh figure of contact emerges in unique response to different aspects/people in the environment

Environment

Self assimilates learning and experiences from each unique contact episode

Self as ground (or sea) with enduring features of consistency, cohesion, flexibility and so on

Figure 7.1 *Self as both changing process and as assimilation and groundedness*

You can shuttle attention between the client's figure of contact and the ground which supports that contact by exploring unique manifestations of self in the moment of contact between you and clients *and* the underlying structures of their life: the value systems, connections and commitments which give meaning and substance to their lives. The discussion on p. 50 illustrates how the counsellor needs to shuttle attention between here and now phenomenology, and the overarching processes of clients' lives (their cultural beliefs and attitudes to self disclosure, for example) and their relationship or contact with the present group.

Sections 26, 27 and 28 discuss ways of supporting clients to develop sufficient consistent and enduring characteristics to function effectively and cohesively in the world; and offer some suggestions for attending to the assimilation into ground over time of episodes of therapeutic work.

Of course as soon as you attend to 'aspects of the ground', these will immediately cease to be ground, for by the very act of turning your attention to them you will reconfigure the field, making them figural for yourself, while whatever you were previously attending to will temporarily recede into the ground. You cannot explore ground without making it figure (Yontef, 1992).

Erving Polster (1995) offers a Gestalt model of the self that could be seen as integrating the poles of variability and consistency in an understandable and practical fashion. He suggests that within our overall sense of self we all have a population of different selves which have their own distinctive and often well established body language, attitudes, priorities, voice tone, values and styles of making or moderating contact. We may for example have a gardener self, a musician self, a kind self, a confident self, a shy self and a panicky self. These internal selves may work in harmony with each other in the interests of the whole self or they may be in discord, each operating in conflict with the other, sometimes with no awareness of the existence of other polarised selves, often with no awareness of the needs of the other selves. Some selves are more manifest than others but the less manifest or less conscious selves are not more or less real than the more manifest ones. Each of us encompasses a population or community of selves that vie for ascendancy.

> When John (introduced on p. 56) was teased by his young son, he flew into a rage. His frightened, raging self temporarily dominated his whole field and he seemed to have no access or bridge to other aspects of self. The therapist worked with John to identify other aspects of self which might be able to help him soothe himself and remind him he was no longer a lonely victim of bullying and could react more lightly to his son's teasing. The therapist and John actively explored how he could remember and evoke these other aspects of himself when stressed by teasing.

Polster's model of self has been sharply criticised by some Geltaltists (Philippson, 1996) who believe that Polster's model departs so radically from Goodman's view of self (as process, creating itself at the contact boundary between self and other in the relational field) that it should be excluded from mainstream Gelstalt theory.

Some clients you see are likely to have a much more fragile sense of self and self organisation than others – see pp. 196 and 245 for a discussion of how to calibrate the Gestalt approach for working with people who have a fragile self process.

Child and self development in Gestalt

Knowledge of theories of child and self development and how they may be relevant to Gestalt counselling and psychotherapy can be invaluable support for therapeutic counselling. Fritz and Laura Perls made some original contributions to child development (Mackewn, 1991b); while more recently N. Friedman

(1992) and other Gestaltists have adopted and adapted the child development theories of Daniel Stern (1985), for Stern's view of several senses of self evolving in relationship to other people from infancy to death is especially compatible with Gestalt views of the self. Other Gestaltists have also explored child development in a Gestalt context (see Mackewn, 1991b; Crocker, 1992). Drawing upon Kohut's (1977, 1984) self psychology and Stern's research into the intersubjective nature of the evolution of the self, Stolorow, Brandchaft and Atwood (1987) have interestingly developed an approach to psychoanalysis known as intersubjectivity theory which shows some important similarities to Gestalt (Jacobs, 1992; Hycner, 1988; Hycner and Jacobs, 1995).

Key point

The self encompasses both variable process and enduring features. It varies, remaking itself afresh in response to new encounters in the ever-changing circumstances of the field; and yet it also manifests background qualities of stability, cohesion and continuity which provide the support for each fresh contact episode. Counsellors and therapists need to pay active attention to both poles of this self continuum. Exploring the counselling relationship provides one easily available means of studying the way clients create themselves in the world and integrate (or fail to integrate) experience.

---

8 Understanding the dialogic relationship and developing a person to person dialogue

The dialogic relationship encompasses several specialised and interrelated aspects of the therapeutic relationship, including a person to person relationship, a working alliance and the transferential relationship. All these aspects of the dialogic relationship inevitably and necessarily encompass both a subjective, person to person ('I–Thou') and a more objective ('I–It') attitude, as well as the rhythmic alternation between the two styles of relating, although the 'I–Thou' attitude is of course more prevalent in the person to person dialogue while an 'I–It' attitude is more prevalent in transferential phenomena.[1]

In this section I discuss the dialogic relationship and its principal components – the person to person dialogue, the working alliance, the transferential relationship and the transpersonal dimensions. I then give an extended example which illustrates how all dimensions of the dialogic relationship are interwoven in practice. There has been much confusion about the meaning of the word dialogic and associated terms; I have therefore summarised key definitions in Box 8.1.

The Gestalt approach proposes that the potential for change and self development arises not through the counsellor or therapist, nor even through the client alone but through what emerges in the meeting or existential encounter between the two of them. Healing and development evolve from the intersubjective realm of the dialogic. The term 'dialogic' does not refer to speech in the ordinary sense but to the fact that human beings are inherently relational (Buber, 1988; Hycner, 1988) – we become and discover who we are through relating to others; from birth to death, our various senses of self emerge in relationship.[2] As discussed in the Introduction and section 6, we grow and develop through contacting and relating to other people and things in our environment and through assimilating those contact experiences.

Dialogic relating, together with the study of the process of relating (or contacting), is the heart of Gestalt counselling and therapy. It provides the medium for the growth of awareness, learning, problem-solving and self development.[3] Your relationship with clients is not ancillary to the therapeutic counselling process but central to it. Dialogic relating can – and does – take place in silence, laughter or play as much as in words.

When two people engage with each other, each constellates the field in their own unique way (see p. 54) and at the same time influences the other and jointly shapes the quality of their

1. 'I–Thou' is used to translate Buber's 'Ich–du'. The translation of 'I–Thou' has a rather more archaic tone than the intimate tone implied by the German.

2. The dialogic approach is not exclusive to any one school of psychotherapy. But Gestaltists have taken a significant role in expounding, discussing, illustrating and applying the dialogical philosophy of Buber.

3. The quality of relationship is central to many other approaches to counselling and has been shown to be an important factor in the outcome of counselling (Highlen and Hill, 1984; Gelso and Carter, 1985).

Box 8.1   Dialogical relationship: definitions*

Dialogical	refers to an approach based on the facts that we human beings are inherently relational; that we become fully human through relationship to others; that we have the capacity and urge to establish meaningful relations with others.
Dialogue or existential dialogue	describes the interaction between people when there is a desire to genuinely meet the other person. It is what happens when two people meet together as persons each being open to, impacted upon and responsible to each other and where each respects and appreciates the uniqueness and otherness of the other. It is not restricted to verbal exchange but may take place in silence, dance or laughter. Encompasses both 'I–thou' and 'I–It' relating and the rhythmic alternation between the two.
Monologue	describes times when a person speaks to themselves in the presence of another, creating an impression that they are open and interested in the other, but having no genuine interest in or appreciation of the other. Much everyday conversation is a form of disguised monologue and does not thus meet human yearning for meeting and confirmation.
Self-dialogue, two-chair dialogue or dialectic	describes occasions when people are in two minds or in conflict about something and each aspect of the self has a different feeling or point of view. Sometimes Gestalt counsellors might suggest that a client hold a 'dialogue' between two aspects of self. This is not the same as the existential dialogue of the therapeutic relationship, for existential dialogue requires two people entering into genuine relationship with each other. The internal or self dialogue could more correctly be called a *dialectic* because dialectic refers to the interaction between two (intrapsychic) polarities.
I–Thou or I–You	refers to a subjective attitude where each person addresses the other as a person and is open to meeting in mutual humanity, accepting and confirming the other as he/she is now, rather than wanting the other to be different, or using the other as a means to an end. Moments of mutual 'I-Thou' meeting have the greatest potential for healing.
I–It	describes a more objective style of relating which is more task and outcome oriented. It includes functions such as analysis, judgement and reflection. I-It relating is essential for life and for counselling if integrated appropriately. In extreme forms, I–It relating can mean treating other people as objects or as a means to an end.

* Drawn from the work of Hycner (1988), Yontef (1993) and Jacobs (1989)

interaction. They co-create their reality in the shared dance of relationship. Each brings their innate preferred styles and all their previous experience of relating and yet each is simultaneously open to the impact of the other. They engage in a dance together which is the product of their joint creativities.

The therapeutic relationship provides a means of studying the ways in which people constellate their reality in fixed ways and thus limit their own possibilities. It also offers people the opportunity to try dissolving some of their established patterns of relating and to experiment with fresh relational approaches.

Developing a person to person dialogue

You can develop a person to person dialogue with clients by adopting an 'I–Thou' attitude towards them. This involves turning your being to their being, addressing them with real respect, being genuinely interested, accepting and confirming of them as they are now and not as a means to an end. It means valuing and appreciating their uniqueness and separateness from you, while experiencing your underlying common humanity; it means risking yourself by living the relationship, showing and sharing yourself, rather than hiding behind the role of counsellor or therapist, being defensive or trying to control the outcome of the session or of the therapeutic relationship; and allowing yourself to be personally affected by and responsive to clients (Yontef, 1980, 1993; Hycner, 1985, 1988, 1990).

Being present and genuine in this way does not of course mean that we share all our spontaneous reactions, because as responsible counsellors and therapists we know that spontaneity at all times would not be therapeutic.

We try to create a 'horizontal' rather than a 'vertical' relationship between counsellor or therapist and client in which we meet as two people who are equal in our humanity even though we bring different qualities and skills to the exchange – clients are experts on themselves and what works for them; while counsellors have been trained in relational skills and theoretical knowledge with which to help clients review their life dilemmas and develop their awareness of new options.

Dialogic relating emphasises joint phenomenological exploration of what is, so we need to speak the same language of present-centred experiencing as clients and give equal value to both perspectives. This horizontal attitude and use of common language is central to the 'I–Thou' dialogue and differentiates Gestalt counselling and therapy from many analytic and psycho-dynamic approaches in which the client and therapist speak different languages (the client free-associates while the counsellor or therapist interprets) and the 'therapeutic' interpretation of the client's experience is largely assumed to have more clarity than the client's perspective.

Differentiate an 'I–Thou' attitude from a mutual 'I–Thou' meeting

The type of person to person relationship which has the greatest potential of all for healing and transformation is the meeting between *two* people both showing and expressing their true selves in a mutual fashion. But Full mutual 'I–Thou' meeting in which each person speaks 'you' to the other is a peak moment of contact and communication in which both will change and be changed. It is inevitably transient. In the evolving cycle of self–other regulation and the ever changing process of the field, a moment of 'I–Thou' meeting will be figural and then it will recede into the background and be replaced by other forms of relating until the next occasion when both client and counsellor are able to risk giving up control and allow another moment of 'I–Thou' contact to emerge from the 'between'.

The person to person dialogue in counselling and therapy is not and cannot be fully mutual. For instance when clients start counselling they are very likely to see you to some extent as a role – a counsellor or therapist who may help them feel better – rather than as a person in your own right. Clients usually start counselling with less holistic support for dialogue, less relational awareness, less interest in 'I–Thou' meeting than the counsellor or therapist. Indeed they are likely to be preoccupied with their emotional problems and the need to alleviate them. Also they may need to work through much unfinished business from their past and archaic or transferential styles of relating before they fully see the counsellor or therapist as a person (Hycner, 1985). For example one client said, 'It was a year before I really thought about the fact that my counsellor was a person with her own feelings too.'

Finally the therapeutic contract is not a fully mutual one because it focuses on exploring the *client's* present functioning, and developing the *client's* awareness and enhancing the *client's* relational stance, not the counsellor's.

However, healing through meeting does imply a certain *type* of mutuality: a mutual humanity, the sense that you are called upon to be present as a person, not just as a competent professional. One person can address another as 'you', whether or not the other reciprocates. So you can have an 'I–Thou' attitude to clients even if they currently have little conscious interest in their relationship with you. Sometimes your 'I–Thou' attitude may be the client's first experience of being seen and confirmed in such a sustained way. Each one of us has a fundamental yearning to be understood and confirmed by another human being. Indeed it is often the absence of such confirmation at crucial points in life that has 'fixed' the individual's creative self regulation and given birth to the dilemmas that they have come to counselling to explore. The sense of being met person to person can restore the natural process of creativity and provide the medium in which clients can once more develop awareness of how they currently are and thus expand themselves.

Appropriately integrating an 'I–It' attitude

As mentioned above, the dialogic relationship encompasses two polar styles of relating – both the 'I–Thou' and the 'I–It' attitude and the rhythmic alternation between the two. It is important to understand the role of an 'I–It' attitude within the therapeutic relationship and to know how to integrate it creatively and appropriately. The 'I–It' attitude is also essential to life and to counselling and therapy. 'I–It' relating occurs when you stand back and think about clients rather than meet them. It is more task and outcome oriented and involves such functions as analysis, judgement and reflection. Everyone needs to objectify sometimes in order to achieve certain goals, learn skills or fulfil tasks, and as a therapist you are no exception to this rule. You may for example need to temporarily objectify clients while you consider their suitability for the therapy you offer (see p. 37), when you consider them diagnostically, when you decide how much to share and how much to withhold in the name of presence, when you imagine possible therapeutic strategies or discuss their progress in supervision.

It is not the existence of an 'I–It' attitude which is damaging to human development but its disproportionate predominance. The materialistic emphasis of the times often leads people to treat each other as a means to an end rather than as human souls yearning for connection, which in turn leads to splits between person and person, between people and nature and to splits within the self. An existential dialogue that prioritises a person to person or 'I–Thou' attitude attempts to heal these splits. Dialogic relating is itself encompassing and holistic. Integrating many polarities, it values the uniqueness and connectedness of both client and counsellor, emphasises individuality and commonality, separateness and relatedness, withdrawal and contact, 'I–It' and 'I–Thou' relating, intrapsychic and interpsychic exploration.

Important though relationship building is, it does not release us from the requirement to learn and develop technical skills. I suggest we look on counselling or therapy as a craft and an art. We develop the skills of our craft, never ceasing to refine our theoretical knowledge, diagnostic acumen, creative range and sense of timing, because these are the disciplines through which we may develop counselling and therapy to art forms where we meet the other person, I to You. Practise the techniques of your craft within the context of dialogic relating, then at the moment when there is the possibility for existential encounter, let all your training and expertise fade temporarily into the background and as a 'mere' human being, meet the other person, with the open wonder and curiosity of someone contacting another for the first time. Buber, the main proponent of the existential dialogic philosophy, has encapsulated this dichotomy with beautiful simplicity: 'Without methods one is a dilettante. I am for methods, but just in order to use them. Not to believe in them' (1967: 154).

Fostering the conditions of person to person relating

We cannot make 'I–Thou' relating happen. Mutual 'I–Thou' contact emerges. It is born of preparation and grace and cannot be aimed for. Indeed if we make 'I–Thou' relating an aim, we paradoxically create a purposeful or 'I–It' attitude (Buber, 1988).

We can, however, learn to nurture the conditions which allow mutual 'I–Thou' relating to evolve. To do this, we need to understand and practise inclusion, presence and confirmation. We need to commit ourselves to dialogue; to non-exploitation and to living the relationship. Each of these disciplines, rather like meditation, is simple and yet not easy. I briefly explain each below but they may take a lifetime to learn.

Inclusion This means entering as fully as possible into the client's subjective world. Without judging or analysing, we try to see the world through the client's eyes and understand the client's perspectives and feelings. For example you may describe phenomenologically what you observe. Or you may make contact with clients and allow yourself to be affected by their experience, while at the same time retaining a sense of yourself.

Presence This means knowing yourself as you are, rather than pretending to yourself that you are something you are not and de-investing in your self image and role, e.g. as a good counsellor. It also involves being aware of how you become defensive and often deliberately relaxing your own defensive reactions. Choose to show yourself by describing your responses, *when you judge this to be in the interests of the client and the counselling process*. This does *not* mean that you share all your thoughts, feelings and problems (as some people mistakenly believe). How much and when to share your self is one of the most important questions to consider in Gestalt or any other approach to counselling and therapy – you need to review various factors within the overall conditions of the field on each occasion. This is a key issue and therapeutic counsellors generally benefit from regular supervision of their practice in order to appreciate the complexity of the factors involved in deciding when and to what extent it is in each client's interests to reveal themselves and how they are responding (L. Perls, 1991; Jacobs, 1989; Hycner, 1985, 1988, 1990; Levitsky, 1993; Friedman, 1985, 1994; Kron and Friedman, 1994; Yontef, 1980, 1993).

Confirmation This means confirming and affirming the being and becoming of the client, even if you sometimes confront or question some of the client's behaviours (Friedman, 1994; Kron and Friedman, 1994).

Key point

Healing and change take place in the meeting between two persons who are wholly present. You cannot make this sort of 'I–Thou' encounter happen but you can foster the conditions which may allow 'I–Thou' moments to emerge from the dialogue between you. All relationship is made up of 'I–Thou' and 'I-It' styles of relating and the rhythmic alternation between the two.

9 Making a working alliance with clients

Start forging a working alliance between yourself and clients from the first contact. Research indicates that the strength and early establishment of a working alliance between client and counsellor is the primary contributor to a successful outcome (Bordin, 1975; Gelso and Carter, 1985).

The working alliance is the adult to adult agreement that you and clients make to work on the client's problems and the client's unfolding development of awareness. It is the alignment which can be created between the 'reasonable' side of the client and your 'reasonable' or working side. It is the commitment to work together even when this seems inconvenient or difficult. This alliance permits the client to experience negative feelings towards the work or towards you, without prematurely ending counselling or therapy. It also permits you to experience similarly negative feelings and to investigate them rather than drop or react destructively to the therapeutic commitment. The working alliance creates a sense of shared enterprise, to which each participant makes a contribution. It is the essential vessel or container which holds the therapeutic process. Without a strong working alliance, meaningful work cannot be integrated. Establishing a working alliance involves allowing the field to be organised in such a way that certain boundaries and structures regarding the background to the therapeutic exploration are in place and can then be taken for granted. It requires both the counsellor and the client to look at and negotiate the field or working conditions that they co-create.

How can you help create a good working alliance? You need to show concern, compassion, respect, professionalism, reasonable consistency balanced with flexibility, together with a real willingness to meet clients and help them face their problems. You also, of course, must be able to negotiate practical and business aspects of the therapeutic contract, clearly and humanely and provide holding for the work. Clients need to be able to invest energy in the therapeutic process and relationship and be motivated to explore their issues.

Reaching consensus on areas for exploration: negotiating the practical aspects

I suggest that you check carefully with clients that you have understood what they want from counselling, so that you and each of your clients *have consensus on the areas for exploration in counselling* (see pp. 33–5). Clients are likely to reveal more intimate, more risky or previously unconscious needs as they build a relationship with you. They may reveal such additional needs indirectly as well as directly, non-verbally as well as verbally. So developing consensus on clients' goals is an ongoing process which needs to be regularly reviewed in your own mind as well as with clients, as you pick up and surface more information and less conscious needs and wishes.

I see the negotiation of the practical aspects of counselling as an important factor in establishing a working alliance. The *manner* in which you negotiate and set up these arrangements (place, time, frequency, fees – if any – arrangements for cancellations, absences and so on) is an essential contribution to and aspect of the creation of an adult to adult agreement between yourself and the clients. I now usually give prospective clients a simple form to think about before deciding to start counselling with me (Dryden and Feltham, 1994).

Fostering a working partnership

It is important to actively foster a working partnership in which clients take some responsibility for the course of their own therapeutic exploration. From the beginning of the process, you can, for example, invite clients to notice what they are doing in the present moment, share your thinking with them and offer choices, so that individual clients become more self supporting, are able to learn to use *your* skills to become more aware of *their* process and can eventually become 'counsellors' or 'therapists' to themselves. For the aim of counselling is not to cure clients but to teach them how to learn about themselves and to send them away with a tool box full of tools, so that they can solve not only present but also future problems (Perls et al., 1994).

The working alliance is a blend of 'I–It' and 'I–Thou' relating. The proportion of 'I–It' to 'I–Thou' relating will depend upon the individual circumstances of the field at the time. For example exactly when you negotiate practical aspects of the counselling commitments or explain aspects of the Gestalt approach must be largely influenced by how each individual presents for the counselling session. Is the person in crisis? Often you will need to meet the human being in distress first and then deal with negotiations or explanations. However if you *only* empathise with the distress and set no conditions, you risk creating an unboundaried situation that the client is not likely to experience as safe or clear enough to work within. In Gestalt there are no prescriptions for exactly when or how to do things because the optimum therapist response or intervention is always field dependent (see p. 49).

You need to continue to nurture the working alliance, while simultaneously exploring the possibilities for mutual trust. Ideally the alliance is strong throughout the therapeutic work. Once established it may become ground rather than figure for a lot of the time but it tends to come to the fore at certain points in the work. Indeed it often needs to be tested and strengthened at all the significant phases of the process – as though to ensure that it is in place before the next step can be taken. Research indicates that the more difficult the problems to be explored in counselling or therapy, the greater the strength of working alliance needed. (Elton Wilson, 1996, has developed a schema showing one view of the role of the working alliance at different stages in the therapeutic journey.)

You can continue to strengthen the working alliance by holding regular reviews, to update clients' goals, to discuss their progress with them, to consult them regarding what has been helpful and what less helpful and what they feel they need next. In these ways you can continue to foster an active partnership and provide boundaries and containment for therapeutic counselling.

I suggest you combine providing therapeutic structural holding with human flexibility and appreciation of the circumstances in which the therapy or counselling is being offered. Counsellors and therapists are generally trained to make initial agreements regarding fees, times, absences and so on, so as to create and maintain safe boundaries in which the therapeutic work can take place. If clients want to change any of these, you might consider discussing the proposed changes in supervision or with a colleague before agreeing, as any change to the agreed conditions represents a change in boundaries of the therapeutic contract and may have a greater significance for the overall process than at first appears.

On the other hand it may be quite unrealistic and overly 'counsellor-centred' to expect all client groups to comply with the therapist's expectations about 'appropriate boundaries'. Counselling and therapy take place in many unconventional settings and are made available to clients who would be unlikely to approach a private counsellor or even the counsellor in a medical practice because of lack of funds or cultural disinclination. Drop-in centres for young people, for example, provide excellent counselling and therapeutic services to people who are often temperamentally unable to commit themselves to regular times but do want to see someone more casually to discuss their lives and problems. In family centres in disadvantaged inner city areas, counsellors and therapists often work in cooperation with social workers, health visitors and other local services. They may pay home visits alone or as a team and they often accept irregular attendance at appointments as the norm or even as a positive advance in the context of teenagers or families who have never previously accepted any support. Counsellors and therapists who have been trained for more formally boundaried work may need to do some unlearning. Again regular supervision with a supervisor experienced in our sort of work can support us in deciding when it is important to be humanely flexible and when it is important to keep a boundary.

Ruptures or mismeetings in the relationship

From time to time therapists will 'let down' or disappoint their clients in some way. These apparent errors often involve a failure to sufficiently enter the client's phenomenological world and to understand their perspective or feelings. Such occasions can be seen as empathic failures or disjunctions between the subjective world of the client and the subjective world of the therapist. Quite frequently these ruptures in the therapeutic relationship echo the ways in which clients were 'failed' by significant others in their life (past or present) and may therefore be additionally charged for the client, provoking feelings of being unsupported or unmet together with possible associated feelings of awkwardness, embarrassment and shame (Lee and Wheeler, 1996).

Although these ruptures in the relational field may be painful they are far from being a catastrophe, because such inter-subjective disjunctions offer the opportunity to reach the heart of the client's internal feeling world and to discuss and explore the relevant experiences and patterns of relating. Such ruptures often trigger old wounds and open fixed gestalts which may in turn allow individuals to be especially available for an alternative experience and deep healing in the present, if these situations are handled delicately and effectively by the therapist.

It can for instance be important to acknowledge occasions when you emotionally miss or misunderstand clients. You might show your acceptance that you have let them down, as you, being human, inevitably will from time to time and then actively work to repair any emotional damage that arises from such mismeetings or disjunctions. It is also usually important to pay particular attention to the level of support (both inner strength and environmental support – see p. 183) that is available to the client, for if the total situation contains no more support than was available at the time of the original empathic failure, the present is likely to be experienced in a similar way as the past; whereas if more support is available, an up to date or more flexible response may be possible. The working alliance is both necessary to and simultaneously developed and strengthened by the surfacing, exploring and repairing of ruptures in the ongoing therapeutic relationship.

If clients have had persistent experiences where their trust was betrayed in early life, then they will have learned to be mistrustful, undoubtedly for good reason. The building of a working alliance, with associated exploration of feelings of lack of trust, exploration of mismeetings and the repair of those relational ruptures may become the central issues in the therapeutic process.

Key point

Both client and counsellor need to make a commitment to working together that will withstand the inevitable pitfalls of the therapeutic process. From time to time misunderstandings or ruptures in this partnership will occur, but if you take care to explore such mismeetings they can help you and clients understand more about their patterns of relationship; while your respectful investigation and repair of misunderstandings can strengthen the working alliance and offer healing for old wounds.

10 Understanding transferential processes within the dialogic relationship

Understanding the role of transference in Gestalt

'You cannot do good therapy [or counselling] without dealing competently with the transference phenomena' (Yontef, 1993). Transferential and countertransferential phenomena inevitably contribute to the way both you and clients understand each other and the clients' problems; while transferential processes often impact upon the development of the working alliance and the person to person relationship. Here I will briefly introduce transference and countertransference in the Gestalt context and then indicate some possible ways of working with transferential processes in the dialogic relationship.

Some people have mistakenly believed (Kovel, 1991) that Gestalt counselling and therapy have no theory of transference. This is untrue. Fritz Perls and other early Gestalt theorists certainly criticised what they saw as the analytic over-emphasis upon the transferential relationship and upon interpretation as the *primary* method of working with transference. However, they acknowledged the existence of transference and had good personal understanding of transferential processes (Robine, 1988; Mackewn, 1991a). Indeed Fritz Perls made an influential contribution to the theory of transference by suggesting that the analyst can accept the client's feelings as valid in themselves and respond to them authentically, rather than dismiss them as mere transference. It has also often been assumed that transferential processes do not affect or are not relevant to short term counselling or humanistic psychotherapy. Gelso and Carter (1985) and Rowan (1983) have cogently argued that this is not the case because transference is a ubiquitous process, affecting all relationships and especially all manner of therapeutic relationships.

In everyday life, everyone does a good deal of transferring a good deal of the time, for all relationship is always a mixture of genuine contact and of transference (Yontef, 1993). When the words transference and countertransference are used in the context of counselling/therapy, they refer to the feelings, behaviours or attitudes of clients and counsellors that belong in the past and are continued in and transferred to the counselling or therapy participants even when the current circumstances no longer call for such attitudes. Transference also refers to the ways of being and relating learned in the past that clients are transferring on to the life dilemmas which they have come into counselling to review (Holmes, 1992).

In Gestalt terms, you could think of transference as the way that individuals inevitably shape their perception of current reality through the lens of their history, their unfinished business, their fixed gestalts rather than merely according to the properties of the current situation. It is the process by which people assimilate their present life experience (including the experience of counselling) into their established patterns of organising and making meaning of their field. In other words transference is one way (often a habitual and fixed way) of organising the field.

The process of transference is complex and largely unconscious (or out of awareness). It usually involves introjection of, and some confluence with past figures or situations as well as projection of such figures and situations on to the present with the spontaneous but often inexplicable reawakening of associated feeling states, body memories, thoughts and sensory experiences:

> Automatic patterns of thinking, moving, feeling, arise as a result of some form of reenactment of a previously unresolved, frozen or fixed gestalt. If, for instance, someone has to confront an abusive person in a work setting, and this evokes or triggers the memory (in or out of awareness) of an earlier traumatic situation (like being shouted at by an angry teacher) – then the old reactions, feeling state, and sense of powerlessness are likely to be at least partially re-awakened. (Parlett and Hemming, 1996)

If transference is seen as the habitual ways in which people organise their perceptual field, clients' responses to current situations and to the counsellor can be seen as a microcosm of important ways in which they organise their psychological world and may thus provide access to their fixed or unaware ways of formulating figure and ground in current circumstances.

When individuals become aware of the fixed ways in which they currently organise their experience, then they can choose whether or not these ways are still useful and necessary to them and (if greater support is available in the current conditions than in the past) they can gradually learn to relinquish the fixed attitudes and remake their perception of reality by reorganising the relationship of figure to ground.

> Alison came into therapeutic counselling feeling lonely and she wanted to make more and better friendships. Exploration revealed the fact that she had been persistently excluded in her family at an early age and often organised her current reality in terms of whether she was being included or excluded. When the counsellor gave Alison warning of a short holiday break, Alison felt excluded from the arrangements and wondered who the counsellor was going with, and so on.
>
> Alison gradually became aware of how her interpretation of most inter-personal situations in terms of how much she was being excluded made her feel miserable and led her to miss opportunities for human contact which didn't fit with her anticipated scenario. Through the therapeutic exploration, she gradually developed a stronger sense of herself and a greater flexibility in the way she formed the figures of interest against the background of her experience – so that when her acquaintances were choosing what to do and who to do it with, she was able to hear that they were often following their own preferences and needs without negative or positive feelings towards her. She discovered that she could ask to be included and if she was turned down, she could soothe any hurt by telling herself there would be other opportunities or people to do it with and in the meantime she could be a good friend to herself. This may not seem like a large external shift but for Alison it represented a really different experience of reality. Alison had slightly reshuffled the way she formed figures of interest against the ground of her experience and thus changed herself and the flavour of her life.

The Gestalt view of transference is of course phenomenological and dialogic and it is not consistent with phenomenological philosophy to see clients' transference (or counsellors' and therapists' countertransference) as merely a 'distortion' of objective reality. From a phenomenological perspective a client's transference is one amongst a multitude of possible subjective interpretations of reality or configuring the field. Further, from a dialogic perspective, the client's process of transferring cannot be interpreted as emanating from the client in isolation but must be seen as emerging as part of an intersubjective relational system or dance. Client and counsellor or therapist actively co-create the shared perceptual field of the therapeutic relationship. When you explore transferential processes in counselling or therapy you therefore need to be prepared to explore your own, as well as the client's, present contributions to perceptions and misunderstandings. So Alison's counsellor considered and investigated what she might have contributed to triggering Alison's response, by the way she announced the holiday break, or by her tone of voice, manner or facial expression.

Countertransference

Proactive countertransference: The first and most important meaning of countertransference is the counsellor's independent or proactive transference on to the client and therapeutic situation. Proactive countertransference means the counsellor's own transference on to the present situation. Proactive countertransference occurs when the counsellor is unawarely transferring material, attitudes or assumptions from their own past on to the client. Proactive countertransference occurs in all counsellors, however well trained and however much therapy they have done. The point is not to try to avoid or overcome countertransferential responses but to be alert for them. If you can become aware that your own unfinished business may have been activated, then you can bracket your personal responses for the moment and explore them in your personal supervision or therapy and thus consider whether or not they are also relevant to the client's work.

Reactive countertransference and projective identification: A second form of countertransference, named reactive countertransference by Clarkson (1992) and objective countertransference by Winnicott (1975), occurs when the counsellor is *reacting* or responding to the client's transferential processes. Attention to and exploration of this form of countertransference can provide valuable clues about how the client may habitually configure the field or about the client's deep and probably unaware feelings. Much useful advice has been addressed to therapists regarding learning about the client's unconscious feelings and dynamics through the study of these interactive transferential patterns, in particular through the phenomena of projective identification in the context of the relational field that is co-created by client and counsellor. Projective identification describes the process whereby a client unawarely conveys his/her feelings by 'giving' the therapist an experience of how he/she feels, rather than by articulating. (The therapist does not, cannot, actually feel the client's feelings but the client evokes similar feelings in the therapist.) (Casement, 1985; Mackewn, 1991a; Parlett, 1991; Staemmler, 1993; Robine, 1988; Stolorow et al., 1987.)

Some ways of working with transferential processes

There is no one way of working with transferential and counter-transferential processes within the dialogical relationship; instead there is a multitude of possibilities. In Gestalt we are more interested in studying the active process of transferring and how that affects the individual's current life than in unearthing the historical origin of the transference, although our phenomenological exploration of the process may well reveal historical insights. Below I briefly mention a range of ways of working with transferential process, which are not mutually exclusive. *Which way you choose to work at any one time will depend upon the overall conditions of the field co-created by yourself and the client (p. 219):*

1. You can adopt an exploratory and phenomenological stance, in which you neither assume that clients' responses are transference, nor preclude that possibility.
2. You can accept clients' descriptions of their own reaction to you or events and persistently explore phenomenologically what in the *present* exchange or in the present field may have triggered the response that the client describes, responding authentically in the present.
3. You can cooperatively explore the possibility that the client or you (or both) may be seeing present events or people through the lens of past experience.
4. You can look for ways to enable clients to study their own transferring and discover when and how they are transferring (organising their field in fixed habitual ways); Gestalt is in the active process of transferring (From, 1984).
5. You can surface unfinished business or make overt the transferential processes. Explore and resolve the pattern of experiences *differently* in the different conditions of the therapeutic counselling – either through re-enactment (see p. 159) of the past or through a vital alternative experience in the present relationship. One vital alternative experience in the counselling situation is of course to be accepted and responded to authentically, as suggested in (2).
6. You can explore the dynamics of the transferential/counter-transferential interactions between counsellor and client as an ongoing aspect of the unfolding exploration of the therapeutic relationship or dance between you. An understanding of projective identification (p. 95) is useful in this context.
7. You can actively try to shake the transference (Perls, 1976).

In highly transferential relating neither client nor therapist is able to really fully apprehend the other person because their perception is so influenced by ways of seeing gained from the past. In this sense genuine mutually contactful relationship is the polar opposite of transferential relationship but full mutual contact is only one moment at a time in the flow of dialogic relating, which encompasses both 'I–Thou' and 'I–It' relating as well as the rhythmic alternation between the two. Mutual person to person relating often only emerges after much exploration of archaic or transferential styles and the investigation of intra-psychic or dialectic phenomena (Hycner, 1985). Examples of transferential phenomena are included in the next section.

Key point

Transference is present in most relationships but is only one dimension of a relationship. You need to be able to understand the complex dynamics of transference and countertransference while also validating what is happening in the person to person relationship between you and clients now.

---

11 Integrating the different components of dialogic relating in practice

This section gives an extended example with commentary which is designed to illustrate how the different strands of the dialogic relationship interweave. A strong working alliance, for example, provides commitment and safety for the persons in the relationship to risk sharing their inner selves (in the person to person relationship) and also to show their unaware archaic, idiosyncratic or transferential styles of relating. Working through those archaic styles of relating in turn strengthens the working alliance and allows a much fuller, more mutual 'I–Thou' meeting of people, the experience of which can help clients develop a more satisfying style of relating to the rest of the world, specifically with regard to the problems they bring. The therapist's authentic person to person relating may sometimes trigger the client's archaic styles of relating – which are then further explored.

Bob, a man in his forties, came for therapeutic counselling saying he had difficulty with intimate relationships and wanted to get better at them. His wife was no longer interested in him and he desperately missed her interest. The therapeutic counsellor, Jane, was interested and empathetic, explained something of her approach and negotiated an exploratory contract or commitment (*thus beginning to create a working alliance*). She also suggested that noticing how Bob and she relate may be a way of discovering more about Bob's style of relating in general. Bob talked hard throughout the first few sessions – and Jane felt ignored and overwhelmed. In supervision Jane realised that Bob was reminding her of her own father and explored and expressed her unfinished feelings towards her father in her own personal therapy (*counsellor's proactive countertransference*).

Jane and the supervisor *also* surmised that perhaps Bob's way of being with Jane was his habitual way of being with others; so the way Jane was reacting (*counsellor's reactive countertransference*) might well be the way others react to him, for we all actively co-create the field in which we live and sometimes we have ingrained fixed ways of doing this. Jane decided to risk sharing her personal response next time she felt 'talked at'.

Jane: I notice you talk fast and I sometimes feel I can't get a word in edgeways. [*Person to person relating – Jane is present and chooses to share a small part of her own ongoing experience.*]

Bob: Well at least that's one way of getting myself noticed. I never could get any attention when I was a child. [*Exploration of the present through dialogic relating enables unfinished business from the past to emerge.*]

Jane: I'm interested. How come? [*Jane is present, shares her own response and invites phenomenological exploration.*]

Bob: Well, my mother was busy, there were seven children, always a crowd around the table. Everyone talked and talked. No-one took any notice of each other. I had to talk. [*Phenomenological enquiry leads Bob to amplify his description of his unfinished business from the past and also to indicate a habitual pattern of behaviour which may suggest a fixed gestalt which is still anachronistically influencing how he behaves now – transferential or archaic style of relating.*]

Jane: I wonder if the way I feel when you talk so fast and loud is at all the way your wife feels? [*Jane is present, sharing her wonderings, inviting the client into phenomenological enquiry.*]

Bob: Perhaps . . . As I was saying . . . [*Bob returns to the story he was telling.*]

Jane: Could you wait a minute? [*pauses*] I feel brushed aside and I'm wondering if there could be a pattern here? I'm imagining that there may be a direct connection between the way I feel, the way your wife feels and the difficulties you have with intimate relationships. [*Person to person relationship – Jane continues to choose to share part of her own experience and invites mutual enquiry.*]

Bob: You mean that perhaps the way I talk may make my wife lose interest?

Jane: I can only guess about your wife, but I do know that when you talk and talk and seem uninterested in my response to you, I feel like giving up on the hope of actually interacting with you. [*Person to person relationship – Jane chooses to share her own experience.*]

Bob: [*is shocked*] I thought if I talked, I'd get people's interest. People have told me I'm a good conversationalist. [*The figure of contact between Jane and Bob is sharpened.*]

Jane: Well talking *is* a very important way of communicating and getting the interest of other people. [*Jane affirms Bob as he currently is.*] But in intimate relationships, people often want more exchange; and I'd be willing to bet that your wife may also need more sense of your interest in her if she is to maintain her interest in you.

[*Bob acknowledges this and soon goes back to talking fast. Jane listens and does not interrupt him because, while developing his awareness of how his style of interaction affects her, she also accepts him as he currently is.*

The following week Bob returned.]

Bob: I don't feel like coming to counselling any more. I can't see any point.

Jane: I'm surprised. You seemed so committed to an exploration of how you relate to others. [*Person to person – Jane is present and chooses to share some of her own responses and also refers to their working agreement, invoking and strengthening the working alliance.*] I'm wondering if anything could possibly have happened last session that has influenced your decision? [*phenomenological enquiry*]

Bob: No, no, I just don't see the point.

Jane: [*suddenly vividly remembers their interaction last week*] I understand and respect that you may want to stop. [*Affirms Bob as he is in the moment.*] At the same time, I am remembering that last time I shared with you how I responded to your style of talking. [*Person to person – shares own response.*] I wonder if you may perhaps feel there's just no point in going on when I respond to your communication in that way? [*Chooses to share a hunch.*]

Bob: Well, I suppose I felt shocked at the time but afterwards I did feel rejected. I felt you weren't interested in me either. [*Bob becomes more fully present, sharing his inner reactions.*]

Jane: And how was that for you? [*phenomenological enquiry*]

Bob: Awful, I felt rejected and angry with you. [*Bob becomes still more present; contact is heightened between Bob and Jane.*]

Jane: I'm really sorry that you felt so bad and I'm extremely glad you have told me how you feel [*presence and confirmation*]. Right now I'm very engaged with you and our exchange. [*Jane is present, choosing to share her own immediate response.*]

Bob: Are you. Why?

Jane explains that she is particularly engaged now because she feels that he and she are having an impact upon each other, are in fact in dialogue. In this discussion they have a brief experience of mutual exchange (person to person relating, temporarily a full 'I–Thou' meeting).

Bob often reverts to his old style and Jane continues to sometimes feel overwhelmed by his speech and unengaged with him. Sometimes she chooses not to share but to bracket her feelings, due to a variety of variable field conditions (including the fact that she occasionally feels her reactions are more to do with her restimulated feelings towards her father than with her current feelings towards Bob; that she sometimes feels that it is more important for Bob to tell his story or experience the support and affirmation of being listened to, without exploratory interventions; the timing is delicate, as just before a break and so on). At other times Jane shares her feelings (as in the example above), due to other variable field conditions. Jane's sensitive sharing of her own authentic reaction allowed Bob to become aware of how she (and others) react when he talks in such a relentless way. Thus he can choose again and again whether to continue to relate in his habitual pattern or whether to try some of the newer ways of relating he has begun to experiment with in short spells.

It is usually important to have a clear working contract with clients (see p. 34) and to have developed a working alliance in which the client has evidence of your empathy, goodwill, trustworthiness and professional integrity *before* you address habitual patterns of relating or share your personal response too openly. If you are working with narcissistically or shame vulnerable people, you may have to build a very strong working alliance and meet their needs for acceptance and mirroring over a considerable length of time before you attempt anything so challenging (E. Greenberg, 1995).

Key point

It is usually wise to allow the therapeutic relationship (like any other relationship) to emerge silently and imperceptibly through the work of addressing the issues that the client has brought for counselling or therapy and the meeting of the two people over time. Occasionally counsellors who have been trained to understand the importance of the counselling dialogue continually refer to the relationship between themselves and their clients. Clients who have come along to solve problems or relieve their distress may feel confused or put off by this mismatch between their expectations and those of the counsellor.

IV

Observing Process,
Developing Diagnostic
Perspectives and
Therapeutic Strategies

12 Observing clients' processes of contact and styles of moderating contact, while developing diagnostic perspectives

As previously discussed, the self develops through contact and relationship. In the interactive cycle of contact and withdrawal, Gestalt offers a model which enables us to finely observe the way we function in the world, relate and interact with each other and thus study in what ways we support our own growth and self development and in what ways we undermine or obscure it. One way to help yourself heighten your ability to notice clients' processes and patterns of relationship comprehensively is to observe (and perhaps describe for yourself between sessions) what you notice about clients in terms of some of these Gestalt maps of processes. You can for example describe clients in terms of a metaphor for their relationship with the environment; or of the cycle of contact and withdrawal; or of their styles of (moderating) contact in relationship to others and to various field conditions; their styles of supporting themselves and so on. This section includes an example which illustrates what such a description might look like in practice for a man called George (Appendix 2 shows a contrasting example for a woman called Rose; while Appendix 3 offers you a form which you can use to do the same sort of thing for one of your own clients.

Metaphor for relationship with environment

You can picture clients in terms of a metaphor or an image which represents the client and his/her relationship to the world, to other people or yourself. Sometimes clients will use images or metaphors to describe themselves. Sometimes counsellors may find that images or metaphors regarding the client emerge spontaneously. Alternatively if a client is asked what images they have of themselves they may respond with a striking and possibly unexpected image. (Of course if the image comes from the

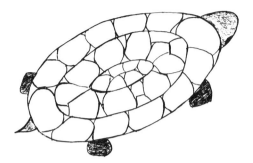

Figure 12.1 *Metaphor encapsulating relationship with environment: George likened himself to a tortoise that was well protected from the environment and withdrew into his shell at the first sign of emotional turbulence.*

counsellor rather than the client, then the counsellor needs to be aware that the image may say as much about him/her as it does about the client – see p. 14.)

Whether the images come from the client or counsellor, they offer a different way of knowing about clients and their situations. The language of metaphor and image can temporarily bypass our logical, rational ways of knowing and allow us to plumb the depths of our imaginative inner worlds, our intuitive wisdom or imaginal knowing (see Reason, 1988, 1994 for discussions of different ways of knowing).

Drawing the metaphor or image can deepen the counsellor's contact with this imaginal way of knowing. In workshops where I have suggested that counsellors spend some time drawing their images or metaphors of clients (or clients' images and metaphors of themselves), participants often discover new insights about the client or the counselling process – insights which emerge only during the process of drawing – for the drawing can harness the intuitive parts of our brains. (Of course, counsellors may also suggest that clients draw the images or metaphors of themselves which arise in the counselling process if this seems appropriate.)

George, for example, described himself as a tortoise (Figure 12.1).

Process of contact and withdrawal

You may describe clients in terms of how they move through the interactive cycle of contact with and withdrawal from the environment (see Figure I.6). As explained on p. 18, every living creature moves through this cycle of contact and withdrawal many times in their life and indeed in each day of their life. The cycles vary in size, significance and type and include both long cycles, such as the 20-year cycle of child raising, or the cycle of grieving a dead friend, and shorter cycles such as celebrating a birthday, eating a meal, breathing in and out or sitting an exam.

Although we all go through these cycles, we have distinctive styles of doing so. Indeed many people have one distinctive style of moving through the cycle when dealing with practical or professional matters and a very different style when approaching emotional or family matters. People's distinctive styles of moving through these cycles of life are significant and may well relate to the issues they want to explore in therapy.

You can develop your ability to notice your client's distinctive style of moving through the process of contact and withdrawal by describing for yourself the process for two or three different clients with regards to a couple of different aspects of their life. George's process of contact and withdrawal is given below as an illustrative example.

George's process of contact with other aspects of the environment

Sensation: George expressed little sensation and feeling in interpersonal matters; seemed rather flat, with low emotional and sexual needs.

Awareness: George seemed vague and absent concerning personal relationships but displayed high cognitive grasp of work-related issues.

Mobilisation: Low energy for personal relationships; higher energy for business matters.

Action: Always carefully thought out; rarely spontaneous. 'Performed well' sexually, 'provided well' for his wife and children. Took carefully planned and extremely effective action in business deals.

Contact: Considerable contact with financial reports and specialist literature. Seemed detached from his children. Limited human interest. Sometimes procrastinates.

Satisfaction: George described measured pleasure regarding his business success; didn't talk of dissatisfaction or satisfaction in personal life.

Withdrawal: George described himself as 'withdrawn'; seemed very familiar with this position. I imagine it has been a useful survival strategy – see metaphor of tortoise.

Styles of (moderating) contact

We all moderate the flow of our contact process awarely and healthily, as our priorities in the evolving circumstances of the field change. Habitual styles of contact, on the other hand, may maintain fixed patterns of behaviour that deny or displace needs or feelings that the individual has for some reason in the past found too problematic to allow. Perls et al. (1994) termed fixed styles of contact, such as confluence, retroflection, projection or introjection 'disturbances to contact' at the contact boundary or 'interruptions to contact'. However Wheeler (1991) has argued that what Goodman and Perls called 'interruptions to contact' could more aptly be called dimensions or styles of contact – because they represent the styles of contact that individuals use to organise their field. Whether they interrupt or support contact depends upon the particular field conditions at any time. Both the 'interruptions to contact' *and* their polar opposites may disturb or support contact:

> while all of them, under various circumstances and for various pur-
> poses, may be essential to the very 'contact' Perls would see them as
> blocking . . . Any and all of these terms may be seen equally as
> resistances to contact, channels of contact, styles of contact, facilitators
> of contact, distortions or blocks in contact and so forth . . . depending
> upon the [client's] flexibility of range along that bipolar continuum
> and the *goals* of the contact in question, under the particular field
> conditions given. (Wheeler, 1991: 123)

For example deflection may sometimes interrupt some forms of contact while at the same time being essential to other forms of contact, because for any given contact to be achieved, other potentially competing needs, figures or ways of organising the field must be temporarily deflected. If I want to write this book, I deflect myself from other enticing possibilities such as going for a walk. But if I wanted to go for a walk, I would equally have to deflect myself from my writing.

Similarly when a client deflects eye contact or tells a story indirectly or in the third person, this may support contact rather than interrupt it, as is illustrated in the example on p. 138 where the counsellor's suggestion that George describe his feelings indirectly (or through apparent deflections) actually supports him to make more personal contact than he has done before. Introjection and confluence too may sometimes interrupt and sometimes support contact. Erving Polster (1993) has shown how introjection and confluence can support community values, promote a sense of belonging and ease social communication and contact, *as well as* clashing with contradictory individual needs.

To say therefore that a client 'retroflects' or 'is confluent' is so general as to be almost meaningless – everyone retroflects, some-times usefully, sometimes less usefully. What is more interesting from a field perspective is to consider *how* and *when* clients moderate their contacting along the bipolar continuum shown in

---

Box 12.1   Polarities (or multilarities) in styles of contact

retroflection . . . . expression . . . . violence, aggression

egotism . . . . spontaneity . . . . impulsivity

introjection . . . . . chewing, destructuring . . . . spitting out, rejecting

deflection . . . . focusing, contact . . . . . . directness, bluntness

projection . . . . . imagination, assumption . . . . owning, literalness

desensitisation . . . . sensitivity . . . . supersensitivity, inability
to protect self

confluence . . . differentiation, separateness . . isolation

Box 12.1, and to investigate with them *of what service* may it be (or have been) to them to do so in *that way, at those times and in those circumstances?* Therapist and client can thus develop deeper awareness of the clients' styles of contact and can review together when current styles of contact are serving the clients' purposes and when they are inhibiting those purposes (see p. 28).

George's styles of (moderating) contact

Retroflection ——— expression ——— violence or aggression: George expressed socially correct feelings of appreciation. He habitually retroflected interpersonal needs and feelings. He knew that he had never mourned the considerable losses of his childhood, came to counselling to learn to do so but found this difficult as his body was controlled and rigid.

Egotism ——— spontaneity ——— impulsivity: George laughed spontaneously and had a wry and witty sense of humour, often at his own expense. Otherwise he was rarely spontaneous in his feelings, words or actions. He considered them all very carefully.

Introjection ——— destructuring ——— rejecting: George had introjected the idea that he would be accepted if he was controlled, hardworking and made no demands. He wanted to change these attitudes but found them difficult to destructure or dismantle.

Deflection ——— focusing ——— directness: George's awarenesses were largely cognitive. Attempts to link thinking with feeling were deflected by a change of topic. He deflected by not answering personal questions and by using rather impersonal language. George was very focused about pursuing his business career, on the other hand.

Projection ——— assumption ——— literalness: George was very literal, showed little imagination regarding other people's experience and when other people talked to him either humorously or metaphorically, he usually took them literally. He seemed to project little, unless he projects his own emotional indifference on to others and assumes they feel as indifferent as he does?

Desensitisation ——— sensitivity ——— over-sensitivity: George was highly sensitive to some social situations where he felt under pressure and occasionally became nauseous, which he took great trouble to hide from other people. Otherwise he reported few sensations except tension headaches after he had been in situations which seemed to be potentially emotionally touching.

Confluence ———— *differentiation* ———— *isolation*: In intimate relationships George tended to keep himself emotionally separate, wondered if he really could love. On the other hand he seemed to retroflect disagreement in order to make himself acceptable.

Gestalt 'diagnosis' of process

The ability to describe the client's processes and current functioning in relationship to other people and field conditions is central to the Gestalt approach. It can also be seen as a Gestalt analysis or diagnosis of process-in-relationship which is not only compatible but actually intrinsic to the Gestalt approach (Melnick and Nevis, 1992). Although there is a common misapprehension that Gestalt eschews diagnosis, even Perls, Hefferline and Goodman argued that Gestalt therapists do need a typology to orient and guide themselves (1994). They emphasised that such a typology must not imply a fixed typology of the person but needs to concentrate on describing unique *processes* of behaviour, because that recognises the ever-changing and evolving nature of the self-in-relationship. The contrasting examples given above and in Appendix 2 show how to put their idea of a typology of process into practice. Appendix 2 discusses the place of diagnosis in Gestalt counselling and therapy and links the Gestalt diagnosis of process with psychiatric diagnostic systems.

Develop differing counselling strategies and evolving plans[1]

Don't expect to work in similar ways with all styles of client. Adjust the Gestalt approach to different clients in different circumstances. Even though Gestalt puts great emphasis upon the present interaction, it is *also* important for you to think about clients' habitual patterns and to be able to conceptualise the

---

1. Although Perls is best known for emphasising the here and now moment and often appeared to dismiss planning and consideration, on at least one occasion he took the trouble to prepare and present a paper on planned psychotherapy (Perls, 1979 – originally delivered 1946 or 1947). Shub (1992) and Melnick and Nevis (1992) have proposed a Gestalt system of diagnosis and treatment planning which gives some direction and structure to the Gestalt process over time, see also pp. 205 and 226–36.

therapeutic work you are doing to address those. You need to take time to reflect upon clients' problems and the behaviour they describe or manifest and to formulate tentative hypotheses and therapeutic plans and strategies for working with people with different diagnostic features, styles of personality and contact.

You can use your observations of the clients' phenomenological processes of contacting and moderating contact in response to others and to field conditions to help you consider them diagnostically and to evolve the best therapeutic strategies for working with this particular style of client. It's important to keep revising your tentative plans and evolving your strategies in the light of the experience of each session; so that you are balancing and integrating attention to the reality of the moment with background conceptualisation, thought and planning. Figure 12.2 illustrates how human meeting, reflection, diagnosis, conceptualisation and development of therapeutic hypotheses and strategies in the Gestalt context can be a developing cycle, which is constantly revised in the light of the human experience. It also illustrates one example of the rhythmic alternation of 'I–It' and 'I–You' styles of relating in the counselling process.

If you compare the description of George's process (above) and that of Rose (p. 238) it will probably be obvious that the therapist needed to work very differently with George than with Rose. For example George's therapist supported George to resensitise himself to his body sensation and gradually to feel and eventually to express his tightly controlled feelings. Rose's therapist on the other hand helped her to slow down, become more aware of herself and reflective about her actions. He actually helped her learn to *hold back* or retroflect her feelings at least until she was in a safe place. Subsequent work with both clients is referred to on pp. 189 and 161 respectively.

Key point

Pay close and detailed attention to how each client functions in the world and to their processes of contact and withdrawal. You can use your observations as the basis for developing diagnostic perspectives and devising individualised therapeutic strategies for working with each client in the future. However, it is also important to keep revising any diagnostic perspectives and tentative plans you make in the light of your ongoing experience of meeting the client person to person and in the light of the phenomenological perspective which invites you to keep an open, fresh 'beginner's mind' (Suzuki, 1970: 21).

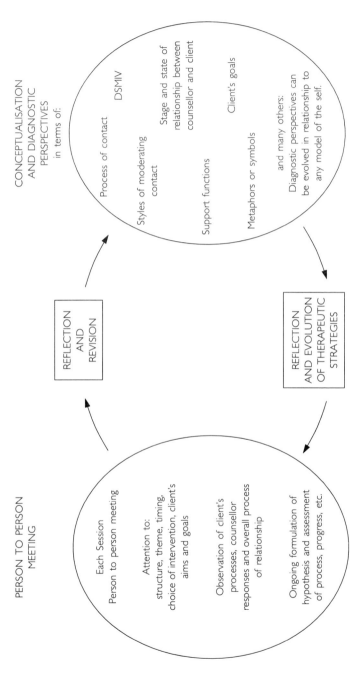

Figure 12.2 *Evolving flow of person to person meeting, reflection, conceptualisation of diagnostic perspectives, therapeutic strategies and human meeting from session to session*

V Exploring Awareness and Contact

13 Exploring and developing awareness and contact

Awareness

In the Gestalt sense, awareness is the holistic process of contact with and withdrawal from others in the field, of self regulation and meaning-making which takes place within our whole person, animates our being and changes us. It is noticing, recognising, being in touch with, and it involves our lived experience of the physical, mental, emotional and spiritual dimensions of our self. It is a whole process engaging the total self in an exchange with the changing dimensions of the environment and it inevitably leads to growth. True awareness is therefore quite different from thinking, ruminating or introspecting, which are primarily cognitive processes that do not necessarily lead to the growth of the person. 'Awareness is like the glow of a coal which comes from its own combustion; what is given by introspection is like the light reflected from an object when a flashlight is turned on it. In awareness a process is taking place in the coal (the total organism)' (Perls et al., 1994: 323). Holistic awareness is rooted in rich somatic and emotional life and encompasses both intuitive hunches and body wisdom.

Awareness is the way in which we understand ourselves and what we need and also the way in which we organise our field and make meaning of our experience. It is our capacity to be in touch with our own existence, to know how we are feeling, sensing, thinking, reacting or making meaning from moment to moment. Awareness is a blessing (Zinker, 1978) because it enables us to perceive and make sense of what is going on inside and outside ourselves and allows us the possibility of ascertaining what we can do to make ourselves, others or the environment better.

Nigel and his partner Janet were discussing the needs of their 10-year-old son and Nigel's recurrent feelings of depression. Nigel (who had prided himself on being a very successful 'house husband' for several years) experienced a moment of self realisation in which he understood that now he wanted and needed to play a more 'manly' role in his family and that his son would also benefit from such a shift in his father's style. His realisation was cognitive, emotional, physical and also very enlivening. He had an image of the new life he wanted to lead, together with a physical sensation that felt almost like mild shock. Janet and his son, Jake, were excited and invigorated in response.

Awareness is the aim of Gestalt exploration

Perls et al. (1994) emphasised that the aim of therapy is increased awareness, contact and integration because these inevitably lead to change and growth. Yontef (1993) has similarly explained that the overall aim of Gestalt is the development of awareness – because paradoxically people change not by willing themselves to change but by becoming fully aware of who and what they *currently* are (see p. 63).

Regaining awareness may sound like rather a slight or simple aim for therapeutic counselling but it is in fact very challenging. Most people who come for counselling and therapy have lost touch with large areas of awareness because we have almost all learned to block out much of our naturally arising awarenesses and our intrinsic self–other regulation and replace them with a sense of how we *ought* to be/respond/feel/act and when we *should* interact or withdraw from others. We have developed deeply ingrained bodily, mental and emotional ways (or fixed gestalts) of maintaining these holes in our awareness (see p. 24). Our habitual ways of keeping aspects of ourselves or our surroundings out of awareness were usually established for what were (or seemed to be) good reasons at the time. For example many people I've worked with have absolutely no awareness of their own potential for anger. Exploration has often revealed that they were violently threatened as children and so they completely cut out of their repertoire all possibilities of angry responses.

Reviewing such fixed gestalts and regaining awareness of aspects of the self which have been denied for such good reasons usually provokes anxiety and a sense of impasse created by an internal conflict between the aspect of self which wants to regain awareness and the aspect of self which wants to avoid painful or uncomfortable feelings. You need considerable skill to help clients stay with and develop awareness of the impasse itself (see p. 171).

Supporting clients to develop awareness of their process of contact and withdrawal

People change and develop through becoming fully aware, in the context of dialogic relating, of who they really are, not by willpower or self coercion (see p. 63). This paradoxical theory of change proposes that supporting clients to develop deep awareness of themselves and their styles of contacting and relating to others will lead to growth. For example, you can find ways for clients to discover experientially how they currently go through the cycle of contact and withdrawal, how they become aware of their needs (or sometimes fail to do so), how they mobilise their energies (and when and how they don't), how they take action to make contact with you or others and how they integrate or learn from their contact experiences. Together you can investigate how clients' current functioning may be supporting or unawarely thwarting their needs and desires.

> Angela became aware that her fear of being judged made her subtly avoid situations, such as learning situations, where she might feel vulnerable. Yet she longed for the stimulus and challenge which further training might provide.

Developing awareness of contact styles at the contact boundary needs to be an exploratory, not a corrective process. This may seem a rather obvious point to make but it is only too easy for counsellors and therapists who have learned about the process of contact and withdrawal to become over-zealous about encouraging clients into contact, rather than exploring *how* the client's present style of contact helps them or exploring what *difference* a different style of contact would make. For example counsellors may routinely invite most clients to make eye contact or speak directly to them in a manner that seems corrective rather than investigative, without apparently understanding the philosophy and methodology of phenomenological investigation and field theory.

Whether certain body gestures or linguistic styles interrupt or support contact depends upon the particular field conditions at any time. Sometimes deflecting eye contact will be an interruption to contact; at other times it may be an aid or facilitator of the clients' process of contact, depending upon the particular field conditions of that client at that time (see p. 219). The idea is to help clients be more aware of how they are interacting with their world (including finding out about their previously unconscious, fixed styles of interacting) and to consider whether and to what extent their present modes of contact are of service to them (so that they have more choice about how they interact in the future). The aim is not to *improve* clients' style of contact so that it fits into some standardised idea of 'good contact' but to help them know about their styles of contact and how they support or hinder the fulfillment of their intentions.

Methods of developing awareness

The holistic methods of developing awareness available to Gestalt counsellors and therapists are limited only by their imaginations and the boundaries of the therapeutic relationship. They include:

- using phenomenological methods of description;
- co-creating experiments or experimental situations;
- focusing upon the dialogic relationship and on the process of the present lived interaction between you and clients;
- working with unfinished situations from the clients' past by focusing upon the internal structure of the present interaction.

Using phenomenological methods

Phenomenological methods of bracketing, tracking, describing and investigating are central to Gestalt and used extensively in Gestalt counselling and therapy as an essential means to increase awareness of how clients are actually functioning, rather than how they or you speculate they *may* be functioning. They can be used to observe, describe and investigate clients' processes of contacting and moderating contact in their dialogic relationship with you. Phenomenological methods are outlined and discussed on p. 59 and illustrated in examples throughout this book.

Co-creating experiments

You can co-create experiments (pp. 131 and 236) expressly designed to heighten clients' awareness of those aspects of themselves which they normally keep blocked out of awareness, of the ways in which they are in intrapsychic conflict, at an impasse, stuck between opposing forces within themselves or

within the field. The theory and practice of using creative experimentation to heighten awareness is discussed and illustrated on
pp. 131–4; while the theory and practice of working with internal
conflict and impasses is discussed on p. 169.

Focusing on the dialogic relationship

You can heighten awareness of clients' styles of contact by
focusing upon the here and now interaction between you – for the
ways clients relate to you is likely to be in some way a reflection or
a microcosm of clients' ways of contacting the world, relating to
others and making meaning of their life. A client's relationship
with you is one of the prime means you both have for studying
their process of organising the field, their styles of making contact
and moderating contact. Through your interaction you can
mutually consider whether and how these processes support
their self development and when and how they undermine it.
Explore and ask yourselves what is going on between you from
moment to moment. Pay attention not only to the client's and your
own words but also to both your whole ways of being – body
structure, gestures, facial expressions, posture and mannerisms –
because people contact and communicate with each other through
their whole being, not just their words.

Frances wanted to be more relaxed and to make friends but she had a
history of relationships where she got rejected and she felt physically rigid
most of the time. In her contact with the counsellor, Frances at first seemed
flexibly available for relationship, showing her vulnerability and appearing to
be open to feedback and empathy. However, soon Frances's initial contact-
fulness was replaced by other physical and emotional responses. Her face
often closed up and her body stiffened. When this happened the counsellor
described what she saw and suggested that Frances experimentally get in
touch with these physical aspects of her response. In doing so, Frances
discovered that she was constantly closing up and cutting off from the
counsellor in lots of small involuntary ways: 'I'm as stiff as a ramrod now.' 'I've
put up a wall between you and me.' 'I'm not taking in your words.' 'I'm
thinking how false and insincere you sound.' 'People who have been nice to
me have always disappeared.' 'I despise myself for minding.' They discovered
that Frances was especially inclined to go rigid when the counsellor expressed
empathy towards her vulnerability or loneliness.

Thus through focusing upon the dialogic relationship and developing
awareness of how Frances was interacting from moment to moment they
found out more about how Frances contributed to her experiences of being
emotionally rejected – by distancing herself, by interpreting warmth and
empathy as false and by rejecting *herself* for her emotional needs. The

counsellor also actively explored how *she* might have contributed in the present to Frances's responses (What was I doing or saying which might have made you feel like that? How might I have contributed to a reaction like that?), thus respecting Frances's reality and making the exploration phenomenological, horizontal and intersubjective rather than assuming that Frances's reactions belonged only to Frances, which would have been more one-sided or hierarchical.

Exploring the past through attention to present process

Although Gestalt therapy and counselling pay particular attention to developing awareness of whatever is happening here and now, this does not mean you have to deny the importance of the past or future. It merely emphasises that although people remember the past and plan for the future, the remembering and planning happen in the present. If you and the client pay careful attention to the internal structure of the present interaction, unfinished situations from the client's past often come into present aware-ness (Perls et al., 1994 and Polster and Polster, 1974). You and clients do not revisit the past, nor would you wish to do so, for revisiting the past without any significant change in the field conditions, particularly the level of support available, would not allow any change and is likely to be re-traumatising. But you can explore elements of the past in the *changed and more supportive field conditions* of the present moment. One of the greatest strengths of Gestalt is that it offers ways of looking for and working with past unfinished situations which are seeking attention in the present. You can often support clients to find a fresh resolution or make a new integration or completion of past unfinished business in the present therapeutic exploration, as is illustrated in the following example.

The session started with Tom's awareness of his tight jaw. His voice had a metallic tone and he turned out his words like a brittle robot. I noticed an odd angle to his jaw and asked him what he felt there. He said he felt tight. So I asked him to exaggerate the movement of his mouth and jaw. He felt very inhibited about this and described his awareness first of embarrassment, then stubbornness. He remembered that his parents used to nag him about speaking clearly and he would go out of his way *not* to. At this point he became aware of tightness in his throat. He was speaking with muscular strain, forcing out his voice rather than using the support which his breathing could give him. So I asked Tom to experimentally bring more air into his speech and see what happened, showing him how to coordinate speaking with breathing by using a little more air and by trying to feel the air as a source of support (see p. 183). His coordination was faulty, though – so faulty as to border on stuttering. When I asked him whether he had ever stuttered, he looked startled, became aware of his coordination troubles, and then remembered what he had until then forgotten – that he *had* stuttered until he was six or seven.

Having recovered the old sensations, his speech become more open and his jaw softened too. He felt relieved and renewed (example adapted from Polster and Polster, 1974).

Key point

Awareness is a holistic process involving people's lived experience on physical, mental, emotional and spiritual levels. Supporting clients to regain fuller awareness and contact with themselves and their surroundings is an effective means of restoring the natural cycle of growth and development. Yet regaining awareness frequently requires the resurfacing and deconstructing of fixed gestalts and is thus often felt by clients as dangerous or risky. When exploring methods for developing awareness you need to be prepared to work respectfully with clients' ambivalence and deep inner conflict.

---

14 Reintegrating disowned aspects or polarities of the self

As already discussed (p. 73), the self is variable and flexible. It encompasses many different apparently contradictory (or polar) processes within the overall self process.

As therapists, we need to be aware of the whole continuum of possible human behaviours and alert to the fact that people who embody a limited range of behaviour or qualities are likely to be denying (or not accepting) large aspects of their conceivable holistic selves. They are almost certainly limiting themselves because of some sense of how they 'ought' to be and they are thus also undermining their genuine self support for awareness, contact and action. People who disown large portions of the spectrum of human qualities are usually in some form of unaware internal conflict, as a controlling aspect of themselves prevents them owning or showing the denied characteristics.

They are also likely to become entangled in interpersonal conflicts or misunderstanding, because if people disown their own qualities they often unconsciously project them on to other people and situations, which leads them to misunderstand those people and situations.

All of us have the potential to embody all manner of human qualities. For example, we all have within us the characteristic of kindness and its polar opposite, cruelty; of foresight and negligence, of liveliness and boringness, of spontaneity and deliberateness. We encompass all possible human dimensions and polarities, although we may not be in touch with them:

kindness	cruelty
liveliness	boringness
spontaneity	deliberateness
foresight	negligence

In theory we are capable of embodying both polarities of these continuums of behaviour and of any positions along those continuums, as we change in relationship to others and in the changing circumstances of our lives. In practice, however, most people have learned to dissociate from those qualities which were forcibly or persistently forbidden or disapproved of by their parents, teachers or cultures. Many children in the United Kingdom are taught that showing off is wrong and manage to block out all experiences of self congratulation and pride. As a counsellor you may, for instance, have learned to value clarity and find it very hard to recognise or value messiness or confusion in your work (see pp. 216–19).

Highly self-aware people are able to respond flexibly and variously to a broad spectrum of different people and situations. They recognise that they need a wide range of human qualities in order to make contact and deal with the complexities of the world in which they live. The more aware the person, the more qualities and apparently contradictory polarities they can accept within themselves and the more they can flexibly acknowledge many facets of their personality. So they may say 'I am usually friendly and easygoing but if I feel someone is trying to hassle me, I'm capable of being fierce and defensive' or, 'It's true I was really unkind to you yesterday.' Of course even very aware people have blind spots and ambivalences so that they are unable to acknowledge certain characteristics in certain circumstances with certain people. But for the most part they can acknowledge many interrelated polarities and can integrate feedback from others about themselves.

Less aware, more disturbed people are less able to acknowledge a range of characteristics and have a much more limited, defensive view of themselves. They tend to be identified with some qualities and alienated from others. They are likely to be rigidly unaware of those polarities which their family, culture or life experience have conditioned them to find unacceptable and to react defensively to feedback which suggests they manifest the denied qualities.

Many people blank out supposedly 'negative' qualities such as cruelty, evil, dullness, clumsiness while others have learned to deny very 'positive' characteristics or polarities (such as being beautiful, brilliant or witty) because they have learned to be embarrassed about their attributes. Other people are fully conversant with both poles of a continuum of behaviours or human qualities, swinging from one to another, but are unfamiliar with the other more moderate positions. For example they are either ecstatically happy or dejectedly miserable, either sugar sweet or coldly angry, and they don't seem to know anywhere in between.

Figure 14.1 shows the idea of polarised qualities. It illustrates how some people have a much greater awareness of opposing forces within themselves than other less aware people, who tend to see themselves in a more rigid or limited fashion.

I have often found it helpful to discuss with clients the idea that everyone has the potential to embody all human qualities and that there is nothing intrinsically wrong with being in touch with any of them as long as they don't *act* on their more dangerous feelings. I have sometimes drawn a simple, blank version of the two illustrations given above and filled them out with individuals or groups, asking them which qualities they know themselves to have and then getting them to fill in their opposites – the opposites are often the characteristics which they don't identify with. Then we've discussed how they would feel about being those opposites. The idea is to explore and discover, not to correct. Such a discussion often surfaces all sorts of interesting stories about clients' background, culture and belief systems.

You can also develop the exploration of polarities in less cognitive and more holistic ways:

> For instance, you can explore how clients have come to exclude certain characteristics from their self definition. You can explore with clients some of the potential advantages of disowned characteristics so that they may begin to see value in qualities which they had previously been afraid of. You could suggest that clients paint, describe or exaggerate the polarity they are already

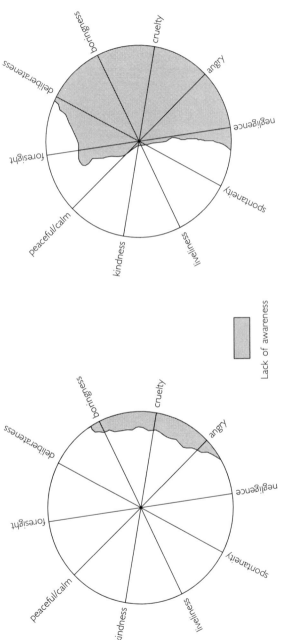

(a) The most aware people can know and accept many opposing forces, polarities and qualities within themselves. They are able to see themselves in a multitude of apparently 'contradictory' ways and experience relationship between these different inner aspects of the self.

(b) Less aware people see themselves in more limited and rigid ways. They tend to know and accept a much smaller range of forces, polarities, qualities and feelings within themselves and to identify with only one polarity along each continuum. So they may accept feedback that they are kind but reject feedback that they are cruel or negligent, for instance. They lack flexibility and breadth of self perception.

Figure 14.1 Differing degrees of awareness of polarised qualities, forces or aspects of the self (inspired by Zinker, 1978)

familiar with and/or paint, describe or exaggerate the one they are fearful of, just to see what it feels like. Alternatively you can suggest that clients choose figures, puppets or objects from the surroundings to represent their known and unknown polarities. You can invite those clients who tend to swing between extremes in their life to imagine what would be the mid-point or middle ground in between their polarities and paint, describe, mime or enact that middle ground.

In addition you can yourself model embracing disowned aspects of the self. A client who suffered from an eating disorder never allowed herself to feel or admit to any fear. She denied fear so adamantly that when the therapist said she sometimes felt afraid, the client thought that the therapist must be no good and briefly reconsidered her choice. However, in the subsequent weeks she gradually began to share her own fears and to resensitise herself to the issues in her life which had contributed to her denial of fear and other feelings and thus to her disorder.

When people either unawarely or awarely disown aspects of their potential whole selves, it is often because their life experiences have taught them to do so. They may be absolutely delighted to expand their self concept and try out new ways of being. But equally they may be quite reluctant to do so because they are deeply attached to their present self concept which is supported by a complicated web of interconnected belief systems. Their belief systems and reluctance are also important parts of their whole selves, so honour and explore them also (see pp. 169 and 188).

Some clients who have emotionally restricting, threatening or abusive backgrounds may not have developed a full range of self functions (see pp. 74 and 201), so they may need to evolve these through the actual process of relationship, rather than just regain awareness of disowned polarities and functions which already exist but have been repressed. Evolving self functions is likely to be a longer and still more delicate task (Kepner, 1995).

Key point

Be aware that we all limit our self concept through disowning certain human qualities. Notice how clients do this and support them to explore a wider range of emotional attitudes and behaviours so that they can respond more flexibly to the world around them.

15 Exploring personal responsibility

Active self and role of responsibility

Gestalt philosophy proposes that individuals are active in the choosing and organising of their lives and reality. Mature people are able to take existential responsibility for themselves, for many aspects of their life and, above all, for the meaning they give their life. Perls (1969b, 1976) often spelt the word responsibility as response-ability to emphasise this point. If one becomes fully aware of events in one's own life, what they are and how they figure in one's functioning, 'then one becomes responsible for them – not in the sense of now having to assume some burden that was not there before, but rather in the sense of now recognising that it is oneself who determines in most instances whether they shall or shall not continue to exist' (Perls et al., 1994: 270).

Existential responsibility does not mean that people are personally responsible for all situations in which they find themselves. People who are starving during a famine or people who are incarcerated in a concentration camp because of their race clearly did not bring about their terrible environmental conditions. However existential theories propose that they can still take some responsibility for how they live out their lives in this environment. Frankl (1973) has described how some of his fellow prisoners in concentration camps remained active in the meaning they gave their lives, even though they were usually unable to change the terrible circumstances in which they existed and died, and Brian Keenan (1992) has more recently shown how he retained his sense of meaning and worth as a hostage.

Although our culture values individualism and self reliance, it places very little emphasis on true self responsibility and what it involves. Many clients come for counselling or therapy wanting to blame others for their predicament, feeling like victims of societal pressures or poor parenting and hoping to get their needs met by someone else – often the counsellor or therapist. They are genuinely ignorant about the whole concept of self responsibility and may have little or no idea that they play an active role in organising their psychological reality (or field) and thus in the way they perceive their experience (see p. 54). Often they don't realise that even though they have not so far been able to change their circumstances, they *are* almost certainly able to change the way they experience those circumstances and the meaning they give to them.

It is important that you hear people's stories and *accept* their current reality, including the current meaning that they give their lives. People often cling tenaciously to *their* version of their story – they have developed ways of being, symptoms and complaints that form a functional whole. They have often invested tremendous personal energy and their self image in their overall way of seeing things. They need, of course, to feel that you accept and respect the self that they currently are.

However, you can also gradually and persistently introduce and model the concept of self responsibility, by exploring whether clients are open to any new perspectives and demonstrating how it is possible to change the whole complexion of an experience by responding to it differently or by perceiving it differently. For change is only possible because the relationship between figure and ground is not fixed (although it may appear so in the light of a fixed gestalt, a habit of blame or a one-sided version of a story).

You may need to respectfully discuss with clients the concept that change comes about when we reshuffle our reality by making new aspects of our field figural or new elements of our story central or by combining different elements of our perceptual field in fresh ways to give new meaning to our circumstances. You can also explain that one small change engenders others so if we learn to change small aspects of our attitudes or behaviour, this usually leads to larger changes and eventually to change in our experience and in our contact with others (see pp. 45 and 192 for examples). Such changes of course lead to systemic change in others, in the sense that if I sing a new tune or dance a new dance, then my partners in the dance of life will almost inevitably respond with a new song or step.

Martin and Janet came for couple counselling construing their present reality in mainly negative terms. They blamed each other and interpreted even the well-intentioned behaviour of the other in mean-spirited ways. The counsellor decided to model the idea that each one of us chooses the meaning with which we endow behaviour by herself choosing not to be confluent with Martin and Janet's negative way of perceiving themselves. Instead she admired both their stances. The counsellor's fresh way of perceiving their reality gently shook their fixed perception and enlivened the contact both between her and them and between the two of them. It also introduced them to the idea that they might create a new world by wearing different spectacles.

The counsellor focused on how they were contributing to staying victimised: how for instance Martin had chosen work which demanded such long hours that he wasn't ever available when his little son was awake; how Janet had chosen not to do paid work and was thus financially dependent on Martin. The counsellor was blunt about the fact that these were real choices. Both Janet and Martin felt uncomfortable experiencing their choicefulness, as if they were losing something important in their view of themselves, and it was only as they found some meaning and dignity to the tenacity with which they had held on to these identities that they began to feel less victimised. After much exploration of this nature, Martin and Janet were eventually able to make some different choices which allowed them to realise a little more of their dream of creating a family unit (Hemming, 1994).

Experimenting with the language of responsibility

An example of the denial of personal responsibility which is so prevalent in our culture is embedded in our everyday language in such phrases as 'It makes me sad when you do . . .' or 'She made me hit her.' In the first phrase an abstract 'it' is made responsible for me, while in the second phrase, someone other than 'I' is responsible for my actions. When we speak in this way, we are projecting initiative and responsibility and thus constantly reinforcing our tendency to experience ourselves in a passive role or as victims.

You could try paying attention to your own use of language and notice whether or not you are using language which reflects your own existential responsibility for your feelings, opinions and the choices and meaning you make in your life. In addition, you can sometimes draw the attention of clients to *their* use of language, *not in a corrective but in an exploratory way*. You may explore with them, for example, whether their attitude to the world changes if they use more direct language which explicitly demonstrates to themselves and others their personal responsibility for their choices in life. You may suggest that at least in the counselling session they try making 'I', rather than 'you' statements or experiment with saying 'I don't want to', rather than 'I can't', or 'I choose to' rather than 'I have to'. 'The aim is to come to realise again that you are creative in your environment and are responsible for your reality – not to blame, but responsible in the sense that it is you who lets it stand or changes it' (Perls et al., 1994: 460).

This sort of experiment in the use of languages involves more than a simple linguistic shift – it is the manifestation of a radical reorientation in the world. Learning what we are responsible for and taking ownership of our feelings and choices is at the heart of Gestalt. This includes a readiness to relinquish responsibility too, to know what cannot be changed. (Hemming, 1994: 72)

When exploring personal responsibility in the ways described above, we need to be aware of differing cultural assumptions and to explore what degree of individual responsibility is compatible with clients' belief systems and cultural values. Gestalt and other humanistic approaches were popularised in the 1960s and tended to glorify the individual and individual responsibility in a way that was heavily influenced by American values of the period (Saner, 1989) and tended to underplay the importance of community and family responsibility in other cultures (Kareem and Littlewood, 1992).

As individuals and as professionals we all have some existential responsibility for the cultural, social and economic field conditions of the age in which we live. The early Gestaltists were radical, political activists and Gestalt can be taken far beyond the bounds of conventional counselling settings. Gestaltists are working in group, organisational, community and political settings and this book includes some examples of instances where Gestalt practitioners have initiated cultural or community action but the vast potential in Gestalt for working in the greater field is still relatively untapped.

Key point

Help clients to experience authorship of their life and to see how and in what ways they are responsible for who they are and how they live, as well as to know what they cannot change and to relinquish responsibility and guilt for those things which are outside their area of influence.

VI

Integrating Experimental, Creative and Transpersonal Dimensions

16 Integrating creative imagination and experiments

Gestalt counselling and psychotherapy are intrinsically creative processes which enable both you and clients to tap into your inherent inventiveness in order to heal the past, expand your experience, transcend the limits you have habitually set upon yourselves and transform your sense of time and possibility. Part VI describes some of the ways in which you can work creatively and experimentally by using your imagination and intuition and introducing metaphor, fantasy, visualisation and play, and synthesising these naturally into the overall flow of the counselling or therapy process.

Creativity and holistic functioning

Many of us have been taught to value very highly the human processes of cognitive deduction, rational investigation, verbal explanation and scientific objectivity – all activities associated with those parts of the brain which favour logic and linear thinking. Important though these activities are, an over-valuation of them can lead – and often has led – to a under-valuation of intuition, play, creativity and subjective experience. The Gestalt approach offers you ways of synthesising rational thinking and intuitive creativity (Ornstein, 1972) in the process of counselling. It allows you to actively evoke and work with the creative and intuitive hunches of both yourself and clients without losing the logical perspectives of theoretical conceptualisation (see Table 16.1). Gestalt thus enables you to work truly holistically to enhance *all* aspects of clients' awareness and to use *all* aspects of your self, in the service of clients' exploration.

Gestalt experimentation

Another unique dimension of Gestalt counselling and therapy is its fresh creative approach. There are several important ways in which it is experimental:

Table 16.1 *Activities associated with different modes of functioning*

Activities associated with logical and linear thinking	Activities associated with intuitive and creative flow
Verbal language: using words to name, describe, define.	Non-verbal: awareness of and working with things, sensations, images, art forms, metaphors, etc.
Analysis: figuring things out step by step and bit by bit.	Synthesis: putting things together to form wholes.
Abstraction: taking out a small bit of information and using it to represent the whole.	Concreteness: relating to things as they are at the present moment: experience-near (as in phenomenological description and investigation of present process).
Reason and Logic: drawing conclusions based on reasons and facts; one thing following another in logical fashion.	Analogic: seeing likenesses between things, understanding metaphoric relationships.
	Non-rational: not requiring a basis of reason or facts, willingness to suspend judgements.
Number: Using numbers as in counting.	
Sequence and Linearity: Thinking in terms of linked ideas, one thought directly following another, and leading to a conclusion.	Intuitive: Making leaps of insight, often based on hunches, sensations, feelings, visual images, dreams, etc.
Temporal: keeping track of time, sequencing one thing after another.	Non-temporal: without a sense of time.
	Holistic: seeing whole things all at once; perceiving overall patterns and structures, leading to multiple possibilities or divergent conclusions.
	Rhythm, music, images, imagination, daydreaming, colour, dimension.
Being in control: certain, serious, curious, intellectual.	Going with the flow: allowing oneself to experience confusion, playing, having a sense of humour.

The whole experience of coming to counselling or therapy is an experiment, a safe emergency in which clients are challenged and supported to look at their familiar patterns of behaviour and their fixed ways of configuring the field in an overall context of safety.

Clients and counsellors are engaged in a dialogic relationship. Neither controls the other or the relationship, but both concentrate upon the unfolding process and in that sense the relationship is experimental from moment to moment. Both allow the outcome(s) to emerge from the cooperative experimental exploration.

You can learn to co-design specific experiments that are intended to focus on either of the preceding two and to heighten clients' awareness and facilitate their action research.

Rationale and aims of Gestalt experimentation

People learn better by doing and by trial and error than merely by talking about something (Lewin 1926, 1935, 1952; Kolb and Fry, 1975). So Gestalt therapy and counselling have developed the concept of experiments, in which clients learn about themselves through active participation and action research within the therapeutic sessions. Active methods of exploration that involve bodily and mental processes are of course highly compatible with Gestalt's holistic emphasis upon the whole of the people involved, not just their words. Gestalt experiments involve the exploration of the client's experience through active, behavioural or imaginative expression rather than merely through internal cognising or verbal explanation. They are creative adventures co-designed and co-developed by counsellor and client.

Gestalt experiments are *not* primarily designed to achieve any specific outcome or to encourage clients into conforming, performing or changing their behaviour (although paradoxically the outcome of experiments *may well be* a change of behaviour *on some occasions*: see p. 63). Instead, the aim of a Gestalt experiment is to support clients to *try things* out in order to do one or more of the following, within the context of the dialogic relationship between client and counsellor:

- to holistically study and *increase their awareness* of their own perceptions of and interactions with others, including the counsellor;
- to develop and explore life themes which are of importance to them;
- to integrate experiential learning and bodily phenomena with cognitive understanding;

- to enable them to explore all the forces which are active within the field and create conditions in which they can see their life as their own creation and responsibility (p. 124);
- to reach their personal impasses and see more clearly what are the different processes which are at work within themselves – both the positive and the 'resisting' forces – at moments of impasse (p. 171);
- to review their repertoire of behaviours and perceptions and thus possibly to choose to enlarge their range of options.[1]

Part VI describes how to design Gestalt experiments and discusses their flexibility and range. Box 16.1 summarises guidelines for when and how to co-design Gestalt experiments.

Range and flexibility of Gestalt experiments

There are almost limitless possibilities for both the type and the scale of Gestalt experiments – the only limit is your own or the clients' imaginations.

You can develop a wide variety, ranging from tiny experiments that concentrate on a detail of behaviour and last a few seconds to large-scale re-enactments involving several people or props and taking considerable time. You can introduce experiments into the current exchange between you and clients. You can suggest experiments which enact real or imagined scenes from the past or the present. Experiments can involve verbal or body language, fantasy, visualisation, movement, dance, enactment or dream exploration. They can take place within the session itself and between sessions. The beauty of Gestalt is that you can move between the laminated layers and levels of the field or life space, switching frames or perspectives and employing a wonderfully creative and varied range of methods of exploration, as needed (Parlett, 1991).

This book gives many examples of Gestalt experiments, as do most other books on Gestalt (see Perls et al., 1994; Polster and Polster, 1974; Zinker, 1978; Perls, 1969a, 1969b; Sills et al., 1995). Box 16.1 gives guidelines for the co-design of experiments and Appendix 5 shows an extended example of co-designing an experiment with a client, together with a commentary which links the practical examples to the theoretical guidelines in Box 16.1.

1. Zinker (1978) has suggested that one of the aims of a Gestalt experiment is to modify the client's behaviour. I suggest that this aim is not fully compatible with the paradoxical theory of change (see p. 65).

Box 16.1   Guidelines for co-designing Gestalt experiments

1. *Precondition*: Clients need to be willing to attend to what they are feeling, thinking and doing and to understand the value of learning actively by trial and error. Counsellors often need to explain the concept of experimentation several times and grade experiments to *tiny* manageable ones if clients are hesitant.

2. *Groundwork and identification of theme*: Listen (holistically) for a central theme in the client's exchange with you. This may be a life theme (one that is central to the client's life and to the problems they have brought to counselling) or it may be a fresh theme emerging in the current session for the first time. Either way, it needs to be a theme which is of immediate interest to the client, something of which he/she is vaguely but not fully aware.

3. *Negotiation*: Negotiate with clients whether the theme you identify is in fact central to their perspective of themselves and whether or not they wish to explore it further. Invite any ideas they have for how they might do so.

4. *Design and clarification of theme*: Propose or co-design an experiment *through the actual doing of which* the client can explore that theme actively and increase awareness, irrespective of the outcome. The nature of possible experiments is very varied but may involve inviting the client to either (a) exaggerate and amplify present behaviour or attitude, or (b) inhibit present behaviour or attitude in the experimental situation.

5. *Grading and negotiating*: In negotiation with clients grade or calibrate the experiment to make it harder or easier so that it is challenging enough to provoke active exploration of the difficulty and yet safe enough to allow the client to attempt it. You can increase or decrease your support as part of the process of calibration.

6. *Impasse*: As contact gets stronger with whatever aspects of the theme are denied (or held out of awareness in a fixed gestalt), clients' excitement or anxiety will inevitably be aroused or mobilised. At that point clients are likely to experience the experiment as some sort of 'safe emergency' or existential crisis and may feel stuck in an impasse between excitement and fear.

7. *Heightening the impasse*: You can stay with the impasse and support the client to really feel their stuckness or conflict and any associated feelings of anxiety or confusion. This often requires the counsellor to tolerate difficult feelings of stuckness or anxiety, as

continued overleaf

Box 16.1 (*continued*)

well. You can also support the client either to fully explore the denied or resisting forces *or* lend energy to the forces within the client which want to push through the impasse (see p. 171).

8. *Significant increase in awareness:* In the safe emergency of the experiment, repressed or unaware attitudes relating to the theme or impasse may come fully into clients' awareness and thus change their experience of themselves and the degree of their own responsibility and choice.

9. *Assimilation and debriefing:* You can attend to these important stages by encouraging clients to chew over and discuss their experience; to review what has been learned and to assimilate any new learning into the ground of self (see Part VIII).

See Appendix 5 for an extended example and commentary which illustrates these guidelines.

Experiments often involve doing things which clients find unusual. As shame reactions are frequently triggered by situations in which people feel uncomfortable or vulnerable, it is possible that some clients may experience some suggestions for Gestalt experiments as shaming; so it is important that you are alert to signs of shame (Lee and Wheeler, 1996 and Appendix 7) and careful not to inadvertently heighten feelings of exposure or embarrassment. Some ways to decrease the dangers of precipitating shame reactions in clients is to constantly monitor the level of support available, to calibrate the process and pace of experimentation finely and to work appropriately with shame experiences if these emerge.

Experiments that introduce an imaginary 'other' or a 'two-chair' dialogue

Some of the experiments demonstrated by Fritz Perls in the 1960s concentrated upon inviting clients to talk to imaginary external third parties (imaginary others) or to hold dialogues between internal aspects of the self (as in the famous 'two-chair dialogue' between two aspects of self). The potential pitfall of that sort of experiment is that it may deflect from the interaction between client and counsellor and therefore dilute the interpersonal focus of the dialogic relationship. Isadore From (1984) and Erving Polster (1995) have suggested that mishandled third party or intrapsychic experiments can reintroduce the 'couch' into counselling and allow the counsellor to hide behind the experiment as effectively as the traditional analysts hid behind their rule of therapeutic abstinence. In some of Fritz Perls's demonstrations, the interaction between client and counsellor was indeed reduced to a minimum – Fritz Perls structured the experiment (which very frequently did have a third party or intrapersonal focus) and instructed the client. The client complied or was asked to return to his seat. Perls actually theorised that experiments should always arise from the unique interaction between client and counsellor but often forgot his own guideline in practice.

If on the other hand you prioritise the sensitive and respectful negotiation between client and therapist regarding the joint design, grading and regrading of the experiment, as illustrated in the example in Appendix 5, then you can ensure that the exploration of the contact process in the dialogic relationship remains central even when working with experiments that have a third party or intrapersonal focus (Zinker, 1978, 1994). The processes of negotiating in these instances may be more valuable focuses of study than the 'official experiment' itself, as the negotiation reveals how clients handle many important aspects of contacting and relationship, such as mutuality, power, assertion and influence in the present exchange. As you negotiate the 'official experiment', you can hold a parallel phenomenological enquiry into the process of negotiation and relationship that happens between you. For example, the counsellor described in Appendix 5 also asked Henry how he felt about being asked to do something new, how he would let her know if he didn't want to proceed, how he felt from moment to moment in relationship to her.

Experiments that focus on the dialogic relationship

It is also possible and may often be preferable to design ongoing experiments that focus directly on and heighten the process of relationship between client and therapist. This book contains a number of examples of exchanges where clients and counsellors have focused upon their relationship in the here and now as a means of developing the clients' awareness of their patterns of interacting and styles of contact (see pp. 138, 141, 161 and 186).

Experiments that focus on the present relationship between client and counsellor also need to be well designed, and finely calibrated to meet the client's current concerns and capacity for contact and self support. For instance the therapeutic counsellor may pursue a simple enquiry into the exchange going on between them by asking open questions such as: 'How are you responding to what I've just said?'; 'What are you feeling? thinking?'; 'What have you not said to me that you wish you had?'; 'How did you feel towards me after the last session?'; 'How might I be contributing to what you are feeling?' and so on.

However, for many clients who have not had any previous experience of direct relationship skills, or who have been shamed in previous relationships, such an enquiry may be too direct and demanding. In these cases the counsellor or therapist can set up all sorts of gentler, less exposing experiments to investigate awareness of the current relationship. For example the counsellor could suggest that clients choose a metaphor to represent their relationship, which they can then develop and explore together (see p. 141 for an example of this). Or the counsellor can suggest that clients paint a colour and shape to represent each participant in the relationship and the link between them. Or the counsellor can invite the client to explore the relationship more indirectly.

George had grown up in a family culture where it was considered unacceptable to tell other people how you felt about them. People were punished or ignored if they did. So he learned to bottle up personal feelings or to talk about people to other people – never directly to their faces. This client found it impossible to discuss his reactions to and feelings for the counsellor directly and yet it was one of the crucial contact skills he wanted to develop. The counsellor suggested that he choose some of the plastic toy figures she kept in her room to represent himself and her. He chose several figures and told a story about how different figures (which represented different sides of himself) felt towards her.

Client and counsellor continued to use this 'indirect' way of exploring their relationship for some time, until George gained confidence about letting her know more directly how he related to her. In this case a form of deflection (that is indirect communication through the toys), was a support to contact rather than an interruption to contact (p. 105).

If the whole experience of coming to counselling or therapy is an experiment, a safe emergency in which clients are supported and challenged to increase their awareness of established patterns of interrelating with others in an overall context of safety, then an equally valid form of experiment is to track, negotiate and debrief the client's experience of being in counselling or therapy, without introducing any further formal structures, exercises or enacted experiments.

Key point

You can use creative imagination and an experimental attitude to help clients increase their awareness and expand their options. Be aware that the whole process of Gestalt counselling and therapy is experimental and exploratory. All therapeutic approaches (not just formal experiments) need to be carefully considered and finely calibrated for each individual client, according to their concerns, character, level of support and the stage of the counselling process.

---

17   Introducing and developing imagery and metaphor

Working with imagery

The use of symbol and imagery can be an important means of reaching the other person in an unexpected and fresh manner and may allow people to contact aspects or depths of themselves which they ordinarily cannot access or which they mask in conventional language or habitual (fixed) patterns of thought. The language of symbol and imagery is the language of the unconscious and the transpersonal, the language of dreams and fairy tales. It enables us to visit our imaginative inner world and find our own deeper intuitive wisdom.

You can notice the images, symbols and metaphors that clients introduce and sometimes draw attention to them or develop them in an experimental way.

Sylvia was having some difficulties adapting to her new job. She sat slumped over, looked despondent and said she felt stupid, even when others reminded her that she was in the middle of a transition and almost anyone *would* have difficulties of adaptation. The therapist enquired how she came to feel stupid just because she was finding her new job a challenge and Sylvia responded, 'Oh I don't know – it's just like I've got a dog barking at my heels all the time – every time I feel a bit better and tell myself some of the things that you're all saying, it starts barking, "There you are, I told you you couldn't do it", then I feel bad again.'

The therapist asked what sort of dog was barking and Sylvia replied, 'a Doberman'. The therapist developed the image, 'Oh a large and powerful dog. What would you need to do if you really did have such a large and powerful dog barking at you threateningly?' Sylvia looked more energised and responded, 'Well that's obvious, I suppose. It belongs outside. I'd chain it up.' The therapist invited Sylvia to develop the image in a visualisation: 'Can you imagine doing that?' To which Sylvia promptly replied, 'Yup, I'm doing it. That's it. It's done already. I've chained it up. It's outside in a kennel.'

The therapist checked: 'So now what's happened to that insistent bark?' 'Well it's stopped, but I'm afraid it'll just start again as soon as I'm alone.' The therapist asked Sylvia what she had done which had contributed to the barking voice stopping. At first Sylvia's mind went blank and she couldn't remember but with support from the therapist she retraced and reiterated her visualised steps and concluded that if the bark started again she would remember what she had done in the therapeutic session and do it again.

You can also notice the images that you yourself are having in response to clients and consider sharing some of them. Images can be like a short cut to the heart of the matter or the heart of the client and may enable you and the client to heighten awareness, develop a theme or precipitate an important impasse or insight which you might never reach through hours of talking around and around the subject. Of course the images you have in response to the client may be more to do with your own life experience (or proactive countertransference: Clarkson, 1992 and p. 92) than with the client. They may also have a powerful impact. So you do naturally need to consider the advantages and disadvantages of sharing your images at any particular time. If you decide to share your image, give careful attention to the way in which you do so, making it clear that the image is your own and that you have no investment in it, as in this example:

Counsellor: This may have no relevance to you or what you are discussing but I had a sudden image of you as a 'penitent'.

Client: How extraordinary, I really feel you put your finger on the spot there – that's exactly what I have always felt like – a penitent, as though I had to apologise for my very existence.

Working with metaphors

Working with metaphors can be vital and revealing. They can enable clients to get around or under their normal inhibitions or blocks in awareness to reach their authentic feelings or attitudes.

Anne came into her regular counselling session and said she didn't know why she was there. The counsellor chose to introduce a metaphor to explore Anne's mood, 'Oh that's interesting – if you were the weather, what sort of weather would you be this morning?' Anne replied, 'Storm at sea' and the counsellor asked Anne to describe the storm. When Anne had really mobilised her energy and given a graphic description of dark louring clouds, low over a black sea, the counsellor enquired who or what the clouds might be louring at? Anne replied, 'Well now you mention it – they're louring at you. When I came in I didn't realise that I had any bad feelings towards you but when I was describing all that blackness and you asked that question, this whole conversation just popped into my head . . . You see I felt unnerved last time when you . . .' and Anne went on to express something she had felt unhappy about in the previous session.

The use of the metaphor helped the client get beneath the crust of her logical and conscious reserve and heighten her vague sense of dis-ease until the figure of her discontent emerged vividly enough to be explored in the dialogic relationship between client and counsellor.

Developing images into metaphors offers the opportunity to connect different aspects of clients' experience in ways in which they have not been connected before and allows a fresh perspective that may permit more room for exploration and manoeuvre in a system that has got stuck or rigid.

A couple, Sandy and Michael, described how they were such complete opposites in every respect that they could never agree about anything, which was ruining their life. The counsellor commented and shared her image: 'It seems almost as though you have made yourselves as different and distant from each other as possible. I have an image of two boxers who have taken up positions in the far corners of the boxing ring and both of you are making sure you keep yourselves there. 'Yes,' they responded, 'we're quite entrenched. We've got our entrenched position and we've dug ourselves in.'

Through the way they developed the metaphor, Sandy and Michael had heightened their awareness of what they were doing and they had an insight into the embattled culture they had created at home.

Subsequently Sandy and Michael continued to develop these metaphors through fantasy, visualisation, exaggeration, enactment and bodily movement, until the impasse they were stuck in finally loosened and allowed more vital relating (see p. 160).

Key point

Notice both the images and metaphors which arise in the client's dialogue and the images and metaphors which occur to you when you are with different clients. See if they provide fresh insights into the client's dilemmas or lifestyle. Be prepared to share some of your images and invite clients to articulate and develop their own, if this is consistent with the overall field conditions.

---

18 Introducing fantasy and visualisation

As we saw earlier, people learn more effectively by doing something other than just by talking about it. If they cannot or do not wish to *do* anything active, then they can learn effectively by doing or exploring something actively in fantasy. Research (Brown, 1973) has indicated that someone who does something in fantasy has similar responses in the brain to someone who actually does it. It is as though they have had actually had the experience. Houston (1982) has demonstrated that athletes perfect their play best by visualising the movements they wish to make *before* doing them. Many people cannot take a new step unless they can imagine it first; so the use of fantasy or visualisation in counselling and therapy is not only useful, it may well be crucial.

Angela, an articulate woman, came to therapy because she had recently been exploited by a senior colleague. Her friends and peers had advised her to stand up for herself but she simply could not imagine doing so. Exploration revealed that she had had an extremely dominant father whom she had never been able to stand up to. In some crucial way, she had missed an experience – she had no internal model of standing up and speaking her own truth to people who had more power in the world than her.

She knew what she wanted to do and yet every time she tried to imagine doing so, her mind went blank: she simply could not get a picture of herself doing so. She wept, she explored scenes with her father, and the therapist offered support, which she appreciated. Yet she was still unable to envisage herself standing up for herself with her boss.

The therapist suggested that they could experiment with a guided fantasy in which Angela sought an inner source of support. Angela agreed and the therapist guided her into a relaxed state and then asked her to imagine walking through a wood until she reached a cave where she would find a source of deep support that was hers and would never leave her. The therapist then carefully encouraged Angela to retrace her steps and return to the beginning of the journey – she checked how fully Angela felt present in the room. Noticing that Angela looked a little vague (as people often do after being in a deeply relaxed state), the therapist encouraged her to take specific steps to ground herself, such as standing up, rubbing her feet against the carpet, naming today's date, her current age and occupation.

Angela reported that she had met a wise woman who was as old as the hills and who moved like a dancer – flexible and strong. This woman had said little but offered to accompany her on her return journey. Angela described a warm sense of having someone behind and beside her. During the following week Angela began to have spontaneous pictures of herself holding the conversation she had known was necessary with her senior colleague. Once she had the picture, she was able to move forward, arranged an appointment with the colleague and began the long-needed negotiations for new conditions.

This example illustrates both the importance of being able to visualise behaviours before undertaking them and the natural introduction of a relevant guided fantasy as an experiment in the counselling session.

I have met many counsellors and therapists, both trainees and highly experienced facilitators, who say that they couldn't possibly use visualisation and fantasy in this way because their clients are either too 'formal' or too 'unsophisticated as clients'. I fully acknowledge that there are certainly clients with whom I would not suggest these techniques. I would not for instance normally use fantasy with clients who have a tenuous grasp on reality and already fantasise only too readily; with clients who regress very easily; with clients who have had previous break-downs; or with clients who seem prone to any form of delusion. I have, however, used these approaches with a wide range of clients in all sorts of settings. I have often found that those clients who are the least used to such processes are the most open to visualisation and fantasy, if it is well explained and introduced from a point of view of 'creative indifference' (or non-attachment) (p. 66) and without investment on my part.

For example I frequently discuss recent discoveries about creative process with groups of senior executives in industry and explain that the most innovative and successful managers deliber-ately develop their abilities to access their imaginal world, as well as hone their logical thinking. I have found such people (who normally have no experience at all of counselling) to be keen to try visualising and guided fantasy in an experimental fashion and to see what happens. As with all Gestalt experiments, I stress that there is no right or predictable outcome, that each of them will have unique reactions and that whatever happens is potentially interesting – even if they fall asleep.

The managers report very different experiences, ranging from minuscule sensations to full-blown visions of forgotten aspects of childhood which throw some light on their present predicaments.

> David had been advised that he could be appointed to the executive board of his company only if he developed 'gravitas'. David was unsure what was meant by this phrase and expressed ambivalence about changing himself in any way – his friendly, jokey manner had served him well, making him many friends and easing his career path so far. After participating in a guided fantasy to meet his wise inner self, he reported having a beautiful vision of many colours and hearing a light clear voice say, 'You are all right. Just ask for what you want.' David seemed softened and stilled by his experience and exuded a new air of quieter confidence – was he spontaneously embodying the very gravitas he sought? Shortly afterwards he was appointed to the board.

Key point

Integrate visualisation into your ongoing therapeutic work. The process of visualising or fantasising a situation, a place or an action can provide inner support and act as either an alternative, a prelude to or a rehearsal for that action taking place in the outer world.

---

19   Working with dreams

Dreams are important. They are a spontaneous expression of the existence of the human being. They are often an entry point to people's inner world, to their deeper intuitive wisdom and their sense of poetry and symbol. What is more they are frequently witty and amusing and contact with dreams can greatly enliven the richness of people's lives. Fritz Perls described dreams as the 'royal road to integration' (Perls, 1969b: 66) and as 'existential messages' (Perls, 1976).

If you want to work with clients' dreams you need first to have developed your interest in your own dreams. If you do not yet have a lively sense of relationship with your own dreams, I suggest you try some of the ideas given here for yourself before you begin doing this sort of work with clients. It is usually important for you yourself to have experienced anything you ask others to experience – we cannot genuinely act as a guide to a process that we have not been through ourselves.

You can nurture people's attention to their dreams by openly expressing your own general interest. You can enquire whether or not clients are aware of dreaming. If clients are also interested in their dreams, you can encourage them to notice their dreams. You can explain that keeping a notebook under the pillow and noting the dream down as soon as you wake up (even in the middle of the night) helps catch dreams which otherwise often evaporate without trace. To support clients' interest you can respond with interest to any dreams they mention and invite them to describe their dream. You can also suggest experimentally exploring their dreams in any of the ways suggested below. If clients feel that they do not dream but would like to know about their dreams, then you can still work with their absent dreams, as suggested below.

Everyone dreams several times a night, although some people have no memories of their dreams. We have many different types of dream, including dreams about everyday issues; dreams that resolve problems; dreams that focus our attention on something we had been forgetting; dreams that highlight or express our feelings; dreams that seem to predict or prepare for the future; dreams that offer guidance about the meaning of our lives or our spiritual quests; dreams that refer to group, community or social issues.

Dream symbols are very personal to the dreamer and the dreamer's current field. What means one thing to one dreamer would mean something else to another dreamer – for example a dream about a car losing its brakes and hurtling down the hill could be a warning to one dreamer that she needs to have her car serviced; while to another dreamer a similar image might be a metaphor for the fact that she is out of control of her life. So although it is often useful to nurture an interest in universal and archetypal meanings of symbols, you also need to be able to concurrently bracket previous assumptions and explore what symbols mean for clients.

Dreams as projections

Dreams are often seen as a spontaneous expression of the dreamer: each part of the dream represents different projected aspects of the personality. The aim in working with clients' dreams as projections is to help clients to identify with and explore all the parts of themselves and their field represented in the dream and thus develop their awareness of what the dream means or symbolises for them and expand their sense of self. Rather than offering interpretations of dreams, you can support clients to explore the meaning of their own dreams through painting or drawing, through retelling, enactment, or movement.

There are many ways of carrying out such an exploration. One good way of beginning is to ask clients to retell the dream, possibly in the present, so as to bring it alive more vividly. You can also enquire about the clients' associations with the dream as a whole and with different aspects of the dream. Working phenomenologically, we try to suspend our prior judgements about which aspects are most important and explore all aspects of the dream field.

Another approach is to ask clients to draw or paint images from the dream, so as to get to know them better. They may then discuss what they have drawn with you but whether or not they talk, the process of drawing or painting can bring them closer to the meaning or sense of the dream. You can suggest that clients draw objects, animals or supernatural forces as well as human beings, because all aspects of the dream can be seen as projected parts of the dreamer.

Alternatively you can suggest that clients close their eyes and visualise the dream sequence in the present. This sort of visualisation is often very real and may bring fresh insight. It is also highly flexible and may lead on one occasion to the dreamer 'finishing' an incomplete dream; on another it may offer an opportunity for the dreamer to imagine introducing a figure, say of support, which wasn't there in the original dream.

You could also suggest that some clients experimentally 'become' each of the dream components in turn; or 'become' the part which has the most interest for them; or talk to certain parts, and so on. 'Becoming' a dream component involves identifying a place that represents that part of the dream and then miming, enacting or dancing that part and speaking or making noises from that part. Sometimes it is valuable to suggest that clients hold a conversation between the different aspects of the dream. These various forms of role-playing often lead clients to unexpected insights about some aspect of the dream or about some aspect of their life dilemmas.

> Meg dreamed about a dog and a couple of rattlesnakes which frightened her. The counsellor encouraged her first to enact the dog and then to dance the rattlesnake. As the dog, Meg tensed until her whole body began to tremble. The counsellor then invited Meg to become the rattlesnake and dance as a rattlesnake. In her dance Meg became acutely aware of anything getting too close to her. 'If you come too close, I'll strike back', she said. Meg thus got in touch with another side of herself which until then she had disowned – one that was able to strike back when threatened. With a little more exploration of her body sensations, she ended the work feeling warm and real, with more confidence (adapted from Perls, 1969b: 164).

In nightmares, people often see themselves as the victim of some monstrous nightmare apparition, such as witches, torturers, bullies, ogres or other terrible creatures. You can see nightmares too as projections of the dreamer: here the monsters represent parts of the self – usually parts which the dreamer finds hard to identify with because they are aspects of the self that he or she has alienated or disowned. However apparently monstrous, such disowned parts of the self may represent important denied vitality so exploration of nightmares may help people reown some of this vitality. Clients may not readily accept the idea that the frightening or horrible creatures and people of their nightmares are parts of themselves. You can invite clients to try describing, visualising, painting or drawing the monstrous part or to experimentally find out what it would be like to play the monster in relationship to you for a while *and just see what happens.* These explorations may allow people to envisage or try behaviours which they would never otherwise try, make noises, play-act and generally discover or regain a lot of energy which they deny in their ordinary working lives. 'If you are pursued by an ogre in a dream, and you *become* the ogre, the nightmare disappears. You re-own the energy that is invested in the demon. Then the power of the ogre is no longer outside, alienated but inside where you can use it' (Perls, 1969b: 164).

If you feel that becoming a dream component might be too challenging or trigger shame reactions, there are many other similarly creative but less active ways you can work: for example invite clients to choose puppets or figures or even pebbles or stones that represent different elements of the dream and allow them to enact their dream or some components of their dream through these. Such deliberately indirect methods are often much safer for people whose sense of self fragments easily or who are easily shamed by play-acting or anything they experience as exposing.

Dreams as intersubjective communication

Dreams may also have an important interpersonal dimension. They may be viewed as unconscious messages from the dreamer to the counsellor or therapist. They may in particular tell the counsellor or therapist something which the client has not been willing to tell directly so they may represent an undoing of retroflection.

Dreams as existential messages and guides

Dreams can be viewed as existential messages, or expressions of the way the dreamer relates to the world or life. Recurrent dreams in particular may be trying to convey a message from the unconscious or intuitive side of the dreamer to the conscious waking part of the self. For example Sylvia often dreamt of a young child who was neglected, starving or drowning. Exploration of these images led Sylvia to realise how she consistently neglected a part of herself that wanted more playfulness and fun in her work-dominated life.

Absent or forgotten dreams

You can work with fragments of dreams, forgotten dreams and the dreams of people who feel that they never dream. For example invite clients to enact a dialogue between themselves and a fragment of a dream or the mood which the dream left upon waking.

If clients can't remember anything at all about their dream(s), you can suggest that they place the fugitive dream(s) upon the empty chair and address them in fantasy. Clients can tell the absent dream(s) how they feel about them. The counsellor or therapist then invites clients to sit on the empty chair and respond as the dreams and thus hold a dialogue between people and their dreams. This is a powerful method which often offers insight regarding the individual meaning of forgetting dreams for that client.

These are only a few of the ways of understanding and exploring dreams. There are many books and workshops which can help you discover more about accessing the wisdom of dreams for the benefit of ourselves and others (Shohet, 1985; Fish and Lapworth, 1994; Sills et al., 1995).

Working with archetypal stories

In recent years I have worked with archetypal stories in some ways which are rather similar to the ways I work with dreams. I have told traditional stories that seem to resonate with the themes that clients are exploring. The storytelling and story-sharing is in itself an important creative medium which often gives clients support. It can make them feel less alone with their life problems to hear similar dilemmas embedded in the symbols of a story that has been told across the world and down the ages and the stories often offer guidance about how to deal with universal problems or life transitions. One client (who felt that she needed to loosen her strong coping persona in order to meet and integrate some more damaged and fragile parts of herself but felt very scared to do so) felt greatly supported by the story of Bluebeard, where the naive woman needs to open the door to the last room and face the horrors therein before she is able to take the next developmental step in her life.

On other occasions I work more actively with stories. I often understand and explain the different aspects of fairy stories or archetypal tales as symbolising different aspects of the psyche. I have experimented with inviting clients in group settings to become all the aspects of the fairy story in turn and enact, mime or dance those different roles. I have also suggested that clients paint the story or the significant symbols of the story.

Key point

Support clients to listen to the voice of their dreams. Help them to enter into their dreams as an active participant who can visualise, represent, explore or become any and every aspect of their dreams, and thus discover their significance for themselves, rather than disown or be fearful of them.

---

20 Opening to the transpersonal and caring for soul

The transpersonal

The transpersonal dimension of counselling and therapy refers to those aspects of the therapeutic process that go beyond the limits of the individual and that connect us with each other and to spiritual traditions and values. This dimension encompasses the belief (or experience) that our existence is grounded and permeated by the spiritual, that we are not isolated beings but part of a larger whole and profoundly interconnected with all aspects of the universe (Hycner, 1988), that we are spirit and soul as well as mind, emotions and body and that our spiritual and soul selves may need nurture and care of a different kind than our bodily and mental selves.

Transpersonal and spiritual matters are inherently difficult to describe because they refer to experiences that go beyond the realm of facts and words. In this section I discuss some of the field factors which may affect how counsellors integrate care for the transpersonal and care for the soul into the counselling process and explore the ways that Gestalt counsellors and therapists may do this. I do not want to be in any way prescriptive. Nor do I intend my discussion to refer to any one set of religious beliefs but to the much broader issues of our place in the world, to our interconnectedness and the meaning we give to our lives described in the previous paragraph.

A sense of connection with the universe or spiritual practice can offer many people support and healing and give meaning to their lives. But counselling and therapy approaches have frequently shied away from discussing the place of transpersonal and spiritual issues in their theory and have hesitated to address or explore spiritual beliefs or needs with clients within the counselling process. With a few notable exceptions (Hycner, 1988; Schoen, 1978; Elkin, 1979, for example), Gestaltists have until recently been rather reticent about integrating spiritual exploration into the overall therapeutic endeavour. Perls and some of his contemporaries in the 1960s and 1970s were often openly dismissive of spiritual matters and this model inevitably influenced some of their descendants. Yet can Gestalt claim to be holistic unless it encompasses attention to spiritual beliefs and needs and to care of the sacred in people's lives and in the world?

Repression of spiritual and soul values

In Western industrial societies, spiritual matters and the needs of the soul have long been dismissed from contemporary affairs and we have largely replaced religious beliefs or spiritual quest with worship of rationality, science and material goods. Our educational systems have concentrated upon developing separate identities and willpower rather than spiritual grace, community or care of soul in the world. The psychological isolation and materialism thus created have opened up a void that yearns to be filled. Since we are no longer skilled in recognising the possibility that our yearnings may be the voice of soul calling for nurture, we find substitutes such as money, drugs, food, sex, consumer goods, work or TV to fill the void. Rather than assuaging our longing, these material items often create fresh craving.

Within our materialistic culture there is considerable emphasis upon the objective, achieving aspect of existence, with the result that many people have learned to objectify themselves, other people and the natural environment. In this objectification they are inclined to see people and natural objects as means to an end to be utilised or exploited to meet their own needs. When we live in this objective and over-rational way, we treat others and ourselves with an 'I–It' attitude rather than opening ourselves to the mystery of being, or to the possible new creation or event which can emerge between us. We strive to assert ourselves or achieve our ends and may know less about the other polarity of going with the ebb and flow of the tides of existence. Life certainly requires choice, commitment, will and discipline but also acceptance and reverence for what is, and a willingness to keep searching for a flow between these two ways or polarities (Hycner, 1988).

Objectification, materialism and loss of connection and meaning have increased people's sense of despair and disassociation and many clients come into counselling complaining of just such a sense of meaninglessness and alienation.

Attending to the transpersonal in the counselling process

Attending to the transpersonal does not mean suppressing or bypassing the personal or getting rid of the ego. We human beings, according to Buber, approach the transpersonal not by trying to transcend the human state but by becoming as fully human as possible, by becoming the people we have the potential to be, by confronting, exploring and recognising our human limits, by struggling to get in touch with what is most central to our existence and by hallowing the sacred in everyday life (Buber, 1958a, 1958b; Hycner, 1988; Moore, 1992). And the discipline of spiritual exploration requires strong personal motivation and ego capacity.

Awareness as a means of knowing our humanity

As we have already seen, the development of awareness is central to Gestalt counselling and therapy. Awareness is a holistic process of contact and withdrawal and meaning-making which takes place within our whole person. It is experiencing and being in touch with our selves and our existence in the world from moment to moment. The development of awareness thus offers us a means to know ourselves (and to support others to know themselves) as human beings. It allows us to discover (and support clients to discover) who we are. The practice of awareness involves feeling our human and personal limits and the limitations of our existential situation, as well as our potential for communion with a greater whole. Knowing our humanity and our human limitedness has the potential to open us up to the unlimited (Hycner, 1988).

It is obviously never easy to know ourselves and to get in touch with our destiny but it is the process of struggling to know ourselves and to become the person we were meant to be that is important.

Awareness as meditative practice

Awareness is developed in many different ways in Gestalt counselling and therapy but they all involve a mindful attention to the present, to the flow of experience, to the unfolding now. Developing awareness often requires a slowing down of people's inner processes which allows them to be in touch with their essential existence. Awareness is *being* in the present, rather than pushing for outcome, action or change:

> There are times with certain clients, and in certain phases of the therapy, that it might be quite appropriate to teach the client to slowly observe all his actions and thoughts without being attached to them. This teaches the client not to be constantly caught up in the flurry of an activity, but rather to just observe it as it is happening. (Hycner, 1988)

This sort of intervention can be especially helpful for people who are overly impulsive and inclined to do things which they later regret but it can also add value to most people's lives. Obviously the timing of the intervention is crucial and will only be experienced as helpful if it is offered with respect and at a moment when it has some meaning or resonance for the client.

A similar awareness is central to many spiritual practices, such as living mindfully or meditating, and can be developed by counsellors as a means of spiritual development in their everyday practices. We can for instance meet clients from a meditative stance, contemplating them with wonder, appreciating the miracle which is embodied in their living and their otherness. We can also sometimes slowly observe all our own actions and thoughts in response to each client without being attached to them or getting caught up in the flurry of trying to help or make better.

Therapists' presence and the 'I–Thou' relationship

Gestalt's emphasis upon the whole being greater than the sum of the parts is a way of recognising that there is something larger present in the therapy situation than just the total of the individuals physically present and that is already an acknowledgement of the 'more than personal' (Welwood, 1983: xii). The I–Thou relationship, with its emphasis upon the 'between', moves us and the people we work with naturally, and often imperceptibly, beyond the narrower concerns of our ego, beyond objectification towards meeting other people and creatures as beings. It thus expands our consciousness and changes our sense of place within the universe.

Clients and counsellors can enter the spiritual domain through an 'I–Thou' or intersubjective meeting with otherness. This otherness is usually thought of as the otherness of the other person or people in the counselling situation, but if we expand our horizons we realise that that otherness may also be the otherness of animals, rocks, trees, a painting, the process of drawing or any aspect of the natural environment. The connectedness we feel in an 'I–Thou' moment with other connects us with the eternal thou of being, takes us to the edge of the sacred, touches our spirit and feeds our soul: 'Man lives in the spirit if he is able to respond to his *Thou*. He is able to, if he enters into relation with his whole being. Only in virtue of his power to enter into relation is he able to live in the spirit' (Buber, 1958b: 39).

Counsellors and therapists cannot make 'I–Thou' meeting occur but they can attend to their own spiritual and personal development so that they approach the client with an 'I–Thou' attitude, attempting to be as fully present as they can be in the therapy situation. This means staying with whatever emerges moment by moment without judgement or pressure, no matter how apparently mundane or fruitless the process might seem. This full non-judgemental presence is an honouring of the being of the other, an honouring of their ordinary experience in all its simplicity and complexity. If counsellors or therapists can offer this sort of presence (at least for some of the time), clients naturally open up more fully to the quality of their own presence and are able to honour more fully their own ordinary experience. In this opening up that emerges between client and counsellor is the possibility for making whole and healing.

Going beyond self absorption to interconnection and care of soul

As both client and counsellor open up in these ways to a greater sense of the miracle of ordinary life, they are hopefully able to go beyond self absorption to a greater awareness of other persons and creatures and the need to be in connection and in the service of others and of the universe. Indeed it could be argued that a therapeutic experience which is predicated upon an intersubjective model of self within a relational field (as Gestalt is) will not only help clients focus very fully and deeply on the self but also support them to go through and beyond preoccupation with the self to evolve in a way which allows them to forget about themselves and experience themselves as part of the unity of the world. If we cannot stretch our conception and practice of counselling and therapy to encompass this movement from individualism to community, therapy may be limited to being a narcissistic endeavour which increases rather than decreases our own and other people's self-consciousness and self-scrutiny and may make us all less rather than more able to cooperate fruitfully with other elements of the universe in which we live.

Care of the soul through imagination and the re-enchantment of everyday life

Tradition teaches that soul lies midway between understanding and unconsciousness and its means of expression and development is imagination. The soul prefers to imagine, rather than to reason, analyse or talk logically. It is nourished by art, beauty, poetry, play, music and creativity (Moore, 1992; 1996). So the counsellor's ability to work naturally and as an integral part of the therapy with creative approaches such as visualisation, imagery, art, play or drama (described on pp. 131–62) can make an important contribution to care of the soul in the counselling process.

To care for soul in ourselves, others or in the world, we need to be familiar with the ways of the soul, we need to observe and discover how the soul manifests itself. For instance counsellors and therapists can listen to and observe people's suffering and symptoms not just as flaws or problems which they want to get rid of but also as revelations of the soul. We can befriend the problems of ourselves and our clients as windows to our soul rather than as enemies. It is not easy to observe closely and discover what the soul is revealing about its yearning through fixations, neuroses and illness but it changes our attitude to one of care and attention rather than cure when we attempt to do so.

The soul is nourished by beauty, friendship, community, tradition, respect for others, re-investing the detail and the tasks of everyday life with meaning and enchantment, reconceptualising the nature of work (Fox, 1994). So counselling and therapy as care of the soul, focus on discovering the aspects of daily life that support and nourish soul and those which disturb or impoverish it. They attend to small details of everyday life at home (Thich nhat Hanh, 1992) and at work, as well as to major decisions, traumas and change. They tend the life of individuals in community.

Anima Mundi or care of the soul in the world

In the ancient world everything in the world, including supposedly inanimate objects, and the world herself had soul. People honoured the rocks and mountains of the world, the trees and creatures of the world as well as the spirit of other people in the world. All things were considered to be alive and to be in relationship to each other. A modern rational scientific perspective explains people's occasional sense that 'inanimate' objects have life as mere projection, which is a very human-centred position. To allow all things to have vitality and personality is an entirely different paradigm which changes the human position from controller and exploiter to participant who can listen and respect the lessons of the trees and waves. We are in need of a rebirth of ancient wisdom and attention to soul in the world. Perhaps the very idea of what we are doing in counselling, therapy and psychology needs to be radically re-imagined to attend more fully to soul in the world as well as in the individual (Abram, 1996; Sardello, 1994).

VII

Working with
Embodiment, Energy
and 'Resistance'

21 Using embodiment, movement and play

The founders of Gestalt were trained in many innovative forms of theatre and expressive movement, so drama, psychodrama, enactment, movement, dance and play are and always have been intrinsic to the Gestalt approach. The rationale for the integration of these creative means of expression comes from learning theory[1] and holism.[2] We human beings learn experientially. We are holistic beings, in which body, mind and soul are united – so any holistic approach to counselling needs to address and involve body, mind and soul in their fullest range.

Movement, dance, sound, enactment and other forms of creative expression are natural aspects of the human repertoire, which almost all children employ all day long for many years in their play and playful learning about life. Many adolescents become self-conscious about doing things like that, dismissing them as 'childish'; yet most people can regain access to these fuller holistic means of expressing themselves with the skilled support of a counsellor or therapist who is familiar and at ease with his/her own creative range of expression. In so doing they regain vitality, contact functions and scope often lost since childhood. Of course some clients had childhoods where very little play of any sort was possible. The counsellor may be able to support these clients in acquiring the ability to play, rather than regaining it. If you are not at ease with your own body process and creative expression, I suggest that you explore the ideas in Parts VI and VII for yourself and gain personal experience of these approaches before trying to introduce them to clients.

You can invite clients to move about within the counselling session, to embody an emotion by miming it, to dance any feeling or any self (from their population of potential selves), to sing their story or make the sounds which express their feelings towards

1. Kolb and Fry (1975); Lewin (1926, 1935, 1952); Johnson and Johnson (1987); Rogers (1969).
2. Smuts (1995); Perls (1969a, 1969b, 1976); Clarkson and Mackewn (1993).

you at that moment; to paint or draw their inner and outer landscapes, to play aimlessly with a piece of clay and see what happens, to demonstrate a significant other person in their life through voice tone, body posture or movement. They can enact or role-play a scene from childhood (or from the office) as they remember it and then re-enact it as they would have liked it to be.

As mentioned in the previous section if clients dislike active embodiment or if you assess that active methods might be too challenging or shame-inducing, you can use visualisation, figures or pebbles for similar purposes of embodiment, enactment and play. These are powerful devices which allow active healing of past wounds and unfinished business in the present and subtle exploration of many aspects of the field and of the therapeutic relationship which might otherwise remain unaddressed.

I love these aspects of Gestalt – they are infinitely flexible, variable, malleable and creative. In the counselling session, client and counsellor can make anything happen in their imaginations, making use of whatever resources lie to hand. In my counselling room I usually have clay, crayons, finger paints, paper, toys, cushions and music available – but I have also worked with creative embodiment, enactment and movement in settings where the only 'props' were two or three chairs, some sea shells and a hard table. Props help but are not essential to the imaginative counsellor-artist.

Space precludes the exposition of more than a small percentage of the possibilities for creative expression and range in Gestalt counselling and therapy. Examples of the use of enactment, psychodrama, embodiment and movement abound (see Perls, 1969b; Zinker, 1978; Sills et al., 1995; Polster and Polster, 1974; Wheeler, 1991; Parlett, 1991 and others). I encourage you to read the relevant sections of the authors indicated and also to attend workshops in the creative aspects of Gestalt, for no amount of reading can convey the enormously increased potential of a therapeutic approach which integrates such media for expression. Here I give a range of examples which I hope will illustrate the scope of the approach and whet your appetite for some active experience of the possibilities.

The couples counsellor suggested that Sandy and Michael (introduced on p. 141) actually take up the entrenched position they described – 'really show yourself and me physically what your inner experience is like'.

The clients took up positions in the far corners. The counsellor encouraged them to find something to represent the trench. Michael said he also felt he barricaded himself in against Sandy's artillery – so the counsellor encouraged him to build a barricade. Sandy fell in with the image and indicated her gun and as soon as Michael peeked up from behind his wall, she fired pot shots at him. Although the imagery and enactment were pretty vicious, their experience was no longer hidden, covert, unavailable for negotiation. Their life as a couple had also lost the frozen, stuck quality which both Michael and Sandy had complained about. They had rediscovered some mobility, spontaneity and playfulness. In subsequent sessions, they were able to remember this turning point and playfully explored venturing into 'no-man's land' to hold a picnic, calling a temporary ceasefire, joining forces and so on – all of which gave them flexibility and range, while still honouring their current reality, which remained for some time a state of war.

Keith was long-term unemployed, persistently moody and unoccupied. He had frequently expressed how depressed and fed up he was with his own moodiness, which infuriated his family. The counsellor suggested that on this occasion they might paradoxically and experimentally explore what Keith's moodiness *did for him*, by both swapping statements about their moods and hazarding guesses about their possible advantages. Keith's energy rose a little in response to the novelty and silliness of the suggestion. The counsellor sang a few lines of a sad melody, to which Keith spontaneously responded with the counterpoint, until the two were singing their feelings to each other in grand operetta style and unexpectedly laughing hilariously. (adapted from Zinker, 1978)

George had a vivid dream in which several people were disagreeing noisily with each other. The therapist suggested that he might like to use some of the figures and toys which she kept on the shelf to explore the dream. George chose various puppets and got each to play their part – one puppet of a soft cuddly bear told a puppet of a large friendly looking dog that he felt comforted by her, while a jack in the box wanted to come out and play. As a touching and lively scene unfolded, the therapist listened and watched respectfully and entranced – George was usually very contained and apparently unemotional and yet using this fresh medium of the puppets he came alive and brought the scene between the puppets alive too. The therapist made few interventions, wanting to allow George to develop the action without interference. After a short period George looked up with tears in his eyes and whispered, 'You know, I think I am both the jack in the box and the cuddly bear and you are the dog.' Although playing with the puppets seemed an apparently indirect way of exploring his dream, it actually allowed his vulnerable and playful feelings to emerge into his awareness and into the relationship between himself and the therapist for the first time.

Jane and Bill came together for a few counselling sessions, knowing that they were splitting up but feeling that they wanted some help to do so. In discussion, it turned out that they both felt guilty and unfinished about a baby of theirs which they had aborted the previous year. After some exploration with the counsellor they decided that they would like to create a ritual which would honour the baby and allow them to let it and each other go. The following week they came prepared with candles and flowers. They lit the candles and made a flower represent the baby. They both talked to the baby in turn, explaining their decision, asking for forgiveness and expressing their sadness. They then responded as the baby. Both wept and were awed by what they had done. Afterwards they felt cleansed and able to say goodbye to each other and to move on to the next phase of their life.

Key point

Integrate movement, dance, sound, enactment, or figures, toys, puppets and other forms of creative expression to represent and explore some of the situations and themes which arise in the counselling process. It is crucial to finely calibrate how you introduce creative media and simultaneously provide sufficient natural support so that you minimise (or work with) any shame reactions which may be triggered by suggesting clients do something unexpected or unusual.

---

22   Attending to body process and energy flow

Attending to body structure, body experience and body process[1]

Attending to bodily experience needs to be an important part of any counselling experience because people's emotional life is largely experienced in and through their bodies. Our feelings arise in our bodily selves and are felt in our bodily selves. Yet the taboos surrounding body process are so great that many counsellors and psychotherapists are not trained to integrate attention to body processes, internal body experiences or body structure into their work.

---

1. The title of this section suggests a duality which is alien to the holistic essence of Gestalt, because Gestaltists are always endeavouring to work with whole persons, body, mind and soul. In this section I am merely making body process and energy flow figural for the moment.

Body process is central to all aspects of Gestalt.[2] In the Gestalt approach to counselling and therapy there is no split between the person and their body or between the body and the person – body, mind and emotions form a whole which cannot be separated without destroying the nature of the total person. Body, mind and emotions function as one whole process – bodily, emotional, mental, verbal and non-verbal experiences co-exist in a synchronous flow of coordinated and collaborative activity in which each part supports the functioning of the other parts and of the whole organism. The body doesn't cause the mind to respond, nor does the mind cause the body to operate. Body and mind cooperate simultaneously. Gestalt therefore proposes a 'unitary' method, in which you shuttle your attention from clients' body process to their words, from your own body sensations, images and thoughts, to the clients' background, to the circumstances in which you are working – in other words, you investigate all the interrelated aspects of the co-created field (see pp. 80–2).

If Gestalt is truly holistic, then I suggest we would be working with body structure, body process and energy flow all the time as an intrinsic part of our approach (Kepner, 1987). For example when we formulate a *Gestalt assessment*, we observe clients' bodily, mental and emotional processes – we notice how and when clients mobilise their energy in relationship; we notice how they move, sit, breathe and support themselves (see p. 103). When we use *phenomenological methods of investigation and description of the field* (see p. 58), we pay attention to all aspects of the concrete experience of clients and ourselves. When we enter into and develop a *dialogic relationship, we use ourselves as instrument* – to do this we need to know ourselves and to stay in touch with our bodily sensations and responses as well as with our energy flow. *In experimental and creative work* (see p. 129) if we introduce enactment, psychodrama, movement, dance, mime, play or puppets we are inviting clients to *embody* psychological experience and explore it through that *embodiment*.

On the other hand nowadays many Gestaltists have had little experience of or training in body work or body process as an

---

2. Particular attention to body process, energy flow and the breath of life are central features of Gestalt and have been since the new integration was first conceived. Both Fritz and Laura Perls trained in various forms of creative movement and active dramatic methods, while Fritz was deeply influenced by William Reich, the grandfather of bio-energetics and body therapies and Laura Perls and Isadore From were trained in phenomenology.

integral part of counselling, therapy or process consultation. Our culture puts enormous emphasis upon cognitive knowledge at the expense of bodily and other ways of knowing with the result that many people who have not actively worked to regain their sense of bodily self are fairly desensitised to it. If you have not had much experience of bodywork exploration, you may like to try out for yourself the ideas that follow and get some training in bodywork before introducing active attention to body structure and process into your practice. For we cannot do with clients anything we do not ourselves fully embody.

Below I give a few examples of the multitude of ways in which you can make body process figural within the therapeutic experience. There are deeply embedded taboos in contemporary life concerning our bodies and our emotions and many people have been shamed concerning the way they look, or humiliated about their emotions (which are, of course, experienced in their bodily selves). People pay little attention to the possible wealth of internal bodily feelings and they may find it hard to do so even if invited because they have so habitually learned to ignore internal sensations. So working with body structure and process in the ways discussed requires discernment and sensitivity to the possible emergence of shame issues (Lee and Wheeler, 1996 and Appendix 7).

Noticing a client's bodily process

You can attend to body process from moment to moment by noticing the flow of clients' gestures, facial expressions, breathing (as well as their words) without interpretation or expectation. Just take in their whole selves with wonder and interest, rather as you might take in the wind in the trees or the clouds moving in the sky. Choose whether or not you describe what you observe about their unfolding process according to the overall conditions of the field at the time. Your observations may of course interrupt the client's words but there is not necessarily any harm in that. Sometimes your interruption will turn out to be relevant, affirmative or helpfully provocative. Other times the client will just experience your observations as interruptive, in which case that will be the next process between you that you explore in the dialogic relationship. Gestalt counsellors and therapists do not of course share all their observations and responses. Whether or not you share your observations verbally, you will gain a holistic sense of clients just by observing holistically.

Supporting clients to experimentally allow their body to speak its mind

You can ask clients what they would do now if they allowed their body to speak its mind. I have found that the answer to this question is very rarely to sit in the same position as they were in before I enquired. Often clients will let out a sigh and take up an entirely or subtly different stance – I've known clients to lie down, sag, turn away with their back to me, start striding round the room. This simple intervention well-timed allows people to contact their inner rhythm and be more aware of what they really want to be or do now. Or it may heighten their sense of how much they are governed by external pressures or established conventions, such as 'In counselling you sit down, face to face with each other.'

Inviting clients to try attending to their breathing while they speak

Attending to breathing can be a revelation – people may realise they are barely breathing, holding their breath, unable to sense their breath, or they may become aware of the sweetness of simply breathing in and out and the grace of the gift of life. You can develop your phenomenological enquiry by describing their breathing, by asking of what value it is to them to barely breathe when they describe emotional or painful events, for instance (see pp. 25 and 118). You can notice and describe your own breathing.

Breathing is central to life. Breathing is the breath of life. After birth, breathing is the first example of the wave of contact with, and withdrawal from, the environment. It is our most essential means of self support. The way we breathe affects our experience from moment to moment. Changing the way we breathe can change our emotional and physiological state and thus change the way we approach and interpret the world. So an enquiry into breathing can have far-reaching results: learning to become aware of and attend to our breathing can transform our lives. Breathing is a link or bridge between body, spirit and soul; attending to our breathing can make us aware of when our bodies, spirits and souls are out of unity and can offer a path to bring them back into harmony.

When we reduce or stop our breathing we reduce our internal bodily sensation, which in turn reduces feelings. In therapeutic exploration, people, often unawares, reduce or lower their breathing and this may be part of a fixed way of organising their bodily structure in response to stress or emotions which were once experienced as dangerous or overwhelming. Sometimes experienced Gestalt body work practitioners may therefore actively instruct a client to breathe more because the practitioner can see that the client has stopped breathing and is thus reducing their internal body sensation to such an extent that they need extra oxygen to pursue the exploration. However, generally there has been much confusion regarding Gestalt's emphasis upon developing awareness of breathing. The aim is *not* necessarily to get clients to breathe more or differently. The aim is to help clients become aware of *how* they breathe and in *what ways* their unaware breathing patterns support or undermine them, so that *they* can then experiment with breathing differently and consciously if they *choose* to do so.

Attending to body structure

We manifest habitual ways of holding ourselves in our body structures. These structures represent a mixture of genetic inheritance and fixed patterns of organising our bodily selves. Our body structures may indicate how we have literally shaped ourselves in ways that pre-organise our availability for awareness and interaction with the world and with others. These patterns of organising our bodies were often formed in early childhood but continue, without awareness of them, in the present – it is as though people literally carry a context with them in their bodily stance. Body structure can be seen as part of the ground of the field from which the individual's current interactions arise.

In a Gestalt approach to body structure we are interested in discovering how people have organised their body structure over the years, in supporting people to fully experience themselves and to discover for themselves the ways they may be unconsciously organising their body structure to undermine present needs for contact and interaction.

Working with energy flow

Gestalt counselling and therapy are lively processes which need energy and 'juice' (Zinker, 1978). We can tell when people are fully engaged with whatever they are doing, whether it is a therapeutic exploration, a conversation between friends or a game of football, by the *way* they engage with it. When people are genuinely interested, their eyes tend to sparkle or be alert, their voice tone is alive, they are absorbed in what they do, they seem excited and vital. When they are not genuinely interested or keen to try something out, their energy will be less, their voice tone may drop, they may yawn or fidget and so on. The words we use – both clients and therapists – easily become habitual or clichéd and may even act as a smokescreen which hides rather than reveals the heart of the person. So if you pay most of your attention to the words of the client, you may get sidetracked and miss the essence. In addition, you can learn to be attentive to the flow of energy in the session, in the client, in yourself.

Use your eyes, body responses, images and hunches. Watch how the energy flows in clients' bodies, where it seems dormant, where it seems blocked and where it is bubbling. You can develop this skill by practising with colleagues in pairs. Notice the energy flow and blocks and try describing to your colleagues what you see and then see what response your description elicits in your colleague. It's often a good idea to start working wherever the energy is already bubbling, while, at the same time, attending to any changes in the energy flow in the client's body, because that is where something new is beginning to happen. Equally, notice where the energy is missing because that may be an area where something new needs to happen. And of course it is equally important to pay attention to the ebb and flow of your own energy and interest.

Even simply noticing energy flow in these ways will have an effect on how you work. In addition there are myriad different ways of working actively with the energy flow. If clients are totally lacking in energy, you can work with that lack in many different ways. For instance, you could describe what you see, and share your own response to their lack of energy. You could enquire what it is like to feel so lack-lustre or empathise and *imagine* what it's like; you could suggest that they sing what they are saying or really exaggerate their flat energy-less voice and state and see what happens.

One therapist described a session in which he explored a number of these approaches to energy flow with a client called Betty. 'She feels flat and immobilised. She feels she cannot survive in this competitive world. She goes on and on. I am beginning to feel drained . . . I watch her body . . . When I bring her attention to her body she says, "I feel tight in my legs and my arms." . . . I ask her to imagine what she could do with her sensations – how she could use the muscles which are stiff . . . She relates an image of running' [This leads to a sequence of unfinished business and a lively re-enactment where Betty unfreezes her energy system to express bodily the sensations and feelings which she was unable to express at the time] (adapted from Zinker, 1978: 27).

Touch – a complex issue

The issue of touch is a complex one for all approaches to counselling and therapy including Gestalt. Nowadays Gestalt counsellors and therapists belong to a professional body and work within a professional code of ethics and practice which expressly forbids touching clients in sexual or exploitative ways. But there is no blanket prescription or formula which either allows or forbids the use of other supportive forms of touch in counselling and therapy – it all depends on the individual client and the overall field conditions. Touch can be communication. Touch can be a conversation, if it is held as such in the consciousness of both participants (Kepner, personal communication). However, if you want to include touch in your repertoire of counselling skills, it is important to be able to assess whether or not touch is likely to be creative, destructive, safe or unsafe with particular clients. Specific training and regular professional supervision can help counsellors and therapists to explore the complexities of the issues involved (Casement, 1985; chapter 7; Kepner, 1987, 1995; Woodmansey, 1988; Zinker, 1978).

Key point

Learn to listen to your own bodily responses in the therapeutic process. Pay as much attention to the client's breathing, body process, voice tone, bodily and facial expressions as to their words. Support clients to become more aware of their own bodily selves as a potential source of wisdom and to discover the different ways in which their bodily selves speak to them and for them.

---

23 Appreciating the wisdom of 'resistance', while exploring the impasse

Gestalt has its own unique perspective on the concept of 'resistance' in counselling and therapy.[1] This perspective appreciates the creative wisdom, as well as the limitations, of 'resistance'; emphasises the importance of moments of impasse between the impetus for growth and resistance to growth; and acknowledges the interpersonal dimension of 'resistance' as it arises between therapist and clients.

Appreciating the creative wisdom of 'resistance'

'Resistance' has been seen as the client's unconscious ambivalence about the therapeutic process, about their own wish for change and/or about the counsellor. Clients are initially likely to embrace the therapeutic counselling process which they have sought but fairly soon demonstrate some form of ambivalence or inner conflict regarding the therapeutic exploration or development of awareness. A degree of ambivalence is not only an inevitable but also a necessary part of effective counselling because if individuals are not in some form of inner conflict regarding problems or issues, they would probably have gone ahead and resolved their problems without seeking the aid of counselling.

Signs of inner conflict may, however, be subtle and even verbally denied because people's ambivalence is often out of their awareness. For example clients may demonstrate ambivalence

---

1. There has been considerable controversy concerning 'resistance' in the Gestalt literature. Perls, Hefferline and Goodman questioned the concept and the term 'resistance' (although they continued to use it), arguing that 'resistance' is the dialectical opposite of 'assistance' and that all forms of current 'resistance' were at some point 'assistance' or creative adjustment in difficult situations. The concepts have continued to be debated by for instance Breshgold (1989); Laura Perls in Rosenblatt (1991); Davidove (1991); and Polster (1991a).

through body posture, energy levels, missed sessions or through an overly compliant attitude. When I suggest a way of exploring a theme, I am sensitive both to the voice tone and to the words with which clients respond. If they say 'I'm fine or OK' with that, I may explore a little deeper and see if they really want to do what I suggest or are just going along with it. Sometimes clients may manifest inner conflict by unconsciously giving you mixed messages – talking enthusiastically about how useful their therapy or counselling has been, while 'forgetting' the insights of previous sessions or continuing self-destructive habits, for example. They may convey negative feelings towards you or the therapeutic process indirectly or metaphorically: when clients describe how other people have disappointed them, you could consider whether they are letting you know (in the only way they know how) that you have done the same thing.

From the holistic perspective of Gestalt, clients' 'resistances' to awareness and their related 'fixed gestalts' are as important and as valuable parts of their whole self process as their commitment to therapeutic exploration and their wish to develop. Their patterns of 'resistance' are highly important, for what may appear now to be a 'resistance' to full awareness was at one time a creative adjustment which helped the individuals cope with the physical and psychological threats of the environments in which they previously lived. So I suggest that you meet ambivalence and fixed or 'resistant' attitudes with compassion and respect for their particular form of wisdom. Understand that they are almost always a manifestation of some hidden vulnerability, a means of self protection against some real or imagined (but seemingly real) threat or deeply felt wound. Far from attempting to dissolve or overcome 'defences', we need to honour and acknowledge the value to the individual of learned 'defences', find out more about the 'resisting' or 'defensive' forces and enable clients to experience that their 'resistance' to the changes they profess to want is as real and potentially valuable an aspect of themselves as their desire for change.

Yet 'resistance' to awareness (together with associated automatic patterns of response) *is* anachronistic in as far as it is not a flexibly aware response to present field conditions but an inflexible response to past conditions as though they still existed in the present. Fixed patterns of self protection seem to offer security but may be primarily defensive rather than genuinely nurturing and supportive. They may protect people from imagined threats but they may also encase people, keeping them stuck as they are, discouraging them from making contact with new experiences and preventing them from growing through such fresh contact episodes.

Working with 'resistance' therefore requires you to develop great sensitivity and fine skills that balance appreciating its creative wisdom with sometimes being prepared to challenge its anachronism and the ways it limits clients' present functioning. 'Resistance' can be most fruitfully explored at the stuck moments of impasse when the forces for and against awareness and growth are in heightened or obvious conflict; so I will now discuss the notion of impasse and give some illustrative examples of valuing and exploring 'resistance' at the impasse.

Recognising and valuing the impasse

The impasse is the point at which the energetic forces within people are equally distributed between the wish to increase awareness and the felt (but often unconscious) need to block awareness. It is the point at which the 'growthful' forces are in conflict with the 'resisting' or blocking forces within the individual–environment field. It is the place where people's organismic urge to uncover fixed gestalts and premature denials of their real needs is met by the pressure of fixed habits and inertia. It is the moment when the natural self-regulating urge to complete the cycle of contact anew in the changed conditions of the present is balanced against the fear and perceived danger of doing so (see Figure 23.1).

Most of us normally avoid experiencing the impasse between our growthful and our 'resisting' sides because to do so involves taking existential responsibility for our own stuckness and our ability to choose to experience things differently and we have often not had sufficient environmental or self support to face these choices. At the stuck point all our available energy is turned inwards: we have no energy available for the outward impulse which might loosen the impasse. We are paralysed by the fear of the unknown. We are either physically tense or excessively limp. Our images and dreams are metaphors which reflect paralysis, confusion or anxiety. The psychological impasse is essentially anxiety provoking.

Even though impasses are confusing and uncomfortable, therapists can learn to look for, welcome and even invite such moments, for much of the individual's psychic energy has accumulated and become lodged in these deadlocked processes.

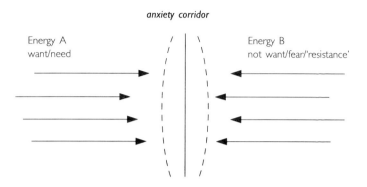

Figure 23.1   *Psychological impasse: the forces of the individual/ environment field are equally divided between the wish to change and the desire to maintain the status quo. This usually stimulates anxiety or confusion (Lubbock, 1996)*

At these stuck points, clients manifest their most deeply embedded patterns of inner conflict (such as the intricate patterns of the introjection–retroflection–projection systems discussed on p. 190), demonstrate to you and themselves the ways in which they fail to meet their needs or resolve the concerns that brought them into counselling or therapy. Thus the impasse is the point at which the most therapeutic leverage or learning may occur, the point at which clients may develop their awareness the most dramatically or resolve inner conflicts experientially. Perls, Hefferline and Goodman suggested that we need to learn to design experiments that precipitate and heighten the impasse because it is the point at which there is the greatest potential for change: 'If these experiments simply sent you about your ordinary business, you would experience little conflict, for in those situations, you know very well how to avoid conflict. *Instead this work is designed with the express purpose of making trouble for you. It is intended to make you aware of conflicts in your own personality*' (1994: 293; italics added).

I suggest that you and clients concentrate upon any so-called 'resistance', staying with the discomfort of their stuck point and fully exploring *both* sides of the internal struggle. This is easier said than done for it requires a high capacity to stay with anxiety. If you yourself are unable to tolerate this discomfort, you will be inclined to unconsciously help clients avoid the psychological impasse or to move them away from it by reassurance, kindly deflection or premature resolution. Try to find a place of 'creative indifference' (see p. 66) within yourself from which you can support clients to explore both sides of the impasse, without yourself getting invested in either part. For if you allow yourself to become invested in the frightened part you may become a rescuer. If you allow yourself to become invested in the client's will to change, you are likely to become a change agent and thus you will no longer be supporting the whole person but only the 'growthful' side of the client (see p. 65).

For example you can invite clients to experimentally become first the side that wants to change and then the side that doesn't and to hold a dialogue between the two (or more) aspects of themselves that are locked in an impasse. Encourage clients to take time to enter holistically into both aspects of the self, so that they really get to know the different bodily, emotional and cognitive feel of both sides. Thus they can experientially increase their awareness of both sides of the impasse and may develop insight into the values and needs of both facets of themselves. Appendix 5 includes a discussion of this sort of 'two-chair dialogue'; the transcripts of Fritz Perls's (1969b, 1976) demonstration work abound with illustrative examples of 'two-chair' dialogue or dialectic, and Section 28 (p. 196) indicates occasions when 'two-chair' dialogue may be contra-indicated.

As discussed previously, some clients dislike or feel embarrassed by being asked to enact or role play. If you find such methods to be unhelpful, you can consider inviting clients to draw or symbolise different aspects of the impasse or invite them to represent different aspects of the impasse through figures or objects gathered from the environment.

Alternatively you can suggest that clients describe, exaggerate or value the side of themselves that 'resists' awareness or change. This sort of novel experiment can be a liberating, enlivening experience that enables the client to reshuffle the relationship of figure and ground and make new meaning of their experience and new configurations of the self.

Explore the client's impasse phenomenologically from all perspectives. First you may choose to explore and/or lend energy to the 'resisting' sides by valuing and hearing them – then you may choose to lend your energy to the 'forces for change'. Or you may shuttle backwards and forwards between the two, heightening the sense of opposing forces, until the energies stuck in the impasse shift in some way.

The way you work will depend upon the client's style of moderating contact, the stage in the cycle of awareness and in the counselling process. I have found that in the earlier stages it is frequently important to give the greatest attention to the 'resisting' forces within the individual. Enter the experiential world view of the other person, find out about the value of the 'resistant' behaviour or interruption to awareness and contact, understand the subjective danger or emotional conflict that makes (or made) the fixed attitudes a felt necessity; for people are usually only able and willing to recognise the self-defeating nature of their own fixed behaviour or interpretations once they feel that their meaning has been fully understood and validated.

However you explore the impasse, you need to be able to come back again and again to a place of creative indifference within yourself where you are not invested in the outcome of the experiment or exploration. This is especially important where the impasse is significant and deeply embedded in the client's character structure because in practice people do not easily break through such an impasse and they need to know that the counsellor is affirming and confirming their whole being, not just their 'good resolutions'. Clients often approach and explore the impasse of significant fixed gestalts (or systems of interrelated fixed gestalts – see p. 24) on several occasions before a shift in energy or perspective occurs.

Appreciating the interpersonal dimension of 'resistance'

Traditionally 'resistance' in therapy and counselling has been seen as a largely intrapsychic phenomenon, arising from the inherent inner conflicts or unconscious ambivalence of the client. The implication of Gestalt's emphasis upon dialogic relating is that 'resistance' must have an important interpersonal or intersubjective dimension. While clients' 'resistances' to awareness can certainly be seen as a manifestation of their fixed gestalts and archaic or transferential styles of relating, they also emerge in the current relationship. They are the product of the interaction between the two of you; so you need to recognise that your interventions or lack of interventions, your words and your gestures, your whole way of being may be contributing to or diminishing clients' 'resistance' to awareness.

And clients' 'resistances' may of course be matched by counsellors' inflexibility, clumsiness or defensiveness; 'client resistance' has even been described as 'therapist error'. Although this is a dramatic swing to the other polarity, it is a thought-provoking reframe, which highlights the intersubjective nature of 'resistance'. When a client's 'resistance' to awareness touches on one of your own raw spots, you may unawarely take up a self-protective or fixed position yourself, creating a mismeeting (see p. 90) in which your defence comes up against their defence rather than a meeting between person and person. So be prepared to explore how you may have contributed to clients' reluctances and ambivalences and to apologise or change your approach if appropriate.

Key point

Keep in mind the inherent paradox of 'resistance'. On the one hand it is something to be respected, since it was at one time a creative adjustment which helped the person cope in difficult circumstances; and on the other hand it may now represent an obsolete or self-limiting pattern or attitude which may be an obstacle to the client's present development. Learn to welcome and explore signs of ambivalence or 'resistance' in clients as real and valuable aspects of themselves and to value and stay with the anxiety of the impasse because it is the point at which there is greatest potential for learning and change.

VIII

Attending to the Background* Features and Processes in Clients' Lives

* As soon as we attend to 'aspects of the structure of the ground', these will of course immediately cease to be ground and become figural.

24 Attending to the ground from which figures of contact arise

In this part of the book I look at the limitations of prioritising highly contactful, episodic pieces of work and the need to address the complexities of the ground from which such work arises. I suggest some ways of helping clients to make connections between episodes of therapeutic work. I discuss the concepts of support and of life themes, introduce the idea of identifying and unravelling interconnected life patterns of perceiving, and I discuss the need to help some individuals to develop greater cohesion, flexibility and continuity.

As soon as we attend to 'aspects of the structure of the ground', these will of course immediately cease to be ground for by the very act of turning our attention to them, we will reconfigure the field, making them figural for ourselves, while whatever we were previously attending to will temporarily recede into the ground. You cannot explore ground without making it figure (Yontef, 1992); in the Gestalt field approach the counsellor is not bound by tracking or staying with the *client's figure* (p. 16) but may make any aspect of the field figural. In shuttling attention between different aspects of the field, we will constantly be reconfiguring the field as we make new elements figural and others ground. Indeed it is the essence of the Gestalt approach to explore the ways in which the client can reorganise the relationship between figure and ground.

Attending to cohesion, continuity and connection in counselling

Gestalt is frequently misunderstood to be primarily (or even exclusively) about helping clients to develop awareness, sharpening their process of figure formation and developing their contact skills. These are indeed fundamental aspects of Gestalt which derive quite naturally from Gestalt's central philosophical stance that growth and change are the inevitable outcome of making full contact with the environment from moment to moment. Historically this emphasis upon the process of present awareness, figure formation and contact were innovatory and exciting and contributed to a major shift in the whole field of counselling and psychotherapy from a preoccupation with the analysis and interpretation of the past to a more vital exploration of the present moment (see Clarkson and Mackewn, 1993).

However, a sometimes relentless emphasis upon the structure of the contact episode, upon present awareness, as well as the many diagrams of the cycle of contact has led to some unintentionally reductionistic misrepresentations of Gestalt by both Gestaltists and non-Gestaltists. Gestaltists[1] have sometimes stressed self responsibility and self support at the expense of caring or responsibility towards the group or community; figure formation rather than figure destruction and assimilation into ground; organismic contact as opposed to organismic withdrawal and so on. As a result of these misunderstandings some Gestalt counselling has until recently tended to be preoccupied with episodic, dramatic contactful work and has paid too little attention to the assimilation into ground over time of those episodes of therapeutic work. Wheeler has suggested that much of the resultant practice of Gestalt has been 'figure bound'.

In different ways many Gestalt theorists and practitioners of the 1980s and 1990s have been energetically attempting to counteract these reductionistic tendencies and misunderstandings.[2] They have re-emphasised the breadth, depth and complexity of field theory and the importance of exploring not just the structure of single momentary episodes of contact in isolated individuals but also the larger processes and sub-processes of individuals as well as the historical and cultural processes from which the individual processes arise. They have strenuously reminded us that the Gestalt approach is as applicable to work with groups, organisations, systems and institutions as it is to individuals. They have sought to find or invent a vocabulary that can be used to examine both individual and social and organisational processes (Nevis, 1987; Farrands, 1995; Luckensmeyer, 1995).

You need to pay attention not just to the structure of each contact episode or 'piece of work' or therapeutic session but also

---

1. Who may have been particularly influenced by distinctive features of 1960s Perlsian demonstration Gestalt.

2. Including Tobin (1982); Greenberg (1989, 1991, 1995); Wheeler (1991); Yontef (1993); Melnick and Nevis (1992); Shub (1992).

to how one contact episode relates to another, to the client's last session, to their previous sessions, as well as to where they are going in their life; to their hopes and aspirations, values, culture, community, job, relationships – in fact to all the interrelated features of their ongoing life structures. Develop a similar phenomenological cooperative enquiry into the background of the problems which bring the client to counselling and the larger processes and sub-processes which impinge upon their life and by which they structure, organise and give personal meaning to that ground.

> Mark, aged 10, came to therapy accompanied by his parents, because he had developed an obsessive routine of basketball shots which he had to go through before going to bed. This routine which sometimes lasted 2 or 2½ hours was causing great distress to himself and his parents. The therapist asked what sense Mark made of his own behaviour. Mark didn't know why he did it but he had to. The therapist shared his belief that behaviour has meaning, even though in this case Mark's feelings, meaning and behaviour appeared to be somewhat disconnected.
>
> Although the therapist did actively explore the figure of the routine with Mark in great detail, he was equally interested in many features of the background to Mark's routine. He wanted to know, for example, what had happened to Mark's parents when they were aged 10 and encouraged Mark to take an active interest in the background of his own routine by keeping daily notes about the routine, any variations in routine and about the events of the day preceding, including interactions at home and school. At the sessions they regularly discussed these notes about the ground from which Mark's routine arose, especially the variations which seemed to offer the most potential for meaning-making (example adapted from Wheeler, 1994).

Of course there were many other features of the ground of Mark's obsessive routine that the therapist could have chosen to explore – there are always myriad possibilities in the background – but the therapist seems to have explored enough to help Mark to reconfigure his field in such a way that six months later he was no longer feeling the need to continue the routine and had returned to the regular pursuits of boys his age. It is quite hard to ascertain exactly which aspects of the work with Mark contributed to his very changed behaviour and attitude – it could have been their joint exploration of the background features, or it could have been the therapist's belief that behaviour has meaning, or his interest in and commitment to Mark, his ability to be jokey, playful and yet serious with Mark, or a host of other unnamed factors. Most probably it was a combination of all of these and more – for human behaviour (and human change) doesn't arise from any single cause but from all the interlocking factors in the field or from the configuration of the field as a whole (p. 49). But the work might well have been less successful if the therapist had *only* attended to an analysis of the structure of the contact episode in the present moment.

> Another far-reaching example of exploring and working with the background features of clients' problems emerged from the work of a family centre in a multi-racial inner city area. A high percentage of the young teenagers who were referred to the centre were skipping school and getting into various forms of trouble. Worried parents (many of whom were single parents struggling to support their families) asked the centre to work with their children but workers often found the young people themselves reluctant to come and resentful of the fact that they seemed to be seen as the problem. In discussion with those young people who did come, the family centre realised that the problems did not belong to the young people in isolation but were intrinsically field dependent and interpersonal. They therefore evolved an encompassing project which involved working actively and systemically with the three groups concerned – parents, teachers and young people – initially in separate groups and later in groups which mixed parents, teachers and young people. Although such work could not resolve all the problems, many of which arose from the larger social and economic circumstances of the area, the response of the young people was much greater. Some of the teachers initially felt quite threatened by the approach which invited them to realise how they had until now tended to see things from their own perspective and have little understanding of the needs of the students.

Key point

While working with the here and now and the contact between client and counsellor, do not overlook the wider context of the client's life. Find out how the background of their lives contributes to who and how they are. Equally explore how clients relate their therapeutic sessions to the rest of their lives and how they integrate the learning of therapy into the overarching processes and structures of their experience.

25 Exploring and developing awareness of support systems

Support in Gestalt

Support is the background from which episodes of awareness-contact-growth and assimilation arise. Background support is essential for the foreground function of contact and people can only make the level or type of contact for which they currently have sufficient support either internally or externally or both. It is therefore important that you and clients attend to their levels of internal and external support and explore how effectively their support systems can underpin their aspirations for action and contact in the world. Support is a central concept in Gestalt counselling and therapy and is differentiated into environmental and self support. So you need to develop an interest in how clients currently support themselves and use the environmental support that is available to them, as well as being alert to how you can use yourself as a means of support and challenge.

Environmental support is the support people can gain from outside themselves. It includes support from friends, relatives, God, animals, nature, daily structures of work, church, temple, synagogue, community, money, social or organised activities, as well as the fundamental supports of the earth beneath the feet, the chair or bed beneath the body, oxygen to breathe, water to drink, food to eat and the natural world.

Self support is the support people can give themselves – it includes all the aspects of the self that the individual can take for granted and draw upon without thinking. Constitutional factors such as health, body, involuntary bodily functions, breathing, acquired habits, posture, belief systems and spiritual practice may all play a decisive role as unconscious or background support to the way an individual functions from moment to moment – the essential background to the figure of their experience. Important acquired habits for self support are the ways people think about themselves and talk to themselves, the ways they assert and defend themselves, the ways they look after themselves mentally and physically, the ways they calm and soothe themselves in times of stress, the ways they organise their field (see p. 54) and the ways they related to the natural environment.

People largely develop their styles of psychological self support through the quality of the environmental support that has been offered them. So if they were generally treated with respect, tenderness and firmness by parents and other adults as children, they will probably have internalised those experiences and as adults they are likely to be able to support themselves in ways that are largely respectful, tender and self disciplined. If on the other hand they were disrespected, humiliated, dominated, bullied, violated or spoilt and set no boundaries, they may well have internalised those experiences and may disrespect, humiliate, bully or indulge themselves in rather similar ways. Counselling and therapy offer an opportunity to review and reorganise these internal patterns of self organisation and fixed patterns of organising the field.

Offering support and challenge

Clients are likely to come to therapy looking for some extra environmental support from the counsellor or therapist. They may be lacking environmental support in their daily life; they often lacked crucial aspects of environmental support in their childhood; and at least initially they almost certainly lack the ability to support themselves effectively in respect of the key areas/problems that have brought them into counselling or therapy.

So our job as therapists includes offering specialised forms of environmental support, such as clarity, boundaries, skills, confirmation, presence, inclusion, creative ideas, challenge, lack of blame and respect. Equally importantly our job involves helping clients develop more effective self support. One of the unique contributions of Gestalt is that it argues that we can best help clients develop self support not by offering continual empathic support alone but by offering a skilful balance of support and respectful challenge (Perls, 1969b). In order to support clients' ability to support themselves, counsellors and therapists may sometimes need to surface and explore clients' habitual patterns of relying on others for support. Challenging habitual patterns need not mean being confrontative or rude (as Perls and some of his followers in the 1960s often were). It means simply not being

confluent with clients' figures of interest, fixed gestalts or expectations of support but bringing them to awareness for
exploration, as illustrated in the examples given in this and
other sections.

Deciding when to affirm and when to challenge is one of the
key decisions in the art of counselling and therapy and you will
of course make individual decisions with each client and at
different points in each therapeutic relationship by considering
various key factors in the field, such as timing, strength or
fragility of the individual's sense of self, your own authenticity,
the manner in which you challenge. Have you got a strong
enough working alliance established to bear challenge? Does the
individual feel accepted and confirmed enough to understand
that you are challenging some of their behaviours or assumptions
not rejecting or blaming their whole self? Will this client be able
to hear your questioning without fragmenting or feeling shamed?

Exploring and developing clients' support systems

Environmental support

You can listen to clients' descriptions of their life and notice what
environmental support they seem to have, keeping an open mind
about what constitutes support. For example some people like
lots of friends around them, while other people like the structure
of a job or a voluntary activity, or an evening class to support
them but they find too much close fellowship more stressful than
supportive.

Discussions with clients about how people need support and
interdependence (giving examples of the sorts of things people
find supportive) can raise people's awareness of the value of
support.

The example of the work of the family centre described on
p. 182 illustrates how counsellors and therapists can put into
practice concepts of environmental support and interdependence.
By working with the teachers and families of the young people
referred to them, they challenged the idea that the problems
belonged exclusively to the young people and helped to increase
the quality of mutual understanding and environmental support
available to teachers, young people and parents.

Watch also how clients use environmental support in the
session – how do they walk on the earth, sit upon the chair,

interpret your gestures, hear your words? Sometimes you may find that clients have similar patterns of responding to and using environmental support in sessions and in the rest of their life. Exploration of this aspect of the dialogic relationship in the present can often reveal fixed ways in which clients fail to allow others to support them or fail to feel nourished by the support that others offer.

> Through exploration of her holistic interaction with the counsellor, Frances (the client introduced on p. 117) became aware of how she distanced herself from the counsellor's support and empathy for fear that the counsellor would disappear in the same way that other people had in her life before. She also realised that she often heard empathy as artificial and false rather than allowing herself to trust the empathy and thus to risk feeling let down again. Once a client has become aware like this of how she habitually configures the supportive gestures of others, she has more choice about whether she continues to do so or not.

Self support

Notice how clients support themselves in their life. How do they look after themselves physically and emotionally, refer to themselves or talk to themselves? Observe how people calm or soothe themselves in times of stress. People's most fundamental means of supporting themselves is the simple act of breathing (see p. 165). You can discover, confirm and affirm the ways that people are already supporting themselves in their life (as long as these are not actively self-harming) and which they may take for granted, like walking the dog, playing bingo, taking half an hour to read a newspaper and so on. And you may explore options for ways they can develop more effective means of supporting themselves.

> Sylvia often talked about herself in the third person – 'that fool Sylvia did it again'. The counsellor wondered aloud if Sylvia had noticed how she disparaged herself. Sylvia hadn't, and anyway it was just the way she spoke. The counsellor accepted this but didn't become confluent with Sylvia's viewpoint. Instead she sometimes winced when Sylvia mocked herself or described what she heard. One day Sylvia said, 'You're really serious about not putting myself down, aren't you?' Gradually she began to notice her own habit. As her awareness grew, the counsellor suggested she experiment with talking about herself and to herself kindly and respectfully just to see if it made any difference. First Sylvia thought this was too silly but one day she decided to try it anyway, if only to show the counsellor it wouldn't make a bit of difference. To her surprise she reported an inner feeling of calm after talking to herself kindly. Sylvia still remained somewhat attached to her old habits of self mockery, and only replaced them grudgingly and sparingly.

If individuals or their lives are temporarily fragmented by stress or events, you may be better advised to design interventions which help them stabilise and organise their field, rather than agitating it further. As Stratford and Baillier (1979) said, some clients need glue, others need solvent. Those who already feel they are coming apart at the seams, or who are disturbed, psychotic or fragile are the ones who need glue. If clients are feeling overwhelmed by change or floundering between too many perceived possibilities, your interventions need to help provide structure, support and orientation, rather than expand their options. Important sources of structure and self support often lie in those aspects of the person's field which are currently out of their awareness, but which still exist in their background if only they can be reached or remembered.

> Robert turned up for a counselling session in deep distress. Almost every aspect of his life was in disarray. The therapist could have chosen to work with the figure of his despair, helping Robert to heighten his feelings, and Robert might easily have wept for the majority of the session, but he was doing plenty of weeping anyway. Instead the therapist decided to try to access what was currently missing in the process of figure formation, that is support. The therapist offered to help Robert to relax (with the help of some guided relaxation suggestions) and then asked him to imagine that he was looking back over his whole life and see if he could notice an instance or person of real hope and strength. Robert's face slightly shifted and the therapist enquired, 'What or whom have you found?' Robert had remembered his grandmother who had been a loving and supportive presence when he was three years old. The therapist then encouraged Robert to review his present life in the company of his grandmother – and Robert was able to find signs of hope, sources of strength and the courage to go on. Robert thus reconfigured his present field through the different perspective of reviewing his life from a supported position (example adapted from Parlett, 1992: 7).

Some clients have a greater tendency than others to fragment psychologically in stressful situations and Section 28 (p. 196) discusses ways of working with such clients.

Actively helping clients internalise your support

There is an important and subtle connection between getting environmental support and developing internal or self support. Ideally one of the outcomes of counselling and therapy is that clients internalise the support and respect they have experienced coming from you and/or the therapeutic process and unconsciously transform these into inner or self support. Section 27 (p. 192) further discusses how counsellors may support clients to internalise the support of the counselling process.

Shame and support within a relational field

Support and shame are interrelated polar opposites within the relational field and both have a specialised function within that field. As we have seen, support allows people to make contact and take risks. Shame allows people to pull back from risks when there is inadequate support available. However when lack of support is severe, shame-binds form and shame may be internalised into basic beliefs about the self. An understanding of the origin, dynamics and present potential for shame is essential for effective, compassionate counselling (see Appendix 7).

Key point

Support clients to develop awareness of external and inner sources of support. Review with them which aspects of their life and inner functioning are genuinely supportive to their current needs and which are undermining. Use yourself as a means of support in the therapeutic process by accepting and affirming clients as they are while simultaneously being prepared to question or challenge some of their belief systems or frames of reference.

---

26 Identifying and unravelling life themes

People's underlying and central life themes are the tenacious and complex themes which emerge again and again in different guises throughout the course of therapy.[1] Life themes are associated with people's fixed beliefs, attitudes and behaviours that are

---

1. I am indebted to Shub (1992) for many of the ideas in this section.

deeply embedded in their character structure. Life themes involve a complex system of interrelated patterns of retroflection–introjection–projection (see p. 190) where one belief, attitude or behaviour sustains another and the whole system interferes with people's ability to express themselves, take action or make contact and relationship *as they now wish to do*. These are themes which often need to be explored repeatedly and systematically.

Unravelling such life themes is mainly relevant to clients who are committed to an exploration of character structure and development of self. In short term, goal oriented counselling you will probably choose not to start unravelling such complex characteristics, but concentrate upon the issues which the client initially wanted to explore. In some instances you and the client may discover that it is difficult to explore the client's specific goals without doing some of this more complex exploration of established beliefs and life patterns. I suggest you discuss such cases in supervision and consider whether or not it would be practical or advisable to recontract with the client for a more far-reaching exploration.

Tracing the introjection system

When you and clients begin to explore such an introjection/ projection system, you may find it helpful to envisage it as a network or web which you are trying to track or unravel patiently and carefully. Look out for and explore those introjects which are deeply embedded in the self–other organisation of the individual and which give birth to interrelated resultant introjects and projections and limit the individuals' options for flexible interaction with the world. Don't try and explore, unravel or undo all introjects – many do not adversely affect people. Indeed many help structure the daily management of people's lives within the culture they live in. Often an individual develops a *core belief* which underlies and organises their other beliefs and their perception of the world.

> At an early age Rose was persistently given the message (both verbally and non-verbally) that her job in life was to take care of her fragile mother and 'look after the little ones'. Rose therefore believed (or introjected the belief) that she was responsible for the health and well-being of others, while also secretly resenting the fact that no one seemed to feel moved to look after her needs.

Such a core introject or belief gives birth to many resultant related introjects.

In Rose's case some of these were:

'Crying is selfish and pathetic.'
'I'm only valuable if I'm looking after people.'
'I have no right to look after and care for myself.'
'No one will ever look after me the way I need.'
'I must not say/do anything to hurt other people – they're fragile.'

Seeing how introjections, retroflections and projections interlink

Such an interrelated set of introjects often gives rise to habitual patterns of retroflection and projection. Resultant retroflections might include people denying or cutting off from feelings; blocking the expression of feelings; turning feelings inwards; or they might involve people doing to themselves what they would like others to do for them and so on.

> Rose often felt sad and tearful and sometimes extremely angry. She frequently started weeping but then stopped herself (retroflected) before her tears brought full relief. Generally Rose bottled up (retroflected) her anger but occasionally it burst forth explosively and somewhat dangerously. Following these outbursts, Rose told herself off viciously (another form of retroflection in which Rose directed her outgoing anger inwards towards herself).

Resultant projections might include unawarely denying or disowning needs, projecting them on to others and looking after the needs in the other; or assuming that other people are feeling the denied feelings instead.

> Rose was unaware of and disowned her own longing for care and attention (as a result of the complex system of introjects described above). She continually projected her need for care on to others and became disproportionately concerned and responsible for *their* physical and emotional needs. She agonised over the rejections she feared her children suffered in the ordinary give and take of school life, even though both the children themselves and their teachers insisted they were happy, self supporting and popular.
>   Even when Rose began to form new relationships, the introjection–retroflection–projection system emerged imperceptibly and unawarely organised her field, structuring all her contact experiences by making them fit in her embedded system of interrelated beliefs and resultant system of

projection and retroflection. For example when Rose met a new friend or potential partner who she thought might share her interests and be able to meet some of her own needs, she almost immediately began to see the needs of the friend/partner and became preoccupied with those rather than exploring the mutual possibilities for contact and support in an open flexible exchange or dance.

This sort of complex web of interrelated introjects, projections and retroflections creates a whole system of rules that can govern people's emotional life, restrict their ability to respond flexibly in the present and colour or distort their understanding of current interactions including, or even especially, the counselling relationship. The different manifestations of such systems are likely to emerge in many ways which may range from clients' descriptions of their relationships with others through the way they support themselves in the session, to the language they use and their relationship to you. You will probably need to work systematically with these different manifestations of the introjection–projection system treating each like a thread in an interwoven rug, tracing or unravelling each and discovering how it is related to the others and how all relate to the core introjects or life themes.

Rose often took up the counsellor's suggestions, thought about the counselling process, kept a journal and painted many pictures between sessions. Less often Rose would be very angry with the counsellor and complain that the counsellor had let her down, not attended to her meaning and misunderstood her. Rose and the counsellor explored these and other aspects of their relationship. They attended to their current interaction and in doing so discovered that although Rose was genuinely committed to counselling, she was also really trying to be a 'good client'. Her striving was fuelled by her underlying belief that she was only worthwhile if she was looking after someone else – in this case she swung between looking after the counsellor and feeling furious with her for being yet another person who let her down and failed to attend to her needs.

You and the people you work with will need time, patience and persistence to identify, track, explore and understand these sorts of system of interrelated introjections, projections and retroflections. Sometimes clients will seem to be attached to the very belief systems that prevent them living as they wish to do. You and they are likely to feel it's uphill work and you may frequently feel stuck at one remarkably similar impasse after another. But persistent exploration of the introjection–projection system can help people begin to sense for themselves when the archaic belief system emerges in the self and starts to colour the current field either in the therapeutic session or in their relationship with other people in their life. Rose, for instance, began to see how often her outdated core beliefs and projections arose and interfered with her present living. She gradually connected the core beliefs and resultant projections and retroflections with her past external environment and gained more choice about whether or not to interpret current events in the light of that past system of perceiving. Thus systematic exploration of and experimentation with embedded beliefs can lead to a reshuffling and remaking of the self, to new ways of organising and perceiving experiences and the field. It can also promote increased self support and an expanded and more creatively flexible sense of self.

Key point

Look out for deeply embedded core belief systems and a network of interrelated resulting introjections and projections, which together make up life themes which may influence all spheres of clients' lives. Help clients to identify, clarify and unravel such webs of belief systems and thus to decide for themselves which beliefs are good for them and which they want to let go or transform.

---

27 Attending to continuity, assimilation and completion

Reinforcement, connection and continuity

Change does not usually occur quickly or immediately. Even when clients have flashes of insight and suddenly reconfigure the way they see themselves or the world, these inspirations often need to be repeated by further similar ones before people assimilate their new perspective. You will often find that clients need to do similar work over time that repeats new emotional experiences and reinforces the insights and learning that they have gained. As Melnick and Nevis tell us: 'The interventions

must occur many times before any long lasting changes occur'
(1992: 65).

You may need to notice and attend to the continuity between
sessions and to the continuity in the client's sense of self, relating
one contact episode to another, this session to the client's last
session and to their previous sessions, as well as to where they
are going in their life, to their hopes and aspirations, values,
culture, community, job, relationships – in fact to all the
interrelated features of their ongoing life structures.

> The experimental session with Henry (described on pp. 236 and 238) did not
> resolve his lack of spontaneity completely. He continued to sometimes feel
> flat and cut off from his own vitality and to fear ridicule. But that experiment
> with his boss did give him a beginning in becoming aware of how he regularly
> and automatically dampened his own vitality in the company of others.
>
> To deepen his organismic learning, Henry and the therapist did other
> sessions where they explored similar material in different ways, repeatedly
> drawing Henry's attention to everyday ways in which he modulated or
> dampened his own being, including in his relationship with the therapist.
> Henry may always be someone who initially stiffens up under certain personal
> threats (real or imagined) but now he can also (usually) notice that he is
> doing so and deliberately relax or change his energy, if he wishes.

At other times clients and counsellor may get *stuck*, in doing
repetitive reworking of childhood trauma for instance. In such
cases counsellors and therapists may conversely need to draw the
repetition to the clients' attention and help them to let go of the
old feelings and identification with those old feelings and move
on to new experiences.

Assimilation and internalisation

Notice and be prepared to explore how clients assimilate and
learn from the experiences of the therapeutic sessions and other
areas of their lives. Western action-oriented culture does not give
a great deal of value or time to the stages of assimilation, satisfaction and completion in life processes. Despite its emphasis
upon the urge to complete, Perlsian Gestalt has also not traditionally given as much time or thought to the processes involved
in demobilisation and assimilation of learning as it has to the
processes of figure formation and contact (Melnick and Nevis,
1992).

Assimilation in the therapeutic process involves the regular
chewing over of experiences to see what has been gained and

what has been learned. The Gestalt approach emphasises observing and exploring, whereas the processes of assimilation and internalisation are largely intrapsychic. They are harder to see and so may easily get ignored or overlooked. In addition, the work of demobilisation and assimilation is not all pleasant and satisfying. It involves the ability to stop, to turn away from something; it necessitates letting go and accepting ending (often associated with death, loss, separation and emptiness) as well as the ability to relax and celebrate.

Like many people who are attracted to Gestalt (as therapeutic counsellors or clients) you may enjoy its lively, exciting quality – so you may possibly find the work of assimilation comparatively dull or boring and may underestimate the time and attention needed for internalisation of the experiences to take place. You may feel that it is the clients' responsibility to draw their own conclusions and learn from the experiences offered in the counselling or therapeutic sessions. Alternatively it may seem 'obvious' to you what the clients' learning or insight from a session or series of sessions is or should be – so you may forget to find out what insight clients have actually had.

In assimilation phases we may encourage clients to reflect on their experiences in the therapeutic sessions and make meaning of them, comparing them to previous life experience and beliefs, discarding what is not useful and retaining what is, until the essence of the useful experience really becomes an intrinsic part of the person and becomes part of their repertoire and their self support system. We may suggest clients experiment with slowing down and take the time to end with one experience, milk the learning from it and rest before embarking upon a new experience. Or we may decide we need to teach them something about the learning process or the need to actively assimilate work done. We may ask them to review the time spent in counselling and tell us what was useful about an experience in the session. We may make links from one piece of learning to another, comparing or differentiating this insight with one they had two weeks or three months ago.

Internalising the therapeutic experience

Ideally one of the outcomes of therapy is that clients internalise the support and respect they have experienced during the therapeutic process and unconsciously transform these into inner or internal support. And indeed many clients do internalise therapeutic support naturally and spontaneously:

> Jessica had a stressful home life. Her husband often criticised her cruelly and her children fought quite viciously. Her familiar pattern had always been to hear this for a few minutes, internal tension mounting, and then to join in and escalate the aggravation and anger by exploding into screeches of rage. She felt she couldn't help herself. After being in counselling for some time, she spontaneously reported to James, the counsellor, that the last time this had happened she took a deep breath and said to herself: Now what would James say to me if he saw me? He'd say something like, Hang on a minute. Take your time. Are you breathing? Are your feet on the ground? What are your options here? Just slowing down like this and consulting her 'internalised James' helped Jessica stay centred and assertive in the difficult situation and feel much better about herself and her ability to handle it.

Sometimes clients don't seem to internalise their therapeutic experiences so spontaneously and you could consider active exploration or stimulation, as in the following example:

> Yvonne worked hard in the sessions exploring all aspects of the field, but nothing much seemed to change in her external life. One day the therapist asked Yvonne what she did with the sessions in between times. Yvonne was surprised by the question, and exploration led to the fact that she tended to keep the sessions in a sort of 'special capsule' isolated from the rest of her life. When she was preparing to leave therapy a year later, Yvonne reported that that simple question was one of the most important interventions the therapist had made – she said it helped her realise she needed to treat their sessions together like a sort of 'compost' and plough them back into her life, if she was going to make her life change (which it subsequently had).

Key point

When appropriate help clients to make connections between one session and another, between the therapeutic process and life. Explore with clients how or to what extent they are assimilating the experience of counselling or the insights they have gained in counselling. If they do not seem to internalise or generalise from the therapeutic process, try exploring this phenomenon and consider adjusting your approach as needed.

28 Calibrating your approach for people who have a fragile sense of self or are easily shamed

Why differentiate people with fragile self process?

There is considerable evidence that more and more people who would meet diagnostic criteria for a disorder of the self (see Appendix 4) or who could be described as having fragile self process (Mollon, 1994) are requesting counselling and therapy in both medical settings and in private practice. Indeed it has been argued (by Lasch, 1979, for example) that we are now a society which by its nature creates people with various kinds of fragile self process. So it is important for you to recognise such people and know either to refer them on or how to work appropriately with them.

True Gestalt is a field approach so a Gestalt counsellor ideally grades every intervention in relation to the degree of self support, stability and internal cohesion of the client as well as to the conditions of the counselling setting. So special guidelines for working with people who are psychologically fragile could *theoretically* be considered redundant because a Gestaltist does not use general techniques but always responds to the individual, taking into consideration his/her ego strength and degree of stability of self organisation. *In practice* many Gestalt therapists (either through inexperience or inadequate training in recognising psychological fragility) do employ some of the approaches which they have seen demonstrated on their training courses or described in this and other books, without realising that all aspects of therapy need to be adapted and graded for individual clients. For example some approaches may not be helpful to psychologically fragile individuals, or people who experience acute shame.

In Gestalt terms the problem of such people is not necessarily that they make poor contact between themselves and the environment but that their sense of self, their self organisation, is not stable through time. 'They are capable of making good contact but they are vulnerable to sudden and severe breakdown of their contact functions in some situations of intimacy or stress' (Beaumont, 1993: 85). During these episodes they experience a loss of their sense of self, saying things such as 'I wasn't myself', 'I don't know what came over me.' They behave in ways that seem justifiable to them at the time but which they find very hard to live with afterwards. To the outsider the situations which trigger these breakdowns of contact functions may sometimes seem trivial in comparison to the emotional thunderstorms, confusion, inner emptiness or loneliness that are evoked.

Gestalt therapy with such people needs to emphasise self organisation and the development of a cohesive sense of self over time; whereas Gestalt therapy which encourages catharsis or heightens contact may be detrimental to them. A number of Gestalt practitioners have taken the trouble to evolve guidelines for adjusting Gestalt for working with people whose sense of self is fragile. It is beyond the scope of this book to define and discuss the vast field of fragile self process. I aim merely to alert you to the need for care, give you a few guidelines and introduce you to some of the authors to whom you can go for further discussion of the issues. Appendix 4 gives the specific *DSM IV* criteria for narcissistic and borderline personality disorders; while Box 28.1 summarises Greenberg's identifying features of people manifesting borderline self process. Please also read Appendix 2, which highlights the need to be very cautious and respectful when considering diagnostic categories of any sort.

Tobin (1982) has made important suggestions for how you can adapt the Gestalt approach to work with people who have narcissistic characteristics; Greenberg has made some equally valuable suggestions for how you can adapt the Gestalt approach to work with people who have borderline character-istics (1989) and narcissistic characteristics (1991, 1995). Almost all of these suggestions involve helping clients strengthen the enduring and cohesive features of the ongoing background self structure (rather than heighten individual contact episodes), which is why I have included this discussion here in this part of the book which attends to aspects of ground. Below I give some guidelines for working with people with borderline traits or self process. They put a tremendous emphasis upon developing cohesion, continuity and stability. For working with narcissisti-cally vulnerable clients I suggest Greenberg's (1995) excellent paper on the subject.

Box 28.1   General features of those with borderline style of self process (adapted from Greenberg, 1989)

1. Core issues revolve around identity and relationship problems
2. Has failed to fully separate and individuate from mother or father; still involved with mother or father or with partners who share characteristics of mother or father
3. Identity – unable to integrate contradictory views of themselves and others; suppressed development of true self; feel incohesive, fragmented, uncertain of who they are
4. Splits by keeping contradictory affective states apart because they 'fear' that the negative affect may overwhelm the positive
5. Oscillate between fears of engulfment and abandonment. When fearing abandonment, may cling and demand love. When fearing engulfment, may keep emotional distance
6. Feel full of overwhelming rage which they experience as dangerous and are often afraid of expressing
7. Has not achieved full 'object constancy', i.e. if they feel angry with someone, they cannot remember their positive affective tie to that person and vice versa
8. Go through life yearning for an intense intimate relationship, the one perfect other who will make them feel better – often projected on to therapist
9. Cannot easily or effectively function as an adult on own – requires others to help them soothe themselves for example

---

Working with people with borderline self process[1]

Creating a safe, consistent environment

The therapist needs to become a steady, stabilising influence in these people's often chaotic lives. So I suggest you try to create a safe and reliable, reasonably consistent environment by giving regular appointment(s) each week on the same day at the same time and consider referring if you cannot offer this sort of stability.

---

1. I am indebted to Elinor Greenberg (1989) and to Stratford and Braillier (1979) for many of the guidelines summarised here.

Fostering auxiliary ego functions and ego development

These people may be very impulsive and regret their impulsive actions afterwards. You can try lending clients your awareness, by helping them to anticipate possible consequences of their actions, for example.

Developing clients' awareness of how to soothe and support themselves

Psychologically fragile clients often don't know how to soothe themselves when they find life stressful. Far from calming themselves they may actually turn impulsively to activities or substances that increase their agitation – they may go on spending sprees, run up debts, gamble, drink pints of coffee or alcohol when they are upset and then tell themselves how awful they are afterwards. You can help these clients explore their options for soothing themselves. You may need to help them to soothe and support themselves in and outside the therapeutic sessions by establishing familiar routines rather than heightening the figure of their distress (which may just lead to further fragmentation, not assimilation). You could suggest they experimentally practise some alternative options with you *in sessions* before they try changing their habits at home (people often need lots of support from the counsellor to try out new ways of supporting themselves before they can do it alone). See p. 186 for further discussion of self support.

Developing cohesion, bridging splits, integrating, interpreting

Under stress these people often 'split' or polarise themselves, other people and experiences into good or bad. You may be able to help them build a more cohesive picture of events by gently reminding them of other ways they have previously described similar people or events. You can support clients to develop cohesion and a sense of a consistent self over time by making links between one session and another, between clients' past and present, etc. With these clients it is sometimes a good idea to suggest interpretations of behaviour and offer explanations that link present behaviour to past experience – for you cannot necessarily rely on them to assimilate insights from experiential work as you do with others (Greenberg, 1989). (This and some other suggestions in this chapter are contradictory to the guidelines for much Gestalt exploration, and are the result of the clinical experience of counsellors and therapists working with clients who manifest a fragile self process.)

Because these people tend to polarise and fragment as a general rule, it is wise to be cautious about introducing two-chair intrapsychic work (see pp. 173 and 236) especially if the client has vicious introjects which can psychologically overwhelm other aspects of their selves. Two-chair work can increase fragmentation in those who already have a fragile self process, and does not necessarily lead to integration and greater wholeness as it usually does with people who already have a more cohesive self organisation. If you do use two-chair, only do so after a solid therapeutic relationship is established and with constant attention to whether or not the client remains grounded in the fact that these are *two aspects of the same self* not two different people, and with attention to whether such work actually leads to greater integration.

It is often important to stress assimilation activities at the end of each session and from one session to another. You cannot *assume* that these clients will make connections over time, link one aspect of themselves to another or assimilate the work done in the sessions.

Avoiding regressive and cathartic work

These clients already have high emotional peaks and may tend to regress spontaneously. So it is often advisable not to heighten emotion but to help them *stay in the present and develop ordinary, grounded ego functioning*.

It is often very useful to help these clients learn to distinguish their overwhelming strong emotions, differentiate and label them; so you will probably want to encourage verbalisation of feeling rather than enactment.

If the clients are angry, it is important to work with rage and anger appropriately, showing that it is safe to be angry with you, that you will not retaliate viciously but also that you will not allow clients to damage themselves or you or your property in any way. You may need to be firm. Sometimes using painting, puppets or figures may offer safer ways for these clients to tell their story or express emotions than more active or less contained approaches, such as sound or movement. Often you need to help these clients *learn* to retroflect rather than teach them to undo retroflection.

Anticipating and dealing with breaks

Breaks in the counselling process (such as those caused by scheduled holidays) may be very difficult for these clients. They often trigger feelings of abandonment, rage or shame and counsellors need to be alert to such possibilities. Sometimes feelings of abandonment emerge and are articulated directly. Other times they may manifest in subtler ways such as a general depression or sense that the therapy is no longer meaningful or worthwhile. Receiving, exploring and understanding these feelings is usually not a diversion from, but central to, therapy.

Once you and a client become aware that breaks precipitate difficult feelings, you may take preventative steps to try and help the client maintain her sense of connection with you and the counselling process during the break (Greenberg, 1989).

Developing self functions

Self functions (Kepner, 1995) involve the capacity to manage and integrate experience and interactions (or contact episodes) and are learned throughout childhood in relationship to other people. If our childhood environment allowed and encouraged us to engage and experiment with a wide range of interactions and feelings, then we develop a broad spectrum of flexible self functions or tools to manage the intensity of experience, to regulate interpersonal boundaries, to rest when we need to, to calm ourselves and be calmed, to form a clear sense of self and other, of how to connect and how to separate. If the childhood environment was rigid, inadequate, invasive or abusive, then people will not have learned (or have only partially learned) essential self functions. The self functions which were not learned will be like missing steps in a staircase of the self. They will be unavailable for use in the present when the individual is in circumstances that make demands for contact that are different from those learned in childhood. If clients have such holes in their functioning, the therapeutic counsellor can look for ways to help them develop the missing self functions by practising relevant skills of managing experience, interpersonal boundaries and so on in the present therapeutic relationship.

Keeping limits and boundaries

Many people with borderline self process have a deep yearning for a perfect other who will give them unconditional love and acceptance, permission for separation, individuation and personal growth and 24-hour devotion within an intense relationship (Greenberg, 1989). They often get angry or even self harming when disappointed. However many practitioners suggest that it is especially important to appropriately challenge destructive behaviour, maintaining clear limits and boundaries concerning cancellations, time, money, telephone calls, etc. with clients of this nature. Within the boundaries of the therapeutic alliance we can still empathise with the client's yearning, accepting them and all their feelings (Masterson, 1985; Delisle, 1989). Such limit setting provides the crucible which brings issues and feelings into the therapeutic dialogue, allowing them to be worked through (see p. 39).

Shame in the relational field

Clients whose sense of self is fragile and who experience the sudden and severe breakdown in self organisation described at the beginning of this chapter are often very vulnerable to shame and I suggest that an understanding of shame dynamics in the therapeutic relationship and in the history of shame-vulnerable clients is essential. Appendix 7 describes shame as a pervasive and evasive intersubjective phenomenon.

Rose (who is described in Appendix 2, and Section 26) demonstrated many of the self-process features of those with borderline self process; the counsellor tried to follow these guidelines for working with people with borderline self process. The therapeutic relationship was lengthy and sometimes threatened to fragment, but Rose did develop a more cohesive sense of herself and an ability to integrate good and bad aspects of herself and others.

Key point

Adjust the way you work to different clients, paying special attention to the needs of those whose sense of self is fragile and whose self organisation and self support is inclined to break down or fragment in situations they experience as emotionally difficult. For these clients emphasising safety, containment and continuity is usually more important and effective than heightening contact or challenge.

IX

Shaping Counselling over Time

29 Shaping therapeutic work over time

Gestalt counselling and therapy require you to be able to stay with the present exchange and explore the unfolding moment without goals, assumptions or direction. You also need to know how to sustain, stay with and shape counselling and therapy over a period of time. The way you do this will be greatly influenced by the type, duration and circumstances of the therapeutic counselling you offer. For example if you are a counsellor within a health centre who is required to limit counselling to six or twelve sessions, this will impose a framework, structure and sense of timing. Such focused counselling can be extremely effective and life changing, especially if the clients are highly motivated to use the opportunity that counselling offers (Stretton, personal communication). But it clearly presents limitations which longer term therapeutic exploration does not.

Although the Gestalt approach emphasises the natural unfolding of the process of exploration, just 'going with the flow' can sometimes make you and your clients feel as though you are going round in circles without direction. So I will briefly describe five possible maps or models for conceptualising and shaping Gestalt counselling and therapy over time and give you some indications regarding where you can find out more about these maps.

- Gestalt counselling and therapy as an exploration of support;
- Gestalt counselling and therapy as interactive cycles of contact and withdrawal;
- Gestalt counselling and therapy as phases;
- Gestalt counselling and therapy as a hologram of healing tasks;
- Contemporary integrative Gestalt as a complex system that is field theoretical and multi-focal.

An exploration of support

You can conceptualise Gestalt counselling and therapy as an exploration of how clients currently support themselves and of how they may develop more effective means of support. Some Gestalt theoreticians have envisaged this development of support systems as a movement from unaware dependence upon environmental support to aware and choiceful interdependence and self support. (Indeed Perls often suggested that the process of maturation involves just such a movement.) You may occasionally work with clients who do move steadily from depending upon environmental support to interdependence and self support. More often clients are likely to move through a complex journey with many twists and turns and hairpin bends. Don't assume that clients' loops 'back' into environmental support are a regression into immaturity (as Fritz Perls sometimes seemed to imply). They may well represent a tremendous growth in trust, confidence and ability to relate. Many clients need to test you to find out that you are to be trusted not to humiliate or reject them before they are likely to risk showing their need for your (or other environmental) support.

Be prepared for the exploration of support even to go in the reverse direction – some clients may start counselling or therapy apparently extremely self supporting (they may in fact be overly self reliant) and may need to *learn* about interdependence and acceptance of environmental support from you, their friends or relatives. Far from being regressive, increased openness to environmental support for these clients may represent a significant surge in confidence. For it can require a good deal of self support to ask for or accept environmental support or interdependence.

Interactive cycles of contact and withdrawal

Another broad way in which you can understand the overall therapeutic process is to see it as an overarching example of the Gestalt wave or cycle of contact and withdrawal. You can for example equate the following phases of each therapeutic relationship with a parallel stage of the Gestalt cycle/wave of contact (see Figure 12.1).

Phase in Counselling and therapy	*Stage in cycle/wave of contact*
Pre-counselling phase	Sensation stage
Initial phase	Awareness stage

Getting going phase	Mobilisation stage
Middle phase	Action stage – often precipitates and includes an impasse stage
Later stage	Full contact stage and resolution of impasse stage
Penultimate phase	Integration, assimilation stages
Final stages and ending	Withdrawal and rest stages

If you want to know more about this model of counselling over time, read Clarkson's (1989) book, but be aware that it treats the 'interruptions' to contact as 'interruptions' and not as bipolar dimensions or styles of contact and the diagrams in the book seem to suggest that certain interruptions to contact mainly occur at certain stages of the cycle or phases of counselling. Experience does not support this idea and indeed Clarkson's text does emphasise that the 'interruptions' she describes may occur at any point in the cycle. All so-called interruptions to contact are complex and interconnected and may occur at any stage of the cycle of contact or at any phase of therapy. This book has argued that whether a particular behaviour or attitude can be described as an interruption or as a support to contact is field dependent (see pp. 106 and 219).

Phases

You can also see longer term Gestalt counselling or therapy as three broad and overlapping phases – initial, mid and later or final – with distinctive tasks associated with each phase (Shub, 1992).

Shub's *initial phase* is concerned with the early diagnostic picture, establishing the client's goals, exploring and building trust, developing awareness and contact skills, working at the contact boundary between client and therapist/counsellor and so on.

Shub's *mid phase* is concerned with identifying ambivalence, life themes and unravelling fixed archaic patterns of behaviour or attitude as embodied in the individual's introjection/projection system (see p. 190), with exploring polarities, reclaiming disowned aspects of self (p. 119) and expanding the sense of self.

Shub's *later and final phase* is concerned with development of increased self support (see p. 183) through self experimentation, fuller exploration of relationship between client and counsellor, integration of introjects, full exploration of ending and all the associated issues (see p. 209).

The phases may vary enormously in length, shape and relative size according to the type of character and self exploration to be done (Shub, 1992). The tasks associated with the initial phase are described in Parts I to V of this book, those associated with the mid phase are described in Parts V to VIII of this book and those associated with the later or final phase are described in Part IX.

A hologram of healing tasks

Self awareness and self development are not a linear but a spiral process. Kepner (1995) has developed a holographic model which identifies and describes four phases of therapy – the support phase, the self functions phase, the undoing, redoing and mourning phase and the reconsolidation phase. The task of developing support is more figural at the beginning of therapy; the task of developing self functions becomes more figural towards the middle of therapy; the tasks of undoing, redoing and mourning become more predominant in the second half of therapy; while the tasks of reconsolidation dominate toward the end of therapy. Kepner's model proposes that while one phase and task is figural or predominant, the tasks of other phases will also be going on concurrently. For example the task of developing support functions may be particularly important at the beginning of therapy but needs attention at intervals throughout the therapeutic process (see p. 183).

Kepner's model was especially developed for working with survivors of sexual abuse, but it offers a conceptual framework for working with a broader range of clients. It is particularly suitable for clients who have a relatively fragile self process as it puts great emphasis upon building support and self functions *before* embarking upon too much expressive or undoing work, in order to ensure that clients have sufficient self organisation and cohesion to be able to assimilate such exploration creatively.

Contemporary integrative Gestalt as a complex system that is field theoretical and multi-focal

In this book I have presented a holographic model for contemporary integrative Gestalt counselling and therapy in which I suggest that the component phases or tasks can be seen as a complex interactive system where development through the phases is not strictly linear and sequential but spiralling, iterative and recursive. See Introduction (pp. 1–4) for a full description of this model.

Key point

Be able to formulate ways of conceptualising and shaping the overall counselling process over time, while remaining flexible, spontaneous and open to the unfolding moment in the present.

---

30 Attending to the final stages and endings

Counselling may be a long or a short process but it is hopefully usually finite, for the aim must be to support clients to live their lives more fully, rather than to be better and better clients. Therapeutic counsellor and client both need to keep some sense of the ending of the process as a supportive framework and real aspect of the work. Psychotherapists, counsellors and clients engaged in longer term work often speak of an increase in intensity and depth of exploration once an ending is clearly envisaged; while those doing shorter term more goal oriented exploration usually describe their work as highly focused (Elton Wilson, 1996). The finiteness and reality of the ending provides a structure and framework which offers an important stimulus to making meanings and completions.

In much focused counselling work the end date is arranged as part of the initial contract. Even in longer term more open-ended therapeutic counselling, some attention still needs to be paid to the reality and process of ending in the initial stages of the counselling. For instance you can discuss a simple leaving contract with clients as described on p. 35. In such longer term exploration, the actual end date is usually negotiated by the therapist and client when they judge between them that the therapeutic work is nearing completion. As part of this negotiation therapists often suggest that clients fix an end date some time in advance and then work towards ending at the date fixed. The duration of the ending period varies according to the field conditions, taking account of such factors as the length of the counselling or therapy process, the practicalities of the client's and counsellor's lives, the significance of endings and leavings in the client's experience, and so on. It is often a good idea to talk through (with a colleague or supervisor) an individual's proposed ending before settling the details – to give yourself an opportunity to review the potential complexity of the issues involved. Agreeing on an end date in advance gives clients and counsellors or therapists time to envisage it and work towards it. There are specific therapeutic tasks or responsibilities associated with ending counselling and therapy which are different from the tasks of other phases (Kepner, 1980; Zinker, 1980).

Responsibilities and tasks of ending

Assimilation and completion

Once an end date is set, counsellor and client can keep the imminent ending in mind and ensure that various themes associated with ending are addressed and explored. Towards the end of therapy counsellors are likely to attend to the activities of assimilation and completion of the whole process in a similar fashion to the way in which they have attended to these phases at the end of individual sessions or in review sessions (p. 192). Counsellors and clients often review the work done, clarifying what has been achieved and what remains undone. Counsellors can help clients to chew over and savour previous work and assimilate insight and learning and changes of attitude or behaviour. They may need to support the client in internalising the experiences of counselling into the ground of themselves and into their repertoire of self functions and self support tools for the future. They can join with clients to affirm and celebrate their achievements, the moments of meeting in the dialogic relationship. They may also want or need to explore and name what has not been achieved or explored and make space for clients to express disappointment or other feelings.

Counsellors also need to help clients envisage what it will be like to *stop coming*. For instance you may feel that it is a good idea to explore how clients are going to get support when counselling or therapy finishes: you may need to help them to consider how to build up their alternative and additional support systems. You will certainly want to explore with clients how they feel about the ending of counselling or therapy and may need to help them to grieve the regular support and the close relationship of the therapeutic process which is soon going to finish. Some clients may of course feel not sadness but joy or relief – be open to the myriad possibilities and help clients explore a range of feelings.

Patterns of ending

People often have fixed attitudes or patterns of behaviour around endings. Look out for these patterns – if a client tells you early in the counselling process that she left friends without saying goodbye, or a previous counsellor without telling her she was dissatisfied, be alert to the fact that she may be revealing her habitual pattern of leaving. The expected ending of the therapeutic process gives you and clients a good chance to find out about, raise awareness of, explore and possibly transform such patterns and the reasons they have arisen.

Association with previous endings and separations

Another important task of ending therapy may be to work through feelings associated with other endings in people's lives. The imminent ending of the therapeutic process often sensitises clients to similar clusters of experience and may restimulate memories of people they have left behind: partings, goodbyes, deaths, separations. Sometimes clients will be fully aware that specific memories have been recalled; other times they may have body sensations or non-specific feelings. Whatever the response, be prepared to explore it and to see if it is in some way connected to ending the therapeutic process or to previous endings.

People often have unfinished feelings concerning previous separations or endings in their life and if the ending of counselling or therapy does surface these, then it can provide a wonderful opportunity to investigate how such feelings can be more fully resolved in the present. Working through feelings associated with separations may be very moving and may require some time – which is one of the reasons that it is advisable to set up a contract that safeguards against precipitous leaving at the beginning and to arrange an end date in advance.

Joan had been divorced several years before and believed herself to be quite reconciled to her divorced status. When she was preparing to leave counselling, she suddenly remembered the time when her ex-husband had been preparing to leave her. She recalled and shared her anguish. She then decided she needed to create a ceremony, which would give her divorce some of the ritual status that her marriage had had. With the counsellor she made a couple of paper figures to represent her young self and her young husband. Later she invited a friend to support her while she placed them upon a small piece of wood and let them float down river – as a symbolic means of letting go her younger self and her relationship. Joan was very moved by what she'd done and reported feeling freer and ready for the next phase of life.

Joanna on the other hand felt powerful but non-specific bodily feelings of heaviness and panic when she contemplated finishing her counselling relationship. Phenomenological exploration of these bodily sensations led to an association with her very early separation from her mother. She and the counsellor decided to allow plenty of time to explore this connection as Joanna had not previously had any sense of vital connection with the first year of her life but had always felt it was relevant to her present patterns of behaviour.

If clients have experienced painful or unsatisfactory separations or difficult goodbyes in the past, it may be especially important for them and the therapist to pay particular attention to the manner in which they end the therapeutic relationship.

Gerald had always been very pleasing and had avoided confrontation or difference. He kept on employees because he could not face dismissing them and stayed in an unhappy marriage because he didn't know how to leave. After much exploration and an increased awareness of this style of relating, he made a definite decision that he would take charge of leaving counselling and felt very good about doing so.

Clients who manifested two very different styles of leaving were Sheila and Jessica. Sheila had never felt that anyone valued her or missed her in her life and was deeply touched when the counsellor showed that she would miss her; whereas Jessica had had clinging parents who tried to make her feel guilty every time she left home (even in her thirties); so during the period she was preparing to leave, she took considerable delight in frequently telling the counsellor that she was going and that the counsellor was not her responsibility.

Counsellors and therapists also need to do most of these tasks for themselves, sometimes with, sometimes without the client. We too need to affirm what we have achieved in this particular episode of counselling and acknowledge what remains undone. We need to review what we have learned from this therapeutic experience and internalise the learning so that we can draw on it in the future, for that is how we build up experience. We need to celebrate our achievements and envisage what it will be like not to see this particular client again. Therapeutic relationships are very real, often involving and affecting both participants deeply, and therapists as well as clients can feel strong feelings, such as loss or relief at the end of any particular counselling process. The more we are aware of this possibility and seek appropriate support from friends, personal therapist or supervisor, the more we will be able to support the client in making the ending he/she needs.

Sometimes it may be important to share with the client how much you value them and show them that you will miss them. Other times you may judge that such self disclosure may be unhelpful. For example with clients, such as Jessica, who had parents who had clung on to her, you may decide to let them see that you value them *and* that you are happy to let them go.

The void

Towards the end of counselling or therapy, both clients and counsellors need to prepare to 'demobilise', finish their relationship – to step into the void of the unknown of the next stage of life. Completion of any experience involves coming to rest, allowing oneself to be at a place in the cycle of experience where one is still, where nothing is happening and nothing is catching our attention – no new figure has yet emerged from the ground of the field. There are no things, only pure being. Many people fear and avoid the experience of nothingness and will engage in all sorts of diversions or busyness rather than face it. This fear of emptiness, of not knowing what will happen, can induce people to stay with painful or toxic patterns of behaviour rather than enter the void. So you may sometimes choose to share with clients your impression that they are afraid of stillness and encourage them to stay experimentally with inactivity or emptiness, while providing them with support to do so. If people can learn to stay with this emptiness, it will sooner or later be transformed as a new genuine figure of interest emerges: 'And we find when we accept and enter this nothingness, the void, then the desert starts to bloom. The empty void becomes alive, is being filled. The sterile void becomes the fertile void' (Perls, 1969b: 57).

Key point

Pay at least as much attention to completing and ending as you do to beginnings, supporting clients to assimilate and internalise the experiences of the therapeutic process and to explore the feelings associated with ending it. Be aware that ending counselling or therapy may reveal people's patterns of endings or trigger feelings associated with previous endings in their life and be prepared to work through these associations. Help clients prepare for ending by discussing what alternative support they will be able to find and discussing what it is like for them to come to an ending.

Conclusion: Simplicity, complexity and paradox in Gestalt counselling and therapy

A paradoxical profession

Gestalt is an encompassing and paradoxical approach to counselling and psychotherapy. On the one hand it is simple and elegant; on the other it embraces complexity and resists reductionism. It is simple in the sense that it is based in simple but profound truths, such as the fact that we human beings are interdependent with our environment; that we grow emotionally and physically through contact with and assimilation of compatible aspects of the environment; that we can discover who we are through person to person relationship; that our best self support is to be fully in touch with ourselves, other people and the natural world around us; that we live more vitally if we live in the present moment. The central method of Gestalt counselling and psychotherapy – the phenomenological method – is also apparently simple, in that it involves concentrating upon what is and describing the obvious, rather than upon making clever interpretations or hypotheses. Simple though it may at first appear, the method is profoundly challenging and allows clients and therapists to strip away assumptions, prejudices and habitual perspectives and experience the other person immediately and freshly from moment to moment, discovering the essential nature of the processes observed.

Paradoxically, Gestalt is also complex, requiring a host of seemingly conflicting human characteristics, qualities and skills and eliciting the tension of powerfully opposing polarities. This book, for example, has suggested that you need to be able to take both an 'I–Thou' and an 'I–It' attitude to clients; that you are spontaneous and imaginative and yet systematic in your work; that you need to enter the internal world of the other and yet stay in touch with yourself; that you need to be practical and theoretical, that you need to suspend previous judgements and yet develop fine assessment skills; that you need to keep an open mind about what is important and yet be able to focus and develop a theme; that you require a substantive body of theoretical knowledge while being able to let go all that knowledge and meet

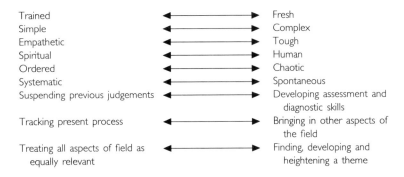

Trained	⟷ Fresh
Simple	⟷ Complex
Empathetic	⟷ Tough
Spiritual	⟷ Human
Ordered	⟷ Chaotic
Systematic	⟷ Spontaneous
Suspending previous judgements	⟷ Developing assessment and diagnostic skills
Tracking present process	⟷ Bringing in other aspects of the field
Treating all aspects of field as equally relevant	⟷ Finding, developing and heightening a theme

Figure C.1 *Polarities within the practice of Gestalt counselling*

the other person as a human being, person to person. The healing process demands great personal involvement together with an ability to maintain an appropriate non-attachment. It requires you to be fully present and yet to be able to reflect on what is occurring. It is both a science and an art.

In the Gestalt approach, the opposites and paradoxes discussed above are not disconnected and irreconcilable but interconnected poles or extremes along a continuum. The whole person theoretically encompasses all human qualities, 'possessing thousands of integrated and interlaced polarities, all melted together' (Zinker, 1978: 197). The healthier the person the more aware he/she is of the huge range of their emotional and cognitive repertoire. The less healthy person is less aware and accepting of a range of human capacities and may deny his or her so-called negative polarities. I propose that Zinker's model of polarities within the whole person can be adapted as a model of the whole counsellor.

Gestalt therapists need to know and embrace contradictory or polar qualities and they need to be able to range flexibly and freely along the bipolar continuums of these qualities as the field conditions of the counselling exchange require. Figure C.1 illustrates just a few of the polarities which Gestalt counsellors need to be able to encompass within their practice.

Less aware therapists may have a restricted, stereotyped view of themselves, knowing themselves to be caring, empathetic, and good at tracking and so on, but perhaps not able to accept that they are also sometimes uncaring, confused, impatient, initiating, distracted, systematic or unpredictable, and finding it hard to see how these latter qualities can possibly have a place in counselling.

More aware therapists can accept most of the polarities within themselves and their practice, including feelings and thoughts which many systems of therapeutic counselling disallow; so they may say to themselves, 'Initially, I treat all aspects of the field as being potentially equally relevant, but I can also swiftly identify a central theme and help the client develop and heighten it' or again, 'I can be creative and spontaneous in the counselling situation, yet I am also willing to reflect upon what I am doing and develop a systematic approach that will enable the clients to reinforce and internalise their insights.'

Qualities, skills and attitudes that counsellors and therapists disallow or disown do not just disappear – they tend to leak out and affect interactions in an unconscious fashion – so the more counsellors recognise and know of their own qualities (both those commonly seen as 'good' and 'bad') the more they can use those qualities flexibly and creatively to do effective therapy in a range of settings with a range of people (see Figure C.2).

Using the self as instrument

The disciplines of counselling and therapy therefore put enormous demands on the person of counsellors or psychothera-pists to know themselves in the fullest possible sense and to manifest themselves in the most flexible and versatile fashion.

Therapeutic counsellors use themselves as instruments: staying in touch with themselves and what they are experiencing, physically, mentally and emotionally from moment to moment while using themselves to tune into what is happening with clients on all these same levels. They need to know their own strengths, weaknesses, wounds and blind spots and recognise how these may impact upon the therapeutic process. 'The person of the therapist or counsellor is incessantly being forced to struggle with his weaknesses, with his blind spots . . . he must incessantly struggle to bring his woundedness into play, yet not make the healing of his own self the focus. In fact it is this struggling which develops the self of the therapist' (Hycner, 1988: 12).

One way for counsellors and therapists to get to know them-selves and stretch their own self image is to be in Gestalt (or other) counselling/therapy for themselves. This can help them to develop their personal awareness and an internal experience or map of Gestalt therapy as well as offering them the support they need in order to grow, change and face the frequently challenging

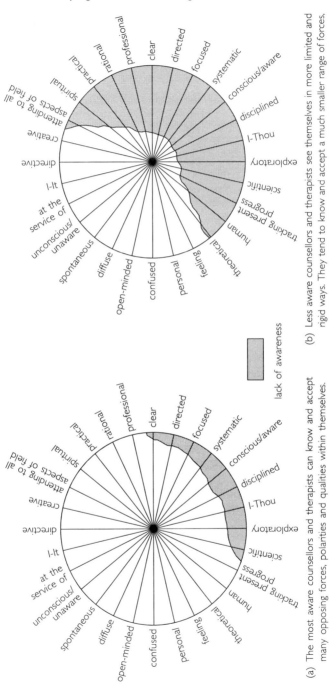

(a) The most aware counsellors and therapists can know and accept many opposing forces, polarities and qualities within themselves.

(b) Less aware counsellors and therapists see themselves in more limited and rigid ways. They tend to know and accept a much smaller range of forces, polarities and qualities within themselves and to identify with only one polarity along each continuum.

Figure C.2   *Polarities in Gestalt counselling and therapy: differing degrees of awareness of polarised qualities or aspects of the* experiences of being a therapist. It can allow them to keep the instrument of the self tuned, clear and true to be responsive to the ever-changing rhythms of the therapeutic exchange.

Counsellors and therapists who work actively with the counselling relationship must be prepared for that relationship to include difficulty and antagonism, as well as magical moments of meeting. All too often I find trainee counsellors and psychotherapists delighting in and depending upon the appreciation of their clients. While it is fine to *enjoy* appreciation, I suggest that counsellors and psychotherapists need to have sufficient support and appreciation from other aspects of their life that they don't *need* the appreciation of their clients – if they need it, they may unconsciously avoid making interventions which would provoke more negative feelings from their clients. I suggest that counsellors and therapists therefore need to consciously cultivate a good network of friends and invest energy in outside non-work activities and interests in order to provide themselves with the requisite level of independent support. Personal counselling/ therapy can also provide the extra support counsellors need in order to allow clients to go through periods of dissatisfaction and offers counsellors an invaluable place to look at their various countertransference reactions to clients.

Choosing interventions in a field dependent approach

Gestalt is a field approach; so there is no 'right way' of intervening; no 'right intervention'. This is not the same as saying that any intervention will do. Some interventions are certainly better than others, at certain points. The choice of approach or intervention depends upon all the field conditions at the time and is a matter of fine discrimination. Factors affecting the choice include the personality type and ego strength of the client and counsellor, the length and aims of the counselling, the circumstances in which the counselling takes place, the holistic energetic process of the client, the recent present and past life experiences of the client, the stage of the counselling process and so on. Developing the ability to be aware of and take account of all these field conditions requires a native interest in and talent for fine observation, experiential and theoretical training, lots of practice and plenty of professional support. Supervision of clinical work by an experienced Gestalt supervisor can help you develop an awareness of field conditions and allow you to discuss possible options for short and long term counselling interventions and decide which approach would be best for each client. It can enable you to develop a substantive knowledge of Gestalt theory while supporting you to learn how to tailor that knowledge for each unique individual and counselling exchange. It can support you to integrate the art and science of psychotherapy and to exploit the creativity of the Gestalt approach. For Gestalt is extraordinarily flexible:

> We can reach deeply into the past in a regressive re-enactment on one occasion, while at another time, in different conditions, we may look purely at the present relationship with the therapist, today in this room now. We can switch from reality to role play, from experiencing something at a physical body level, to visual fantasy, to searching for metaphor, to telling the story. (Parlett, 1992: 8)

Appendices

1 Examples of Gestalt intake sheet and initial contract form

Client intake sheet

This sheet is meant to be filled out by the counsellor (not the client) *after* the session. It is designed to support counsellors in conceptualising their work in Gestalt terms. **It is important not to turn the initial sessions into an interrogation in order to acquire this information.** Much of the information can be gathered by fine phenomenological observation. When completing the intake sheet after initial sessions counsellors often find that they do not yet have some information so they have to leave gaps. The gaps – the places where clients have not yet shown themselves – may be as significant as the portions that can be filled in easily. And the gaps can be filled in gradually as you gather the information.

Date of interview	Referred by	Name

Sex	D.O.B.	Occupation	Relationship status

Children	GP: Name and Tel. No.

Medications (if any)

Health and any psychiatric history

Presenting problems

Why now?

Client's preferred outcome(s)

Contracts

Medical and psychotherapeutic history

Family background

Use of drugs (e.g. alcohol, nicotine, caffeine, other)

Self support

Environmental support

Contact functions

Styles of contact

Identified polarities

Identified unfinished business

Relevant symbolism and metaphors

Therapist's responses to client

Operational diagnosis of client in terms of Gestalt processes such as contact and withdrawal; support; internalisation, etc. and/or in terms of psychiatric diagnosis if considered relevant

---

Rationale for diagnosis

Initial hunches re. therapeutic direction and strategies

Example initial contract form

This initial contract form is meant to be filled out by the client. It needs to be modified to suit the needs and circumstances of different practitioners in different contexts or settings.

Name address and phone number of Practitioner

Please complete this form

NAME. . . . . PHONE . . . .

ADDRESS . . . .

. . . . POST CODE. . . . .

GENERAL PRACTITIONER'S NAME . . . .

GENERAL PRACTITIONER'S PHONE NO . . . .

ARE YOU ON ANY MEDICATION?   Yes/No

IF YES, WHAT?. . . . .

ARE YOU SEEING ANY OTHER THERAPIST, PSYCHOLOGIST OR PSYCHIATRIST?   Yes/No

NAME . . . . PHONE . . . .

HAVE YOU ANY MEDICAL PROBLEM WHICH I MAY CONSIDER IMPORTANT TO KNOW?   Yes/No

IF YES, WHAT?. . . . .

TREATING PRACTITIONER . . . . PHONE . . . .

ANY HISTORY OF DEPRESSION OR PSYCHIATRIC TREATMENT. . . . .

. . . .

I wish to undertake Gestalt therapeutic exploration

. . . .

I consent to my work being presented for professional supervision.

Although I expect . . . . to keep my work with him/her confidential in general, I understand that he/she has a right and duty to break confidentiality in situations where I or members of the public are at risk if he/she does not do so.

I consent to personal information being recorded on computer for research purposes (with a guarantee that no information other than statistical will be used publicly without my express consent).

SIGNED. . . . . DATE . . . .

2 Integrating Gestalt and psychiatric diagnosis

Gestalt diagnosis of process

Traditionally Gestaltists have diagnosed in the way described in Part IV – identifying the points of difficulty by paying attention to the unfolding phenomena in the moment. Indeed much of the practice of Gestalt counselling consists of a careful cooperative exploration of contact, the creating and destruction of figures, the development of clients' awareness of how they form figures of contact and withdrawal effectively and how they have learnt to disturb or moderate that contact in ways that make them less able to support themselves and enjoy their lives.

In the past Gestaltists, along with many humanistic practitioners, have been wary of psychiatric diagnosis because they felt that it was often used to objectify clients and treat them more as a case than a person. On the other hand, ignorance of diagnostic procedures has sometimes led counsellors to take on clients who need more support than they can offer; and to work in a similar way with all clients irrespective of ego strength, personality style or character structure, which has unfortunately at times precipitated further fragmentation or even breakdown in clients whose sense of self was already fragile (Merian and Tillett, personal communications).

Linking diagnosis of process with psychiatric diagnosis

Recently Gestaltists have argued that it is equally important to observe and work with the client's *habitual* patterns of behaviour and the structure of their ground, as with their moment by moment process. Some Gestalt theoreticians have judiciously assimilated diagnostic and treatment planning skills in order to improve the safety and efficacy of the approach without losing sight of the need for mutual respect and spontaneity, or of the evolving, changing nature of people within the ever shifting field (see Tobin, 1982; Yontef, 1988, 1993; Greenberg, 1989, 1991, 1995; Delisle, 1988, 1991, 1993b; Melnick and Nevis, 1992; Shub, 1992; Wheeler, 1994).

This is an innovative leap in the field of humanistic counselling, which counterbalances the possibility of Gestalt counselling over-concentrating upon the here and now without an acknowledgement of the patient's *habitual* patterns of behaviour. The ability to correlate our Gestalt system of assessment with psychiatric disorders can also facilitate communication with other professionals in the psychological field and can open to the Gestalt practitioner the vast array of research and theory available through the publications of other orientations.

Delisle (1988, 1991) in particular has worked out a thorough system of Gestalt diagnosis based on the careful observation of the processes described in Part IV and has linked this systematically and creatively with the American Psychiatric Association's *Diagnostic and Statistical Manual of Mental Disorder*, known as the *DSM IV*. Read Delisle's systematic, creative and humane work and decide for yourself whether or not you find his approach compatible with and enhancing of the Gestalt approach.

The challenge for Gestalt counsellors is to learn to use assessment and diagnostic procedures and the information they afford and yet set them aside in order to open themselves to the uniqueness of the unfolding moment by moment interaction between counsellors and clients – for at the moment of meeting, diagnosis and theories of treatment planning must recede into the background (Hycner, 1985, 1988).

At a minimum you need to know how to recognise someone whose sense of self is relatively fragile and either refer them to a therapist experienced with working with people with self disorders or fragile selves (Mollon, 1994) or adapt your Gestalt approach along the lines suggested by Tobin (1982), Greenberg (1989, 1991, 1995), Yontef (1988) or Beaumont (1993). Significant evidence suggests (Philippson, 1994; Lasch, 1979; Kahn, 1991) that increasing numbers of clients are presenting in counselling agencies who would meet criteria for borderline and narcissistic personality disorders. 'If you're working in independent practice you should at least acquire enough diagnostic skills to know who you can safely work with' (Fry, 1993: 78).

Developing different counselling strategies and evolving plans[1]

Don't expect to work in the same or similar ways with all clients or styles of client. Adjust the Gestalt approach to different clients in different circumstances. Even though Gestalt puts great emphasis upon the present interaction, it is also important for you think about and to be able to conceptualise the therapeutic work you are doing. You need to take time to reflect upon clients' problems and the behaviour they describe or manifest and to *formulate* tentative hypotheses and develop tentative short and long term therapeutic plans and strategies for working with people with different styles of personality and contact.

Use your observations of the clients' phenomenological processes of contacting and disturbing contact to help you consider the best strategies for working with this particular style of client. Discover the clients' strengths, build upon them and become more aware of their individual point(s) of difficulty. You can often share your thinking and discuss your reflections with the client; so that you are inviting clients into active partnership with you.

Keep revising your tentative plans and evolving your strategies in the light of the experience of each session, so that you are balancing and integrating attention to the reality of the moment with background conceptualisation, thought and planning.

Figure 12.2 (p. 110) illustrates how human meeting, reflection, diagnosis, conceptualisation and development of therapeutic hypotheses and strategies in the Gestalt context must be a developing cycle, which is constantly revised in the light of the human experience. It also illustrates one example of the rhythmic alternation of 'I–It' and 'I–Thou' styles of relating in the counselling process.

Below I give a brief description of the process and contact styles of a client called Rose in order to offer a contrast to the description of the client called George offered on pp. 105–7.

It is probably obvious from the description of both clients' process, that the counsellors needed to work very differently with George than with Rose. For example George's counsellor supported George to resensitise himself to his body sensation and to gradually feel and eventually express his tightly controlled feelings. Rose's counsellor, on the other hand, helped her to slow

1. See fn 1 in Chapter 12 (p. 108) which is equally relevant here.

herself down, become more aware of herself and reflective about her actions. He actually helped her learn to hold back or retroflect her feelings at least until she was in a safe place. Subsequent work with both clients is referred to on pp. 189 and 161 respectively.

Contrasting example of description of client's process: Rose

Metaphor
A waterfall over jagged rocks
or game of push-me, pull-me

Rose: *cycle of contact and withdrawal*
Rose's energy cycle seemed erratic. She would speak in a great rush and then fall silent. She would make animated contact and then turn her head to the wall. She reported occasional binge drinking episodes followed by vomiting. She expressed great bursts of rage with her intimate family, followed by remorse. In the next breath or the next session her family was wonderful.

Retroflection   Expression   Violence, aggression

◄——————————————————————————►

Rose expressed feelings of both rage and sadness volubly and erratically. Sometimes she expressed rage violently and in situations where she was doing herself a disservice (as when she raged at her boss) or where it could be dangerous or damaging to others (as when she swore and threw dishes around her children).

Egotism   Impulsiveness

◄——————————————————————————►
                   Spontaneity

Rose was spontaneous to the point of impulsive. She spent money without any idea of what her assets were, she raged, laughed and cried. She did display a type of self-monitoring egotism – but almost always after the event, when she told herself off, in a way which did not prevent the next risk of impulsive behaviour.

Introjection   Rejecting

◄——————————————————————————►
                  Destructuring

Rose tended to spit out and reject the experiences that life offered. She sometimes binged on alcohol, vomiting afterwards. If she got close to someone, she destroyed the pleasure by telling herself off and shaming herself afterwards. She seemed to have some highly active, vicious and rather split off parental-style introjects which told her she was wicked or unworthy of love and attention.

Desensitisation ◄———— Sensitivity ————► Over-sensitivity

Rose was desensitised to physical pleasure and pain but she was highly sensitised to possible social slights and injuries and would withdraw hurt and angry.

Confluence   Isolation

◄—————————————————————————————►

Differentiation
Separation

Rose swung from idealising confluence with friends and family to angry isolation. When she was angry with people she had no recollection of her previous warm feelings. When she idealised people, she could not imagine that they had the smallest flaw and felt completely let down and furious when they turned out to be ordinarily human.

3   Form to support Gestalt diagnosis of process and psychiatric diagnosis

One possible approach to diagnosis in the Gestalt context is to consider the individual in terms of Gestalt processes, such as his/her process of contact, his/her styles of moderating contact, supporting self, etc. For example you can consider individuals in the following terms:

I   metaphors or images which represent particular individuals and their relationship to the environment and to other people;
II   their process of contact;
III   their styles of moderating contact;
IV   their contact functions;

V   their styles of supporting themselves through environmental or self support systems;

VI   their processes of internalising and assimilating contact episodes into the enduring features of self or into their support systems;

VII   their polarities and unfinished business;

VIII psychiatric diagnosis (if relevant)

I Metaphor or image which could represent this individual and their relationship to the environment or to other people:

II Observations re cycle of awareness/process of contact:

Sensation:

Awareness:

Mobilisation:

Action:

Contact:

Assimilation or integration:

Withdrawal:

Rest:

III Observations re individual's styles of moderating contact on the following dimensions of contact:

How and when does he/she moderate contact on the continuum of: **confluence** . . . **isolation**:

How and when does he/she moderate on the continuum **introjection** . . . **rejecting**:

How and when does he/she moderate contact on the continuum **projection** . . . **owning**:

How and when does he/she moderate contact on the continuum **retroflection** . . . **expression**:

How and when does he/she moderate contact on the continuum **deflection** . . . **bluntness**:

How and when does he/she moderate contact on the continuum **egotism** . . . **impulsivity**:

How and when does he/she moderate contact on the continuum **desensitisation** . . . **supersensitivity**:

IV   Observations re contact functions:

(i)   Appearance:

(ii)   Verbal, voice, sound:

(iii) Seeing, eyes, etc.:

(iv)   Hearing, *how* and *what* does he/she hear/mishear:

(v)   Smell:

(vi)   Taste, eating, etc.:

(vii) Movement, mobility, touching, etc.:

V   Observations re support systems:

How does he/she use:

(i)   Interpersonal support systems:

(ii)   Cognitive support systems in therapeutic session and elsewhere:

(iii) Biological support system (e.g.: breathing, posture, etc.):

(iv)   Use of environmental support – use of room, chair, etc., in session; and other environmental support outside session:

VI Observations re this person's processes of internalising and assimilating contact episodes into the enduring features of themselves or into their self support systems:

How do they assimilate therapeutic experiences into their self concept?

How do they remember previous therapeutic sessions with you?

How, if at all, do they internalise the support of either the therapeutic process or the therapist?

How much do they integrate fresh life experiences into their sense of self and the way they describe themselves or tell their life story? Or how fixed (and impervious to fresh contact episodes) is their self concept or narrative sense of self?

How integrated are different aspects of themselves?

VII Observations re polarities and unfinished business:

VIIII Psychiatric diagnosis (in terms of DSM IV for example):

Rationale/criteria to support psychiatric diagnosis:

4 Diagnostic criteria for those with borderline and narcissistic self process

General features of those with narcissistic style of self process (adapted from Tobin, 1982)

1. Low self-esteem, inadequacy, shame, emptiness (sometimes hidden behind defensive grandiosity).
2. Lack of realistic goals (either denigrate and under-strive or exaggerate abilities and strive for unrealistically high goals).
3. Problems with ideals (sometimes very high).
4. Feel disconnected from past (may have 'blanks' about past/childhood).
5. Lead disjointed, fragmented lives or overly controlled (both types tend to *feel* disjointed).
6. Alternating grandiosity and depression.
7. Lack of pleasure over success.
8. A tendency to fragment psychologically (see Kohut and Wolf, 1978 for definition of self-fragmentation).
9. Difficulties in forming and maintaining satisfying relationships.
10. Vulnerability to narcissistic hurt (may be deeply wounded, feel destroyed by criticism or even mild personal failure or may defend against the wound by fury).
11. Great fears of loss of love or abandonment.
12. Tendency to split self and object images; that is, they are acutely aware of only one aspect of their reality at any one time and rigidly hold other aspects out of awareness.
13. Have vicious 'superegos', or parental introjects (Greenberg, 1991, 1995).

DSM IV diagnostic criteria for 301.81 Narcissistic Personality Disorder

A pervasive pattern of grandiosity (in fantasy or behaviour), need for admiration, and lack of empathy, beginning by early adulthood and present in a variety of contexts, as indicated by five (or more) of the following:

1. has a grandiose sense of self-importance (e.g. exaggerates achievements and talents, expects to be recognised as superior without commensurate achievements).
2. is preoccupied with fantasies of unlimited success, power, brilliance, beauty or ideal love.
3. believes that he or she is 'special' and unique and can only be understood by, or should associate with, other special or high status people (or institutions).
4. requires excessive admiration.
5. has a sense of entitlement, i.e. unreasonable expectations of especially favourable treatment or automatic compliance with his or her expectations.
6. is interpersonally exploitative, i.e. takes advantage of others to achieve his or her own ends.
7. lacks empathy: is unwilling to recognise or identify with the feelings and needs of others.
8. is often envious of others or believes that others are envious of him or her.
9. shows arrogant, haughty behaviours or attitudes.

(American Psychiatric Association, 1994: 661)

DSM IV diagnostic criteria for 301.89 Borderline Personality Disorder

A pervasive pattern of instability of interpersonal relationships, self-image and affects, and marked impulsivity beginning by early adulthood and present in a variety of contexts, as indicated by five (or more) of the following:

1. frantic efforts to avoid real or imagined abandonment. (Note: Do not include suicidal or self-mutilating behaviour covered in Criterion 5.)
2. a pattern of unstable and intense interpersonal relationships characterised by alternating between extremes of idealisation and devaluation

3. identity disturbance: markedly and persistently unstable self-image or sense of self
4. impulsivity in at least two areas that are potentially self-damaging (e.g. spending, sex, substance abuse, reckless driving, binge eating). (Note: Do not include suicidal or self-mutilating behaviour covered in Criterion 5.)
5. recurrent suicidal behaviour, gestures or threats, or self-mutilating behaviour
6. affective instability due to a marked reactivity of mood (e.g. intense episodic dysphoria, irritability, or anxiety usually lasting a few hours and only rarely more than a few days)
7. chronic feelings of emptiness
8. inappropriate, intense anger or difficulty controlling anger (e.g. frequent displays of temper, constant anger, recurrent physical fights)
9. transient, stress-related paranoid ideation or severe dissociative symptoms.

(American Psychiatric Association, 1994: 654)

5   Co-designing Gestalt experiments with clients

This appendix gives an extended example of an experiment which involves speaking to an imaginary other, together with a commentary which links the practical example with the theoretical guidelines for co-designing experiments which is given on p. 135.

Henry knew himself to be inhibited and wished to be more spontaneous. He spoke about his previous boss whose memory still 'bugged him' (*Stages 1 and 2: preconditions, groundwork and identification of theme*). The counsellor asked whether or not Henry wanted to explore these feelings towards his boss more actively. Henry giggled and looked a bit embarrassed and said yes (*Stage 3: negotiation*). The counsellor explained that people often learn a lot by talking 'directly' to the other person in an imaginary scenario rather than just talking about the other person (*Stage 2 groundwork*). She suggested that Henry might be willing to imagine he was an uninhibited friend of his and be that person talking to his boss (*Stage 4: clarification of theme and design of experiment*). Henry looked anxious and mumbled something about not being sure if he could do it (*Stage 6: a mini impasse*).

Responding to Henry's hesitancy, the counsellor 'graded the experiment down' a bit by suggesting that Henry keep his present chair to represent 'his ordinary self' and come back to that chair whenever he wanted (*Stage 5: grading and negotiating*). She also emphasised that she had absolutely no expectations of the experiment – the idea was to try something out and see what happened. Henry therefore couldn't possibly get it wrong – because there was no wrong or right way of doing it (*Stage 1: re-emphasising the preconditions – which contributed to a further grading of experiment – Stage 5*). Henry expressed relief and chose another chair to be an 'uninhibited person' talking to his boss. From here Henry 'spoke' angry words rather quietly to his boss, jerking his arms backwards and holding on to his hand. The counsellor listened to his words and described what Henry was doing with his body.

Henry was surprised and interested – he hadn't noticed these things, although he knew he often twitched if he felt excited. He then paused reflectively and added, 'I associate holding on to my hand as a way of holding myself back' (*Stage 8: significant increase in awareness*).

The counsellor suggested that if Henry wanted to take the experiment further he could repeat some of the things he'd already said to his boss, while doing the opposite of holding back – leaning forward, for example, and making outward gesticulations with his arms. Henry did this with more energy and some embarrassment. He said he felt silly (*Stage 6: impasse*) and with the counsellor's support he went back to his 'ordinary self' chair for a break. (*In making this suggestion, the counsellor was also offering environmental support and supporting Henry to recontact his self support: see p. 183.*) Back in his 'normal chair' Henry described his feelings of silliness and the counsellor encouraged him to explore and value these feelings. It turned out that fear of 'being silly' had kept him from attracting negative attention in many viciously teasing environments in the past. The counsellor imagined that his past decisions to avoid attracting attention in such circumstances were wise (*Stage 7: heightening the impasse and exploring and valuing so-called 'resisting' forces: see p. 169*). Henry said he felt lighter.

The counsellor asked if Henry now felt finished with the experiment or wanted to do more. Slightly to the counsellor's surprise, Henry said with energy that he'd like 'one more go'. This time from the 'uninhibited chair' he spoke fluently, using his words, voice and arms more freely. After completing this, he returned to his own chair again, where he reported feeling much lighter and clearer in his chest, more alive and very pleased with himself.

The counsellor asked Henry what he had discovered. He said that he had learnt that he could be more spontaneous and playful than he had ever expected. The counsellor asked him how he had achieved this, to which Henry responded, 'Imagining I was someone else helped me be spontaneous; knowing that there were absolutely no expectations helped me feel safe enough to try.' The counsellor enquired whether any of these insights were things that Henry could use in other circumstances of his life. He thought a bit. 'Yes I think that noticing what I'm doing with my body and sometimes choosing to do something different might make a real difference. And imagining I'm someone else at meetings might help me to loosen up' (*Stage 7: significant increase in awareness and Stage 9: assimilation, internalisation and debriefing*).

6 Complex cycles in individual, group and systemic process

Complex cycles in lives of individuals

The cycle of contact and withdrawal described and illustrated on pp. 19 and 21 is (like all models) somewhat simplified. Life is, of course, more complex and people are going through a series of interrelated and crisscrossing cycles of contact and withdrawal all the time, so I may be engaged with writing a book, then take time out to write a book review, take time out again to see a friend and eventually get back to the larger cycle of contact and withdrawal with the book. Meanwhile I have gone through hundreds of cycles of breathing in and breathing out and many cycles of sleeping (Figure A6.1). Authors such as Zinker (1994) and Nevis

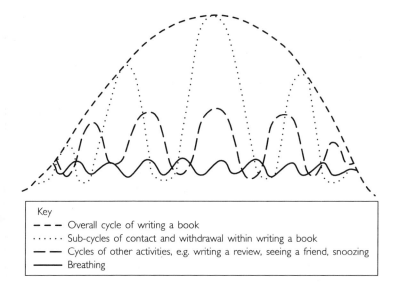

Key
- – – Overall cycle of writing a book
- · · · · · Sub-cycles of contact and withdrawal within writing a book
- — — Cycles of other activities, e.g. writing a review, seeing a friend, snoozing
- ——— Breathing

Figure A6.1   *Complex interrelated cycles of contact and withdrawal*

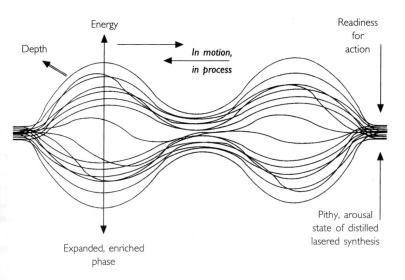

Figure A6.2   *Dynamic state of awareness (Zinker, 1994)*

(1987) have developed models and illustrations of the individual's process of contact and withdrawal which try to do more justice to the complexity of real life: 'The process (of awareness) must be multiplied several times, since we are quite capable of organising a number of our experiences simultaneously, letting go of some while holding onto others at the same time' (Figure A6.2) (Zinker, 1994).

Complex cycles in group process

The cycles of contact and withdrawal in group process are even more complex. Zinker (1980) developed a description of the stages of group development which suggests that groups go through the phases of Superficial Contact and Exploration; Conflict and Identity; Confluence and Isolation; High Cohesiveness. Zinker's model shows some similarities both to Tuckman's (1965) stages of forming, storming, norming and performing and to Elaine Kepner's (1980) alternative Gestalt model of the development process of a group (see Box A6.1).

Mitchell and Broughton (1995) have significantly developed Zinker's description into a more comprehensive and flexible Gestalt model of group development. They describe and illustrate (Figure A6.3) group process as a series of waves of contact and withdrawal through which there is a rhythmic ebb and flow of energetic surges and rest and consolidation. Each stage or wave provides the necessary ground for the next emergent figure of group development. Bentley (1997) has clearly described Mitchell and Broughton's model in relation to team development.

Although these models are very helpful for understanding group dynamics and stages of group development, even these are inevitably simplifications. Individual members of groups engage with the group's process in different ways and with differing tempos. Nevis (1987) and Zinker (1994) have tried to illustrate the differing and complex cycles or waves of energy which may co-exist in a group or small system (Figures A6.4 and A6.5).

Group process is made up of many cycles and is thus a complex process. Each individual member and each sub-system of a group follows and creates their own energetic patterns and waves. The awareness of each member and energetic processes of each sub-system will be unique, depending upon many factors. What each will be able to attend to will vary, and what each will allow to come into awareness will be different. The energy

Box A6.1 Comparison of several approaches to developmental process of a group

Tuckman	Zinker	Kepner (Elaine)	Mitchell and Broughton
(1965) in Bion	from *Beyond the Hot Seat* (1980)	from *Beyond the Hot Seat* (1980)	from Bentley (1997)
Forming	*Superficial Contact and Exploration* Disjointedness, lack of contact, withholding, ANXIETY, exploration of implicit/explicit rules. Need: find out what I can do and who I can trust.	*Identity and Dependence* Anxiety re identity of self re process, leader, etc. Need: to establish relationship contact, safety, boundaries, clarify approach.	*Superficial Contact* High anxiety, stereotyped behaviour. Therapist's role: modelling, setting boundaries, developing safety and a climate where anxiety and exploration at all levels is accepted.
Storming	*Conflict and Identity* Testing and probing. Individual identity shaped by conflict with others.	*Influence and Counter-Dependency* Issues of influence, authority and control. Intrapersonal, interpersonal and group challenge.	*Conflict and Identity* Challenge, dissatisfaction, pushing of boundaries, subgrouping. Therapist's role: supporting expression of difference, holding firm boundaries, survival while continuing to confront and be confronted.
Norming	*Confluence and Isolation* Sharing and support. People get stuck in role stereotypes within community. Need: to become aware of these confluent and fixed roles, take responsibility for how each co-creates stereotyping, break stereotypes down and mobilise energy to create fresh and more flexible possibilities for each person.	Establishment of norms which increase safety but limit behaviour. Roles played out at this stage are often projection of disowned parts of personality. Need: to bring limits and stereotyping to awareness and challenge.	*Consolidation of Roles* Freezing of roles, non-discriminating support and/or hostility without much warmth or contact. Therapist's role: generally staying with, supporting cohesiveness and acknowledging usefulness of the stage.

continued overleaf

Box A6.1   (continued)

Tuckman	Zinker	Kepner (Elaine)	Mitchell and Broughton
Performing	*High Cohesiveness* Real interpersonal trust. Capacity for caring *and* confrontation. Each person valued for the special different qualities he gives and takes. Group can now recreate and transform self.	*Intimacy and Interdependence* Real contact now possible based on differentness and separateness of individuals. Interdependent behaviour relying on each other for understanding, support *and* challenge.	*Role Destructuring* Conflict in open, more risks with self and other, vulnerability and awkwardness as roles crumble. Therapist's role: heightened awareness of roles and structures and becoming more of a consultant. *High Cohesiveness* Similar to Zinker. Therapist's role: consultant, facilitating differentiated contact and eventual closure.
		N.B. Differentiation or high cohesiveness is an advanced stage and many groups do not reach it. Short-term groups cannot usually reach it.	
Mourning	(Rest, resolution withdrawal – no full stage)	(Need for closure mentioned – no full stage described)	*Mourning* Facilitating closure and acknowledging unfinished business are included under high cohesiveness.

The stage of internalising and mourning is often omitted in theory and in practice because people in the West can be 'addicted to action' and avoid facing satisfaction, celebration, completion., endings, goodbyes and mourning *and* demobilisation, emptiness, withdrawal, void. When these last stages are omitted, they may leave awareness and learning unassimilated and important business unfinished.

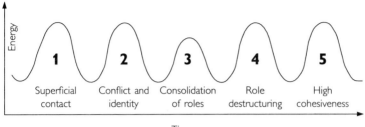

Figure A6.3   *A Gestalt model of group process (Mitchell and Broughton, 1995)*

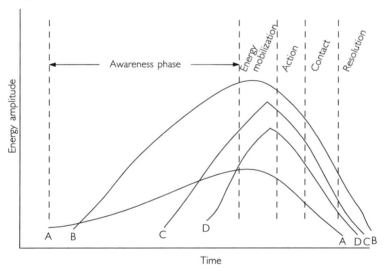

Figure A6.4   *Gestalt interactive cycle showing weak joining around a group figure (Nevis, 1987)*

available for dealing with any phase or issue will also vary, sometimes greatly. At the same time all the unique cycles of individuals or sub-systems will interact and influence each other (Figure A6.6).

The group counsellor and process consultant needs to be able to attend to these complex interactive cycles and energetic patterns and especially to the divergence and convergence of such processes. Failure to appreciate these realities and to deal with them effectively is an important reason why groups do not function at optimal levels of effectiveness. Such failure may also contribute to difficulties in gathering and honouring divergent

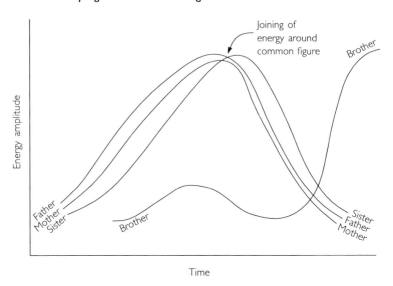

Figure A6.5(a)   *Gestalt interactive cycle as applied in a family system (Nevis, 1987)*

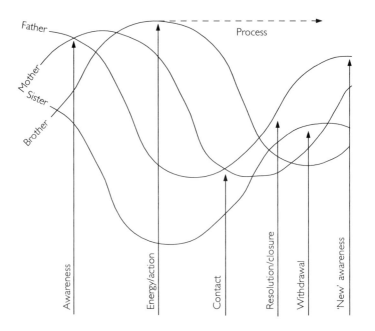

Figure A6.5(b)   *Gestalt interactive cycle in a family system (Zinker, 1994)*

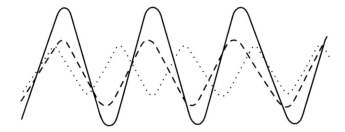

Figure A6.6   *Complex cycles of individuals or sub-systems interacting in group or systemic process*

views and identifying times of convergent energy when special opportunities for group and individual development often exist.

Complex cycles in systems and organisations

Obviously this picture of interactive cycles becomes even more complex when you are talking about an organisational system which consists of many sub-systems (made of several or many people). Each sub-system generates an equally complicated picture of interaction (Figure A6.6) and the pattern of interaction of each sub-system is interrelated to and influencing the pattern of interaction in each other sub-system. If we could imagine superimposing several illustrations of this sort one upon the other, we might get some idea of the sort of processes we are trying to study when we manage or consult to an organisation.

7   Shame in the intersubjective field

Shame and the creation of shame-binds

Shame is a pervasive phenomenon of the field, a regulator of contact, which may arise from a trivial misunderstanding, from exposure to judgement, from rejection, from neglect, from physical, mental or sexual abuse. It involves the whole self and may manifest through blushing, silence, withdrawal, a desire to disappear or hide, averting eyes, stillness, self scrutiny or various forms of shame avoidance, such as rage, vivacity, defiance and so on.

Shame becomes embedded in a person's self organisation by the creation of shame-binds, a process which is fairly similar to Perls's description of introjection. Shame-binds form when a person's feelings and needs are seriously unsupported by others or the environment. Both shame-binds and introjects evolve in the context of relationship – for example when an aspect of one's functioning is disapproved of by significant others, one may experience a threat of abandonment and so disown the disapproved aspect of the self through shame thus maintaining the needed relationships at a cost of loss of self. Shame has a function and that is to help the organism pull back from interest – excitement that is perceived to be inappropriate or dangerous to a needed relationship. The need that is not received by the other is disowned and made 'not me', establishing a linkage between shame and the need which is not supported or received by the environment.

Such shame-binds are formed less through verbal injunctions than inferred from accumulated (often non-verbal) childhood experiences. The sense of shame in shame-oriented people goes back before the age of clear memory and is based in the earliest interpersonal experiences of the infant and toddler. In the interactional field between infants and their caretakers, infants learn to support, enhance or interfere with their self functions. Verbal and non-verbal interactions occur constantly between infants and others in the family system and this largely non-verbal interaction helps shape both the infant's response repertoire and sense of self. This child rearing can be done with a message of firmness combined with love and respect for the whole distinct person that the child is ('That was a very creative idea. I am sorry it did not work out'). Or it may engender a sense of chronic personal shame or guilt ('You are stupid'). Shame induction at this period can be intense and brutal or subtly devastating as when a parent turns cold, seems consistently absent, recoils from the infant or looks disgusted. Not being able to make sense of why the parents react as they do, infants usually conclude that they are defective or not worthy of love. They frequently withdraw from the emotional reaction of the parent and split into the self-that-identifies-with-the-rejecting-parent and the self-in-need. The child turns in on the needy self the anger that was originally directed at the parent, as if the pain and anguish of deprivation and unrequited love were because of the need rather than the parental (or field) response. This retroflection is the birth of the shaming process – infants shame themselves for their needs because they were not receivable to their caretakers (Yontef, 1996).

The shame is generalised to a shame-bind such as 'my crying is dangerous to relationships' or 'my body is untouchable' – so that aspect of the self is assumed to be unacceptable in all circumstances. With low levels of frustration this may be a temporary linkage and another way of pursuing the need may be found. With more severe frustration and shame (stemming from greater or more persistent lack of receptivity for the felt need) a permanent linkage is made between shame and the unacceptable need with consequent loss of access to the need. The need loses its voice. The shame linked need does not disappear. Anytime it emerges unawares, the person experiences shame, both in order to continue to experience the need as 'not-me' and in order to continue to live in harmony with an environment perceived as not supporting the need.

Shame and support within a relational field

Shame and support are interrelated polar opposites within the relational field and both have a specialised function within that field. Support, for example, allows people to accept themselves, make contact and take risks. Shame allows people to pull back from risks when there is no support or inadequate support available. It is thus a regulator or modifier of contact and can be positively useful. On the other hand when lack of support is severe enough, shame-binds form and shame is internalised into basic beliefs about self. Thus fixed gestalts learned in a particular field become blueprints with which to interpret experience, restricting the person's flexibility.

The place of shame is very different in an intersubjective model of the self in the field than in an individualistic one. From the perspective of the individualistic model of the self, remaining vulnerable to shame (or field-dependent) is understood as an issue of arrested development. So in that individualistic model, I will cover up such feelings even from myself and try to achieve the level of stable autonomy and independence which the model prescribes. The model of maturity associated with the individual-istic model insists that adults should be self reliant, adequate, responsible, dependable rather than dependent. It glorifies the lonely hero and shames adults (particularly men) for having feelings (big boys don't cry, cowardly, cowardly custard . . . the litany is endless), being vulnerable, shy or experiencing shame. Shame plays an active part in holding in place an individualistic, competitive and macho social system. Because shame itself is shameful, people can't even identify its function in their own process. Women are for example unlikely to say they breast fed their babies or paid their son's way through university for fear of shame. And men don't often boast that they went to war or got drunk for fear of shame.

On the other hand in an intersubjective field model, where self is created at the boundary between self and other, then a sig-nificant break in the field, in the natural connectedness between me and my surroundings, will be felt as a break in the cohesion of the self that gives rise to shame. From this perspective shame can be seen not as a deficiency in myself but as a lack of fit between me and my environment.

The place of support in an intersubjective field model is also very different. In the individualistic paradigm, support is a crutch, something you need if you are not autonomous, a badge of shame. Whereas under the field paradigm, support represents connectedness in the field, an essential condition for development of self, self process and contact.

Exploring and healing shame in relationship

Reorganisation of the field without shame requires more than undoing of retroflection and reowning of aggression. It requires an experience in which the client's shame and shame-linked need is received in conditions of felt support. Processes that heal shame therefore start with the formation of a reciprocal relationship. The linkage between shame and parts of self that are felt to be unacceptable were found in relationship – so can only be de-constructed in relationship. In therapy they can be explored in the context of the therapeutic relationship and through the explora-tion of contact, support and shame dynamics in that relationship. The construction of a supportive relationship is not a preliminary stage but is the essence of the therapy itself. The goal of therapy could be seen as the transformation of the experience of shame into the experience of connection in the field. We aim not to rid the self of shame but to live it differently – in connection, rather than isolation (Wheeler, 1996).

Jacobs (1996) highlights how extraordinarily difficult it is – for both client and therapist – to contact and bring into awareness the feelings, thoughts and perceptions about which one feels ashamed. She explains how certain elements of the therapeutic situation lend themselves to evoking shame in the client. These elements include the fact that the therapist is often more important to the client than vice versa; that the client reveals more of himself than the therapist does; that the therapist is in a relatively powerful position to the client and the fact that the therapist has a human tendency to avoid her own shame through such unaware defences as denial, defensiveness, explanations and subtle attempts to transfer blame on to the client.

To some extent all of us have developed character patterns designed to reduce our potential for feeling shamed. However therapists who are predominantly organised around avoiding experiences of shame will often be highly constricted in their therapeutic approach. A major problem of course is knowing whether or not we are such a therapist because the character style of these therapists operates largely outside of their aware-ness – so as to avoid shame. Therapists can unawarely but perfectly legitimately avoid their own shame in the therapeutic encounter, as for example when a Gestalt therapist *consistently* explores the client's responsibility for his or her feelings (for example, how are you confusing yourself?), rather than exploring how the feelings arise intersubjectively or between the two of them, or when the therapist invariably thinks of clients as 'projecting', 'distorting' or 'transferring' rather than validating the clients' reality.

In an intersubjective approach the therapist necessarily con-siders that shame is present-based as well as being historically rooted and is genuinely open to exploring how he or she may have contributed to triggering a shame experience in the dialogue between them. So the therapist's questions will not be only 'Who shamed you in the past?' but also 'How am I shaming you right now?' 'What am I missing or misunderstanding or failing to hear loudly and clearly enough?' 'What am I failing to appreciate the importance of?'

Jacobs (1996) gives detailed examples from her own cases which illustrate how easily the client's shame is triggered in the therapeutic dialogue, how difficult that can be for the therapist to spot, how inevitably the therapist's own defensiveness is

activated and what sensitivity, delicacy and openness is often
needed to unravel the impasses that thus occur.

> David was intense and easily injured. He was coming to me for a
> period of three months while his therapist took a maternity leave. In
> our first meeting he asked whether we could arrange a regular weekly
> session time. He said it would help anchor him during this difficult
> time. He was feeling bereft and abandoned by his therapist, and
> frightened that the therapist's new baby portended a loss of his place
> in his therapist's heart and mind. As our discussion unfolded, I told
> him that although there would be occasional exceptions, we could
> meet regularly on Friday mornings.
> A few weeks later, I told him, in a rather matter-of-fact tone, that I
> would have to reschedule three of our subsequent sessions. In our next
> session, he expressed hurt and righteous anger at my casual attitude.
> He said it meant to him that I did not take our interim work seriously,
> that I was just biding my time with him. Frankly, I was surprised by
> the intensity of his reaction. I felt a flash of reciprocal righteous anger,
> saying to myself, 'How dare he attack me. I have gone out of my way
> to accommodate him. Surely, he must know it was not easy to carve
> out a regular time on such short notice!'
> My angry reaction was defensive. I had experienced his right-
> eousness as shaming to me, and I wished to defend myself against my
> rising shame by shaming him for shaming me! I also recognised that I
> had presumed he was aware of the demands he had made on my
> schedule. I had simply been so absorbed in my own perspective that I
> had not noticed his vantage point was quite different from mine. In
> the course of our explorations he described how he had never had any
> impact on his parents and on how they treated him. They were
> dismissive of his aims and desires. I asked how I had dismissed him.
> He said I ignored his need to plan and his feelings about needing an
> anchor and needing me to see our work as important. He said he felt
> like just a flat line, someone I did not need to contend with. I told him,
> appreciatively, that he had now brought himself to me as someone to
> contend with. I also said I had been insensitive to his needs and had
> been preoccupied with my own. He was excited and relieved that we
> could work/fight this problem out between us. (Jacobs, 1996: 302–3)

Non-verbal aspects and approaches to shame

Shame originates in the interactional field of early infancy largely
through non-verbal interpersonal exchanges. It is therefore largely
non-verbal in nature. Yontef is especially skilled at evoking the
pervasive but evasive nature of existential shame in which the
individual has some sense of being flawed or defective, a process
that is 'largely preverbal, operating largely in the background . . .
and virtually automatic in shame-oriented people. Before shame-

oriented therapy, this process is usually successfully hidden from consciousness' (Yontef, 1993). 'Initially a person might only be aware that he or she regards him or herself as inadequate, unworthy, not a joy or just plain ok' (Yontef, 1996).

Shame is built into habitual body structure, held through body tension, often manifests in eating habits, breathing patterns, in excruciating body pain, twisting, turning, self damage, bruising, cutting, as well as through the subtler signs of blushing, withdrawing or wishing to hide. Although the more inchoate manifestations of shame may not always be shown in the therapeutic hour, they are frequently the ways in which chronically shame-oriented individuals manifest their shame and self loathing when alone at 3 or 4 in the morning.

If therapeutic work is primarily verbal it often misses some of these deeper non-verbal levels of shame and may offer little to help people explore and relieve their chronic bodily experiences of shame. Working mainly verbally may leave clients hiding these shameful secrets, even from the therapist. And thus deep down they assume (but may never articulate) that their 'real' selves (which they experience as shameful) can still not be received or valued in the therapeutic relationship. Body experiences of shame and bodily-held shame patterns need to be met and explored in non-verbal as well as verbal ways within the therapeutic relationship.

I propose that evoking and receiving non-verbal dimensions of the self requires us to create a non-verbal space and work through non-verbal media. In order to evoke such a space, I may work with a range of art materials, paper, clay, collage, musical instruments, voice, movement, puppets, toys, sandtray, as well as attention to and investigation of breathing, body structure and energy patterns, contact with the natural environment, meditative disciplines and spiritual practices. Of course such media and approaches must be carefully chosen (p. 219) and integrated and finely calibrated to meet the needs of individual clients and the stage of the therapeutic relationship and I suggest that therapists who work with deep pre-verbal shame issues benefit from thorough training in integrating a full range of non-verbal approaches into their exploration of shame and support.

References

Abram, D. (1966) *The Spell of the Sensuous*. New York: Pantheon Books.

American Psychiatric Association (1994) *Diagnostic and Statistical Manual of Mental Disorder: DSM IV*. Washington: American Psychiatric Association.

Beaumont, H. (1993) 'Martin Buber's "I–Thou" and Fragile Self-organisation: Contribution to a Gestalt Couples Therapy', *British Gestalt Journal*, 2(2): 85–95.

Beisser, A.R. (1970) 'The Paradoxical Theory of Change', in J. Fagan and I. Shepherd (eds), *Gestalt Therapy Now*. Palo Alto, CA: Science and Behavior Books.

Bentley, T. (1997) *Sharpen Your Team Skills in . . . TEAMWORK*. Maidenhead: McGraw-Hill.

Bohart, A. and Todd, J. (1988) *Foundation of Clinical and Counselling Psychology*. New York: HarperCollins.

Bohm, D., Hiley, B. and Kaloyerou, P.N. (1987) 'An Ontological Basis for Quantum Theory', *Phys Reports*, 144(6): 323.

Bordin, E.S. (1975) 'The Generalizability of the Psychoanalytic Concept of the Working Alliance', *Psychotherapy: Theory, Research and Practice*, 16: 252–60.

Breshgold, E. (1989) 'Resistance in Gestalt Therapy: An Historical/Theoretical Perspective', *Gestalt Journal*, 12(2): 73–102.

Briggs, J. and Peat, F.D. (1989) *Turbulent Mirror*. New York: Harper & Row.

Brown, B. (1973) *New Body, New Mind*. New York: Harper & Row.

Brown, D. and Pedder, J. (1991) *Introduction to Psychotherapy: An Outline of Psychodynamic Principles and Practice*, 2nd edn. London and New York: Tavistock/Routledge.

Buber, M. (1958a) *Hasidism and Modern Man*, ed. and trans. M. Friedman. New York: Harper & Row.

Buber, M. (1958b) *I and Thou*, trans. R.G. Smith. New York: Charles Scribner & Sons. (Original work published 1923.)

Buber, M. (1967) *A Believing Humanism: Gleanings*. New York: Simon & Schuster.

Buber, M. (1988) *The Knowledge of Man: A Philosophy of the Interhuman*, ed. M.S. Friedman, trans. M.S. Friedman and R.G. Smith. Atlantic Highlands, NJ: Humanities Press International.

Buckroyd, J. (1979) *Eating Your Heart Out*. London: Macdonald.

Carlock, C.J., O'Halleran, K. and Shaw, M.S. (1992) 'The Alcoholic: A Gestalt View', in E.C. Nevis (ed.), *Gestalt Therapy*. New York: Gestalt Institute of Cleveland Press and Gardner Press Inc.

Casement, P. (1985) *On Learning from the Patient*. London: Routledge.

Chia, R. (1994) 'Management Research as Speculative Knowledging'. Paper, Anglia Polytechnic University.

Clark, N. and Frazer, T. (1987) *The Gestalt Approach*. Horsham: Roffey Park Institute.

Clarkson, P. (1989) *Gestalt Counselling in Action*, 2nd edn. London: Sage.

Clarkson, P. (1991a) Keynote address at British Gestalt conference, London, July.

Clarkson, P. (1991b) 'Individuality and Commonality in Gestalt', *British Gestalt Journal*, 1(1): 28–37.

Clarkson, P. (1992) *Transactional Analysis Journal*, 22(4): 202–9.

Clarkson, P. and Carroll, M. (1993) 'Counselling, Psychotherapy, Psychology and Psychiatry: The Same and Different', in P. Clarkson (ed.), *On Psychotherapy*. London: Sage.

Clarkson, P. and Mackewn, J. (1993) *Fritz Perls*. London: Sage.

Clayton, S. (1997) *Sharpen Your Team Skills in . . . DEVELOPING STRATEGY*. Maidenhead: McGraw Hill.

Crocker, S. (1992) 'A Philosophical Framework for Understanding Developmental Issues'. Paper prepared for *The Gestalt Journal*'s Annual Conference, Boston, MA.

Davidove, D. (1991) 'Loss of Ego Function, Conflict and Resistance', *Gestalt Journal*, 14(2): 27–43.

Delisle, G. (1988) *Ballises II: A Gestalt Perspective of Personality Disorders*. Montreal: Le Centre d'Intervention Gestaltist, Le Reflet.

Delisle, G. (1991) 'A Gestalt Perspective of Personality Disorders', *British Gestalt Journal*, 1(1): 42–50.

Delisle, G. (1993a) *Personality Disorders: A Gestalt Perspective*. Highland, NY: Gestalt Journal Publications.

Delisle, G. (1993b) *Les Troubles de la Personnalité*. Quebec: Les Editions du Reflet.

Dryden, W. and Feltham, C. (1994) *Developing the Practice of Counselling*. London: Sage.

Dublin, J.E. (1977) 'Gestalt Therapy, Existential-Gestalt Therapy and/versus "Perlsism"', in E.W.L. Smith (ed.), *The Growing Edge of Gestalt Therapy*. Secaucus, NJ: Citadel Press. pp. 124–50.

Duker, M. and Slade, R. (1988) *Anorexia Nervosa and Bulimia: How to Help*. Milton Keynes and Philadelphia: Open University Press.

Elkin, E. (1979) 'Towards a Theory of Transpersonal Gestalt', *The Gestalt Journal*, 2(1).

Elton Wilson, J. (1996) *Time Conscious Psychological Therapy*. London: Routledge.

Farrands, B. (1995) 'Contact and Leadership'. Paper presented at New Orleans Contact and Leadership Conference (April).

Fish, S. and Lapworth, P. (1994) *Understand and Use Your Dreams*. Bath: Dormoss Press.

Fodor, I. (1996) 'A Woman and her Body: The Cycles of Pride and Shame', in R. Lee and G. Wheeler (eds), *The Voice of Shame: Silence and Connection in Psychotherapy*. San Francisco: Jossey-Bass.

Fox, M. (1994) *The Reinvention of Work*. San Francisco: HarperCollins.

Frankl, V.E. (1973) *Man's Search for Meaning*. London: Hodder & Stoughton.

Friedlander, S. (1918) *Schöpferische Indifferenz*. Munich: Georg Müller.

Friedman, M.S. (1985) *The Healing Dialogue in Psychotherapy*. New York: Jason Aronson.

Friedman, M.S. (1994) 'Reflections on the Buber–Rogers Dialogue', *Journal of Humanistic Psychology*, 34(1): 46–65.

Friedman, N. (1992) 'The Infant Research of Daniel Stern and its Implications for Gestalt Therapy'. Paper presented at *The Gestalt Journal*'s Fourteenth Annual Conference, Boston, MA.

From, I. (1984) 'Reflections on Gestalt Therapy after Thirty-Two Years of Practice: A Requiem for Gestalt', *Gestalt Journal*, 7(1): 4–12.

Fry, M. (1993) in J. Hemming, 'Beyond Right and Wrong: An Interview with Marianne Fry', *British Gestalt Journal*, 2(2): 77–84.

Gelso, C.J. and Carter, J.A. (1985) 'The Relationship in Counseling and Psychotherapy: Components, Consequences, and Theoretical Antecedents', *Counselling Psychologist*, 13(2): 155–243.

Goldstein, K. (1939) *The Organism*. New York: American Book Company.

Gray, A. (1994) *An Introduction to the Therapeutic Frame*. London: Routledge.

Greenberg, E. (1989) 'Healing the Borderline', *Gestalt Journal*, 12(2): 11–55.

Greenberg, E. (1991) 'The Diagnosis and Treatment of Narcissistic Disorders'. Paper for Gestalt Center of Long Island conference.

Greenberg, E. (1995) 'Gestalt Therapy and the Narcissistically Vulnerable Client: When Insight Hurts'. Paper for the Association for the Advancement of Gestalt Therapy conference.

Harris, C.O. (1992) 'Gestalt Work with Psychotics', in E.C. Nevis (ed.), *Gestalt Therapy*. New York: Gestalt Institute of Cleveland Press and Gardner Press Inc.

Hellinger, B. (1991) 'For Love to Flourish: The Systemic Preconditions for Love'. Lecture given in Munich.

Hemming, J. (1994) 'Contact and Choice: Gestalt Work with Couples', in G. Wheeler and S. Backman (eds), *On Intimate Ground*. San Francisco: Jossey-Bass.

Highlen, P.S. and Hill, C.E. (1984) 'Factors Affecting Client Change in Individual Counselling: Current Status and Theoretical Speculations', in S.D. Brown and R.W. Lent (eds), *The Handbook of Counseling Psychology*. New York: John Wiley.

Holmes, P. (1992) *The Inner World Outside, Object Relations Theory and Psychodrama*. London: Tavistock/Routledge.

Houston, J. (1982) *The Possible Human*. Los Angeles: J.P. Tarcher.

Hüsserl, E. (1931) *Ideas: General Introduction to Pure Phenomenology*, Vol. 1. New York: Macmillan.

Hüsserl, E. (1968) *The Idea of Phenomenology*. The Hague: Nijhoft.

Hycner, R.H. (1985) 'Dialogical Gestalt Therapy: An Initial Proposal', *Gestalt Journal*, 8(1): 23–49.

Hycner, R.H. (1988) *Between Person and Person*. Highland, NY: Gestalt Journal Publications.

Hycner, R.H. (1990) 'The I–Thou Relationship and Gestalt Therapy', *Gestalt Journal*, 8(1): 41–54.

Hycner, R. and Jacobs, L. (1995) *The Healing Relationship in Gestalt Therapy*. Highland, NY: Gestalt Journal Publications.

Jacobs, L. (1989) 'Dialogue in Gestalt Theory and Therapy', *Gestalt Journal*, 12(1): 25–68.

Jacobs, L. (1992) 'Insights from Psychoanalytic Self Psychology and Intersubjectivity Theory for Gestalt Therapists', *Gestalt Journal*, 15(2): 25–60.

Jacobs, L. (1996) 'Shame in the Therapeutic Dialogue', in R.G. Lee and G. Wheeler (eds), *The Voice of Shame: Silence and Connection in Psychotherapy*. San Francisco: Jossey-Bass.

Jacoby, M. (1984) *The Analytic Encounter*. Toronto: Inner City Books.

John-Wilson, D. (1997) *Kuumba/Umoja or Creativity and Unity: An Afrocentric Approach to Family Therapy*. M.A. Dissertation, London Gestalt Centre.

Johnson, D. and Johnson, F. (1987) *Joining Together: Group Theory and Group Skills*. Englewood Cliffs, NJ: Prentice-Hall.

Kahn, M. (1991) *Between Therapist and Client: The New Relationship*. New York: W.H. Freeman.

Kareem, J. and Littlewood, R. (eds) (1992) *Intercultural Therapy*. Oxford: Blackwell Science.

Keenan, B. (1992) *An Evil Cradling*. London: Vintage.

Kempler, W. (1973) *Principles of Gestalt Family Therapy: A Gestalt Experiential Book*. Norway: Nordahls.

Kepner, E. (1980) 'Gestalt Group Process', in B. Feder and R. Ronall (eds), *Beyond the Hot Seat*. New York: Brunner/Mazel. pp. 5–24.

Kepner, J. (1987) *Body Process: A Gestalt Approach to Working with the Body in Psychotherapy*. New York: Gardner Press.

Kepner, J. (1995) *Healing Tasks: Psychotherapy with Adult Survivors of Childhood Abuse*. San Francisco: Jossey-Bass and Gestalt Institute of Cleveland.

Koffka, K. (1935) *Principles of Gestalt Psychology*. New York: Harcourt, Brace & World.

Kohler, W. (1970) *Gestalt Psychology: An Introduction to New Concepts in Modern Psychology*. New York: Liveright (first published 1947).

Kohut, H. (1977) *The Restoration of the Self*. New York: International Universities Press.

Kohut, H. (1984) *How Does Psychoanalysis Cure?* Chicago: University of Chicago Press.

Kohut, H. and Wolf, S. (1978) 'The Disorders of the Self and Their Treatment: An Outline', *International Journal of Psycho-analysis*, 59: 413–24.

Kolb, F. and Fry, D. (1975) 'Towards an Applied Theory of Experiential Learning', in C.L. Cooper (ed.), *Theories of Group Processes*. Wiley.

Kopp, S. (1977) *Back to One: A Practical Guide for Psychotherapists*. Palo Alto, CA: Science and Behavior Books.

Kovel, J. (1991) *A Complete Guide to Therapy*. Harmondsworth: Penguin (first published 1976).

Kron and Friedman (1994) 'Problems of Confirmation in Psychotherapy', *Journal of Humanistic Psychology*, 34(1): 66–83.

Lasch, C. (1979) *The Culture of Narcissism*. New York: W.W. Norton.

Lee, R. (1995) 'The Foundation for a Clearer Understanding of Field Dynamics', *British Gestalt Journal*, 4(1): 14–23.

Lee, R.G. (1996) 'Shame and the Gestalt Model', in R.G. Lee and G. Wheeler (eds), *The Voice of Shame: Silence and Connection in Psychotherapy*. San Francisco: Jossey-Bass.

Lee, R.G. and Wheeler, G. (1996) *The Voice of Shame: Silence and Connection in Psychotherapy*. San Francisco: Jossey-Bass.

Levistky, P. (1993) 'Techniques and the Field: Analytical versus Gestalt Techniques', *British Gestalt Journal*, 2(1): 63.

Lewin, K. (1926) 'Vorsatz, Wille und Bedürfnis [Intention, Will and Need]', *Psychologische Forschung*, 7: 440–7.

Lewin, K. (1935) *A Dynamic Theory of Personality*. New York: McGraw-Hill.

Lewin, K. (1952) *Field Theory in Social Science: Selected Theoretical Papers*. London: Tavistock (first published 1951).

Lieberman, M.A., Yalom, I.D. and Miles, M.B. (1973) *Encounter Groups: First Facts*. New York: Basic Books.

Lubbock, P. (1996) Unpublished case study (GPTI).

Luckensmeyer, C. (1995) 'Bringing us Together: Paradoxes and Polarities'. Paper presented at American Association of Gestalt Therapy Conference, New Orleans (April).

Mackewn, J. (1991a) 'Transference and Countertransference: A Gestalt Perspective'. Paper presented at Metanoia Psychotherapy Institute, London.

Mackewn, J. (1991b) 'Child Development in Early Gestalt Literature'. Paper.

Mackewn, J. (1995) 'Gestalt Psychotherapy', in M. Walker (ed.), *Peta: A Feminist's Problem with Men – In Search of a Therapist*. Buckingham: Open University Press.

Mackewn, J. (1996a) 'Working with Archetypal and Transpersonal Dimensions'. Working Paper.

Mackewn, J. (1996b) 'Modern Gestalt', in S. Palmer, S. Dainow and P. Milner (eds), *Counselling: The BAC Counselling Reader*. London: Sage.

Mackewn, J. (1996c) 'Psychotherapy as Care of the Soul'. Working Paper.

Mandelbrot, B.B. (1982) *The Fractal Geometry of Nature*. San Francisco: W.H. Freeman.

Melnick, J. and Nevis, S. (1992) 'Diagnosis: The Struggle for a Meaningful Paradigm', in E.C. Nevis (ed.), *Gestalt Therapy*. New York: Gestalt Institute of Cleveland Press and Gardner Press Inc.

Melnick, J., Nevis, S. and Melnick, G.N. (1995) 'Living with Desire – An Essay', *British Gestalt Journal*, 4(1): 31–40.

Merian, S. (1993) 'The Use of Gestalt Psychotherapy with Clients Suffering from Bulimia', *British Gestalt Journal*, 2(2): 125–30.

Mitchell, J. and Broughton, V. (1995) in T. Bentley (ed.) (1997) *Sharpen Your Team Skills in . . . TEAMWORK*. Maidenhead: McGraw-Hill.

Mollon, P. (1994) *The Fragile Self*. London: Whurr Publishers.

Moore, T. (1992) *Care of the Soul*. New York: HarperCollins.

Moore, T. (1996) *The Re-enchantment of Everyday Life*. London: Hodder and Stoughton.

Nelson-Jones, R. (1982) *The Theory and Practice of Counselling*. London: Holt, Rinehart & Winston.

Nevis, E. (1987) *Organizational Consulting: A Gestalt Approach*. New York: Gardner Press.

Nevis, E., Lancourt, J. and Vassalle, H.G. (1996) *Intentional Revolutions: A Seven Point Strategy for Transforming Organisations*.

Ornstein, R.E. (1972) *The Psychology of Consciousness*. San Francisco: W.H. Freeman.

Ovsiankina, M. (1928) 'Die Wiederaufnahme von Interbrochenen Handlungen', *Psychologische Forschung*, 2: 302–89.

Papernow, P. (1993) *Becoming a Stepfamily*. San Francisco: Jossey-Bass.

Parlett, M. (1991) 'Reflections on Field Theory', *British Gestalt Journal*, 1(2): 69–81.

Parlett, M. (1992) 'Field Theory'. Plenary lecture at European Gestalt Conference, Paris (May).

Parlett, M. and Hemming, J. (1996) 'Developments in Gestalt Therapy', in W. Dryden (ed.), *Developments in Psychotherapy: Historical Perspectives*. London: Sage.

Pedersen, P.D., Draguns, J.G., Lonner, W.J. and Trimble, E.J. (1989) 'Introduction and Overview', in P.D. Pedersen, J.G. Draguns, W.J. Lonner and E.J. Trimble (eds), *Counselling across Cultures*, 3rd edn. Honolulu: University of Hawaii Press. pp. 1–2.

Perls, F.S. (1948: 573) 'Theory and Technique of Personal Integration', *American Journal of Psychotherapy*, 2: 565–86.

Perls, F.S. (1969a) *Ego, Hunger and Aggression*. New York: Vintage Books (first published in South Africa in 1942).

Perls, F.S. (1969b) *Gestalt Therapy Verbatim*. Moab, UT: Real People Press.

Perls, F.S. (1976) *The Gestalt Approach, and Eye Witness to Therapy*. New York: Bantam (first published 1973).

Perls, F.S. (1979) 'Planned Psychotherapy', *Gestalt Journal*, 2(2): 5–23 (originally delivered at the William Alanson White Institute, New York, 1946 or 1947).

Perls, F.S., Hefferline, R.F. and Goodman, P. (1973) *Gestalt Therapy: Excitement and Growth in the Human Personality*. Harmondsworth: Penguin. (Originally published in New York by Julian Press in 1951; reprinted by them with new Author's Note, 1969.)

Perls, F.S., Hefferline, R. and Goodman, P. (1994) *Gestalt Therapy, Excitement and Growth in the Human Personality*. New York: Gestalt Journal Press.

Perls, L. (1991) *Living at the Boundary*. Highland, NY: Gestalt Journal Publications.

Philippson, P. (1994) 'Gestalt Therapy and the Culture of Narcissism', *British Gestalt Journal*, 3: 11–14.

Philippson, P. (1996) 'A Population of Gestalt Therapies', *British Gestalt Journal*, 5(1): 64–8.

Polster, E. (1987) *Every Person's Life is Worth a Novel*. New York: W.W. Norton.

Polster, E. (1991a) 'Response to "Loss of Ego Functions, Conflict and Resistance"', *Gestalt Journal*, 14(2): 45–65.

Polster, E. (1991b) 'Tight Therapeutic Sequences', *British Gestalt Journal*, 1(2): 63–8.

Polster, E. (1993) 'Individuality and Commonality', *British Gestalt Journal*, 2(1): 41–4.

Polster, E. (1995) *A Population of Selves*. San Francisco: Jossey-Bass.

Polster, E. and Polster, M. (1974) *Gestalt Therapy Integrated: Contours of Theory and Practice*. New York: Vintage Books.

Polster, M. (1993) *Eve's Daughter*. San Francisco: Jossey-Bass.

Reason, P. (ed.) (1988) *Human Inquiry in Action: Developments in New Paradigm Research*. London: Sage.

Reason, P. (ed.) (1994) *Participation in Human Inquiry*. London: Sage.

Reason, P. and Rowan, J. (eds) (1981) *Human Inquiry: A Sourcebook of New Paradigm Research*. Chichester: Wiley.

Rebillot, P. (1993) *The Call to Adventure, Bringing the Hero's Journey to Daily Life*. San Francisco: HarperCollins.

Robine, J.M. (1988) 'La question du transfert en Gestalt-therapie'. *Paper: Former pour la Gestalt-therapie*.

Rogers, C.R. (1969) *Freedom to Learn: A View of What Education Might Become*. Columbus, OH: Charles E. Merrill.

Rosenblatt, D. (1991) 'An Interview with Laura Perls' [1982], *Gestalt Journal*, 14(1): 7–26.

Rowan, J. (1983) *The Reality Game*. London: Routledge & Kegan Paul.

Saner, R. (1989) 'Cultural Bias of Gestalt Therapy: Made-in-USA', *The Gestalt Journal*, XII(2): 57–71.

Sardello, R. (1994) *Facing the World with Soul*. New York: HarperCollins.

Schoen, S. (1978) 'Gestalt Therapy and the Teachings of Buddhism', *The Gestalt Journal*, I: 2.

Shohet, R. (1985) *Dream Sharing*. Wellingborough: Turnstone Press.

Shub, N. (1992) 'Gestalt Therapy over Time: Integrating Difficulty and Diagnosis', in E.C. Nevis (ed.), *Gestalt Therapy*. New York: Gestalt Institute of Cleveland Press/Gardner Press.

Sills, C. (ed.) (1997) *Contracting in Counselling – A Mutual Commitment*. London: Sage.

Sills, C., Fish, S. and Lapworth, P. (1995) *Gestalt Counselling*. Bicester: Winslow Press.

Smuts, J.C. (1995) *Holism and Evolution*. Highland, NY: Gestalt Journal Publications (first published 1926).

Spinelli, E. (1989) *The Interpreted World: An Introduction to Phenomenological Psychology*. London: Sage.

Spinelli, E. (1994) *Demystifying Therapy*. London: Constable.

Stacey, R. (1995) *Creativity in Organisations: The Importance of Mess*. University of Hertford: Complexity and Management Centre.

Staemmler, F.M. (1993) 'Projective Identification in Gestalt Therapy with Severely Impaired Clients', *British Gestalt Journal*, 2(2): 104–10.

Stern, D. (1985) *The Interpersonal World of the Infant*. New York: Basic Books.

Stolorow, R.D., Brandchaft, B. and Atwood, G.E. (1987) *Psychoanalytic Treatment, an Intersubjective Approach*. Hillsdale, NJ: Analytic Press.

Stratford, C. and Braillier, K. (1979) 'Gestalt Therapy with Profoundly Disturbed Persons', *Gestalt Journal*, 2(1): 90–103.

Suzuki, S. (1970) *Zen Mind, Beginner's Mind*. New York: Weatherhill.

Thich nhat Hanh (1992) *Being Peace*. London: Rider.

Tobin, S.A. (1982) 'Self Disorders, Gestalt Therapy and Self Psychology', *Gestalt Journal*, 5(2): 3–44.

Truax, C.R. and Carkhuff, R.R. (1967) *Towards Effective Counselling and Psychotherapy*. Chicago: Aldine.

Tsoukas, H. (in press) 'Forms of Knowledge and Forms of Life in Organised Contexts', in R. Chia (ed.), *In the Realm of Organisation: Essays for Robert Cooper*. London: Routledge.

Tuckman, B. (1965) 'Developmental Sequences in Small Groups', *Psychological Bulletin*, 63: 384–99.

Von Bertalanffy, L. (1950) 'The Theory of Open Systems in Physics and Biology', *Science*, 3: 23–9.

Walker, L.G. and Patten, M.I. (1990) 'Marriage Guidance Counselling: II What Counsellors Want to Give', *British Journal of Guidance and Counselling*, 18(3): 294–307.

Welwood, J. (ed.) (1983) *Awakening the Heart: East/West Approaches to Psychotherapy and the Healing Relationship*. Boulder, CO: Shambhala Publications Inc.

Wertheimer, M. (1925) 'Gestalt Therapy', in W.D. Ellis (ed.), *A Sourcebook of Gestalt Psychology* (1938). London: Routledge and Kegan Paul. pp. 1–11.

Wertheimer, M. (1938) 'The General Theoretical Situation', in W.D. Ellis (ed.), *A Sourcebook of Gestalt Psychology*. London: Routledge and Kegan Paul. pp. 12–16.

Wheeler, G. (1991) *Gestalt Reconsidered: A New Approach to Contact and Resistance*. New York: Gardner Press.

Wheeler, G. (1994) 'Compulsion and Curiosity: A Gestalt Approach to Obsessive-Compulsive Disorder', *British Gestalt Journal*, 3(1): 15–21.

Wheeler, G. (1996) 'Self and Shame: A New Paradigm for Therapy', in R.G. Lee and G. Wheeler (eds), *The Voice of Shame: Silence and Connection in Psychotherapy*. San Francisco: Jossey-Bass.

Wheeler, G. and Backman, S. (eds) (1994) *On Intimate Ground – A Gestalt Approach to Working with Couples*. San Francisco: Jossey-Bass.

Winnicott, D.W. (1975) 'Hate in the Countertransference', in *Through Paediatrics to Psychoanalysis*. New York: Basic Books.

Woodmansey, A.C. (1988) 'Are Psychotherapists out of Touch?', *British Journal of Psychotherapy*, 5(1): 57–65.

Yalom, I. (1985) *The Theory and Practice of Group Psychotherapy*, 3rd edn. New York: Basic Books (first published 1970).

Yontef, G.M. (1980) 'Gestalt Therapy: A Dialogic Method'. Unpublished manuscript.

Yontef, G.M. (1988) 'Assimilating Diagnostic and Psychoanalytic Perspectives into Gestalt Therapy', *Gestalt Journal*, 11(1): 5–32.

Yontef, G.M. (1991) 'Recent Trends in Gestalt Therapy in the United States and What We Need to Learn from Them', *British Gestalt Journal*, 1(1): 5–20.

Yontef, G.M. (1992) 'Considering *Gestalt Reconsidered*: A Review in Depth', *Gestalt Journal*, 15(1): 95–118.

Yontef, G.M. (1993) *Awareness, Dialogue and Process: Essays on Gestalt Therapy*. Highland, NY: Gestalt Journal Publications.

Yontef, G.M. (1996) 'Shame and Guilt in Gestalt Therapy', in R.G. Lee and G. Wheeler (eds), *The Voice of Shame: Silence and Connection in Psychotherapy*. San Francisco: Jossey-Bass.

Zeigarnik, B. (1927) 'Uber das behalten von Erledigten und Unerledigten Handlungen', *Psychologische Forschung*, 9: 1–85.

Zinker, J. (1978) *Creative Process in Gestalt Therapy*. New York: Vintage Books (first published in 1977).

Zinker, J. (1980) 'The Development Process of a Gestalt Therapy Group', in B. Feder and R. Ronall (eds), *Beyond the Hot Seat*. New York: Brunner/Mazel. pp. 55–77.

Zinker, J. (1994) *In Search of Good Form*. San Francisco: Jossey-Bass.

Index